REVOLUTIONARY POETICS

Revolutionary Poetics

THE RHETORIC OF THE BLACK ARTS MOVEMENT

Sarah RudeWalker

The University of Georgia Press   Athens

© 2023 by the University of Georgia Press
Athens, Georgia 30602
www.ugapress.org
All rights reserved
Designed by Erin Kirk
Set in Arno Pro

Most University of Georgia Press titles are
available from popular e-book vendors.

Printed digitally

Library of Congress Control Number: 2022049677

ISBN 9780820362007 (hardback)
ISBN 9780820363967 (paperback)
ISBN 9780820361994 (ePub)
ISBN 9780820363974 (PDF)

Contents

Acknowledgments vii

INTRODUCTION Don't Call It a Comeback *The Rhetorical Successes of the Black Arts Movement* 1

CHAPTER 1 "Art for All Our Sake" *Frameworks for Assessing Black Arts Writers' Rhetorical Legacies* 11

CHAPTER 2 "Our Distaste for the Enemy, Our Love for Each Other" *The Radical Rhetoric of Blame and Praise in Black Arts Movement Poetry* 43

CHAPTER 3 "A Tradition of Beautiful Talk" *The Black Arts Poet-Rhetor and the Black Is Beautiful Movement* 78

CHAPTER 4 "Most of My Heroes Don't Appear on No Stamps" *Toasts, Hip-Hop, and the Black Pride Movement* 116

CHAPTER 5 "Woman Power / Is / Black Power / Is / Human Power" *Resistance Rhetoric of Black Arts Women Poets* 152

CODA "A Language That We Been Speaking" *Twenty-First-Century Echoes of the Black Arts Movement* 189

Notes 199
Bibliography 207
Index 223

Acknowledgments

This book has been a long time in the making, and I owe thanks to many along the way who have helped me bring it to fruition. First and foremost, the book would not have been possible without the invaluable mentorship I received over the course of three degree programs at two different institutions. I am deeply grateful to have had two outstanding graduate school mentors at Penn State University, Keith Gilyard and Bernard W. Bell, who will always be my teachers and who have become my family. They challenged me to do the deep study necessary to be a scholar of the African American literary and rhetorical traditions, and they taught me to "historicize, contextualize, and problematize," to take risks, to hear critiques with good humor, to celebrate the victories, and to put in the work. I am honored to have my research be part of their amazing legacies as scholars and teachers.

While at Penn State I also benefitted from the teaching and guidance of other brilliant scholars, including Cheryl Glenn and Deborah F. Atwater, who served on my committee and provided invaluable input into both the big-picture and minute aspects of the project; Debbie Hawhee, Aldon L. Nielsen, and Suresh Canagarajah, in whose graduate seminars I developed some of the book's key arguments; and Shirley Moody-Turner, Linda Furgerson Selzer, Jack Selzer, and Julia Kasdorf, whose teaching enriched the range of texts and methodologies that informed my work. I want to thank also the members of my talented graduate cohort in the African American Literature and Language Program at Penn State, Phyllisa Deroze, Grégory Pierrot, Micky New, Nadia DeLane, Laura Vrana, Susan Weeber, Ersula Ore, David Green, and Alex Lockett, who encouraged me, inspired me, and challenged me to get on their level. I am especially grateful for the talents of Nadia DeLane, who created the cover art for this book.

But the project I brought to graduate school actually had its beginnings in my undergraduate work as a double major in the Political and Social Thought

Program and the Modern Studies Program in English at the University of Virginia. I am indebted to Scott Saul for introducing me to the Black Arts Movement in his seminar on the literary avant-garde and for advising my undergraduate honors thesis as if it were the work of a graduate student. I am also deeply grateful to Michael J. Smith and the Political and Social Thought Program for giving me the intellectual freedom to do interdisciplinary work and for having great expectations about the kind of scholarship an undergraduate can produce. I hope that I can nurture the same kind of growth and intellectual victories for my undergraduate students.

I am a proud member of the faculty of the illustrious Spelman College, and I would not have been able to fully realize this project without the support of my colleagues and my institution. Thank you especially to Stephen Knadler, Alex Lockett, Akiba Harper, Lynn Maxwell, Pushpa Parekh, Deanna Koretsky, Michelle Hite, Sharan Strange, Michelle Bachelor Robinson, Trish Ventura, Melanie McKie, Opal Moore, Tikenya Foster-Singletary, and Tarshia Stanley for your support, collegiality, and friendship as I faced the challenges of being both a junior scholar and a new mom. Their support for my professional endeavors and their embrace of my family as part of the Spelman English family serve as exemplars of cultivating academic environments that truly support faculty in all aspects of their work.

My Spelman students have also been invaluable contributors to this project, and I want to thank them both as students for their investment in the legacies of Black Arts poetics and the rhetorics of Black Power and as leaders for showing me what it looks like to love as hard as you fight. I am particularly thankful to Destiny Reese and Morgan Howell for their work as student research assistants for this project.

I could not have completed my research without two very valuable resources: the archives and time to write. I am grateful for the assistance of the archivists at the University of Virginia, Penn State University, Emory University, Spelman College, and Atlanta University Center libraries, whose dedication to supporting researchers is commendable. I also want to thank Spelman College for awarding me Junior Faculty Research Leave and Cynthia Spence and the UNCF/Mellon Program for awarding me a Faculty Residency Fellowship to complete this project. I am grateful to Andra Gillespie and the James Weldon Johnson Institute for the Study of Race and Difference at Emory University for hosting me as a researcher during my fellowship.

I am delighted to be publishing this book with the University of Georgia Press, and I want to extend deep thanks to Walter Biggins, who believed in the promise of the project and had infinite patience with me as I persevered through childbirth and health issues. I am grateful to my editor, Patrick Allen, who inherited the project from Walter, and who also has had infinite patience with me as I persevered through a pandemic. I also want to thank the two anonymous readers who reviewed my manuscript for the press. Your critiques and insights have made this a stronger book.

Thank you to all of the people who read drafts of the book in various forms over the years, including the members of my English department and Center for Democratic Deliberation writing groups at Penn State, both of which were led by Cheryl Glenn: Heather Brook Adams, Sarah Summers, John Belk, Mark Hlavacik, Fabrice Picon, and Jessica Kuperavage. I appreciate the feedback I received from members of the African American Literature and Culture Society, who heard early versions of chapters as conference presentations, and from my collaborators in the Rhetoric Society of America summer workshop. My mom, Anne Rude, also provided rich editorial advice on the manuscript, as she has since I learned to write, as did my husband, Mat RudeWalker, who has given me invaluable feedback at every stage of the project since we met in our first graduate seminar at Penn State.

I am most deeply indebted to the love of my friends and family, who support and encourage me unwaveringly. Thank you to my lifelong friends Susana Duarte, Jenne Pross, Drew Protacio, Stephanie Osborn, Katie Owens-Murphy, Nadia DeLane, and Ernest Jackson, who have shown me that family goes beyond blood. Thank you to my parents, Anne and Lawrence Rude, my first and always teachers, and my siblings, Chris and Jenn Rude, for loving me all my life, and to Debby Walker, Craig Walker, and Tiffany Boswell for welcoming me as if I have always been family. Most of all, I am grateful beyond words to my children, Ani and Kai, who challenge me to be the best teacher and to love in ways I could have never imagined, and to the love of my life and partner in all things, Mat RudeWalker, whose strength is my strength, and to whom this book is dedicated.

REVOLUTIONARY POETICS

INTRODUCTION

Don't Call It a Comeback

The Rhetorical Successes of the Black Arts Movement

Less than a year before his death, and a little over a year after the murder of Trayvon Martin,[1] Black Arts Movement (BAM) founder Amiri Baraka published a piece in the May 2013 issue of *Poetry* magazine, the hundred-year-old journal of the Poetry Foundation, in which he reviewed the recently published *Angles of Ascent: A Norton Anthology of Contemporary African American Poetry*. Edited by Charles Henry Rowell, the founder and editor of the noted African American literary and scholarly journal *Callaloo*, the anthology collects selected poetry by Black authors written from 1940 on.[2] As anyone familiar with Baraka would expect, he does not mince words in the review. In the opening lines, he charges, "This is a bizarre collection. It seems that it has been pulled together as a relentless 'anti' to one thing: the Black Arts Movement." Although Baraka objects, as do most critics of anthologies, to Rowell's decisions about whom to include and exclude, he directs his most impassioned critique at Rowell's introduction, which he characterizes as a text "aimed at rendering the Black Arts Movement as old school, backward, and fundamentally artless" ("Post-Racial Anthology?" 166). He calls one particular passage from the end of the introduction an "icy epilogue" that "is too comic to be tragic, though it is both," portraying Rowell's argument as "a cold class dismissal by would-be mainstream Negroes on the path to mediocrity." Rowell's text here reads, "Without the fetters of narrow political and social demands that have nothing to do with the production of artistic texts, black American poets, since the Civil Rights Movement and Black Power Movement, have created an extraordinary number of aesthetically deft poems that both challenge the concept of 'the American poem' and extend the dimensions of American poetry" (qtd. in Baraka, "Post-Racial Anthology?" 172). Baraka responds sharply to the contention here that "narrow political and social demands" served as inhibiting "fetters" that kept writers of the Civil Rights and Black Power eras from creating poems that are "aesthetically deft" or that innovate the American poetic corpus. He quips, "This is poppycock at its poppiest and cockiest. You mean the struggle for our humanity is a *fetter* (to whom? Negroes seeking tenure in these white schools who dare not mumble a cross word?). Why is the struggle for equal rights and self-determination narrow? To whom? Racists?" ("Post-Racial Anthology?" 172).

The blurb Norton uses to advertise *Angles of Ascent* reinforces this provocative implication: that the seemingly "apolitical" poetry included in the anthology demonstrates a general improvement in the aesthetic quality of African American writing since the 1960s. Norton presents the book as "a gathering of poems that demonstrate what happens when writers in a marginalized community collectively turn from dedicating their writing to political, social, and economic struggles, and instead devote themselves to the art of their poems and to the ideas they embody. These poets bear witness to the interior landscapes of their own individual selves or examine the private or personal worlds of invented personae and, therefore, of human beings living in our modern and postmodern worlds" ("Angles of Ascent"). Baraka has no patience for this text either, which he calls "imbecilic garbage." Addressing the problematic aspects of the blurb in his review, he observes, "You can see how that would be some far-right instruction for 'a marginalized community,' especially one with the history of the Afro-American people: *We don't want to hear all that stuff... make up a pleasanter group of beings with pleasanter, more literary lives than yourselves and then we will perhaps consider it art!*" ("Post-Racial Anthology?" 166).

This conversation about the relationship between politics and aesthetics, and particularly the nexus of these concepts in African American writing, is not new. Norton's blurb and Baraka's response could have been point and counterpoint in New Negro Renaissance–era discussions of art as "universal" versus art as "propaganda," with George Schuyler siding with Norton's writers and Langston Hughes and W. E. B. Du Bois getting Baraka's back,[3] and it echoes the main points of contention among the thirty-eight opinions featured in the "Writers Symposium" in *Negro Digest* in January 1968.[4] The Black Arts Movement in particular has been subject to criticism like the dismissal implicit in Rowell's introduction well before the publication of this particular anthology, and the judgment of BAM as a "failure" because of its inherently political—and, as I discuss in this book, inherently *rhetorical*—mission has been the prevailing attitude about the era among literary critics from as early as the 1980s.

One particularly influential dismissal of the Black Arts Movement appeared in *Time* magazine's issue from October 10, 1994, which included an article titled "Black Creativity: On the Cutting Edge" by Henry Louis Gates Jr., one of the world's most prominent scholars of African American literature. Written in support of the contemporary African American literary renaissance headlined by writers like Toni Morrison and August Wilson (the fourth such renaissance declared in the twentieth century), the article begins with a characterization of the preceding three eras of African American literary production. Gates identifies the four eras as follows: (1) the New Negro Movement at the turn of the twentieth century, which included Paul Laurence Dunbar, Charles Chesnutt, Pauline Hopkins, W. E. B. Du Bois, and Anna Julia Cooper; (2) the Harlem Renaissance of the 1920s and 1930s; (3) the Black Arts Movement of the 1960s to the 1970s; and (4) the flowering initiated by women novelists of the 1980s.[5] But he squarely critiques the Black Arts Movement's legitimacy, describing it as a so-called renaissance "[e]rected on a shifting foundation of revolutionary politics" that caused it to be "dead" by 1975. Calling into question the artistic commitment of movement activists, Gates asserts that Black Arts writers failed literarily by "view[ing] black art as a matter less of aesthetics than of protest," a charge that paints the movement more as an era of misdirection than a time of meaningful artistic production.[6] This critique of BAM, a view Gates articulated as early as 1987 in his monograph *Figures in Black: Words, Signs, and the "Racial" Self*, stands as a notably influential example of the ways the movement was historicized in the decades following its ebb, and the appearance of the critique in *Time* demonstrates that the reach of this negative history extended through not only academic but also popular circles.[7]

In recent years, however, Gates seems to have revised his stance on the relevance and aesthetic worth of the Black Arts Movement—a change that is timely in an era in which concepts of the "post-racial" have proven ridiculously naïve and in which a vigorous and much-needed Black Lives Matter (BLM) movement has inspired a new generation of politically conscious Black art. In an advertising blurb for a 2016 international conference on BAM sponsored by Dillard University and the Hutchins Center for African and African American Research at Harvard University, the second such conference in three years,[8] Gates goes so far as to recognize the contributions of the movement as "cultural genius": "We are in the midst of what can be seen as a second wave of appreciation and exploration of the cultural genius of the Black Arts Movement. Amiri Baraka, Larry Neal, Haki Madhubuti, Sonia Sanchez, Askia Toure, Kalamu ya Salaam and countless other voices moved us toward new understandings of Black identity in the late 60s and early 70s. Now we find ourselves in a moment in which their art and their thought were never more relevant" ("Black Arts Movement Conference"). Although the forum through

Introduction 3

which Gates articulates this critical stance certainly reached a significantly smaller audience than his previous publication in *Time*, his pivot from painting the movement in broad strokes as a failure to articulating the movement's wide-ranging successes anecdotally marks a watershed moment in changing attitudes toward the Black Arts Movement.

But while Gates's revisionism is significant, he is far from the first to call for a more nuanced understanding of the successes and legacies of BAM. In the early 1990s, a small cadre of scholars began the "second wave" of appreciation and exploration of the movement that Gates references above. A major voice for reassessing the Black Arts Movement-as-failure narrative was poet and Africana Studies scholar David Lionel Smith, who issued a call in a 1991 *American Literary History* article for more—and more thoughtful—scholarship on Black Arts works. In the opening of "The Black Arts Movement and Its Critics," Smith declares that literary critics of the 1980s and early 1990s have held Black Arts Movement writing in "low esteem," and he indicts scholars for the "paucity of scholarly literature" on the era's substantial body of work. The problem Smith identifies with the existing history of the movement is not that scholars have emphasized problematic and controversial aspects of the Black Arts project but that they have reduced the movement in historical and critical accounts to consisting *only* of these problematic impulses. Critics of Black Arts, fairly in some cases, Smith asserts, level the following charges against the movement: "[Black Arts Movement writing] often confuses social theory with aesthetics, failing to articulate the complex relationship between the two; much of it is predicated upon crude, strident forms of nationalism that do not lend themselves to careful analysis; and too often the work is marred by the swaggering rhetoric of ethnic and gender chauvinism." The result, according to Smith, of focusing Black Arts criticism only on these "egregious extremes" of the movement's writing is that "we may come to equate all the work of the movement with its worst tendencies." Although it is appropriate and necessary to critique these extremely problematic aspects of Black Arts writing, critics should not reduce the movement solely to these attributes. Smith rightly calls for scholars to address the work of the movement more comprehensively, asserting that "even the most rudimentary work in this area is yet to be done" (93). He cites the fact that no single scholarly or journalistic book had at the time been written about the movement by critics *outside* the movement as evidence that it had not been thoughtfully treated.[9] Indeed, this remains a crucial area of need in literary, rhetorical, and African American Studies—one that is vital and timely and that has implications for art and activism beyond the ivory tower as well.

In the more than two decades since Smith's article, a range of scholars have risen to the challenge he presents, including Joyce Ann Joyce (1996), Aldon Lynn Nielsen (1997 and 2004), Julius E. Thompson (1999), Margaret Ann Reid (2001), Tony Bolden (2003), Melba Joyce Boyd (2003), Keith Gilyard (2003), Cheryl Clarke (2005), James Smethurst (2005 and 2021), Margo Natalie Crawford (2006 and 2017), Lisa Gail Collins (2006), Amy Abugo Ongiri (2009), Daniel Widener (2010), Meta DuEwa Jones (2011), Howard Rambsy II (2011), Evie Shockley (2011), Jean-Philippe Marcoux (2012), Carmen L. Phelps (2012), Michael S. Collins (2013), Virginia C. Fowler (2013), Kathy Lou Schultz (2013), Jeffrey B. Leak (2014), Carter Mathes (2015), La Donna Forsgren (2018 and 2020), Jonathan Fenderson (2019), and Casarae Lavada Abdul-Ghani (2022). Perhaps the most significant and nuanced comprehensive literary and historical analysis of the Black Arts Movement so far is James Smethurst's *The Black Arts Movement: Literary Nationalism in the 1960s and 1970s* (2005). Smethurst echoes Smith's concern about the relative dearth of Black Arts scholarship, especially in relation to the significant and lasting impact Smethurst believes 1960s and 1970s literary nationalist movements had on academic and popular culture. "Even now," he notes, "academic assessments of the Black Arts and Black Power movements are frequently made in passing and generally seem to assume that we already know all we need to know about these intertwined movements and their misogyny, homophobia, anti-Semitism, and eschewal of practical politics for the pathological symbolic" (4). Smethurst focuses his own work on interrogating the inevitable questions and contrasting histories of the movement's "success," stating that his book "echoes the set of questions that scholars of the New Negro Renaissance have raised since the 1980s: Was the movement a 'failure' in something other than the sense that all cultural movements (whether British Pre-Raphaelite, Russian futurist, German expressionist, U.S. abstract expressionist, or Brazilian tropicalian) ultimately 'fail' to achieve their most visionary aims—and simply end? Who says so? And why do they say it?" (7).

In this book, I take up the work of revising the narrative of the Black Arts Movement by reassessing its successes specifically as a *rhetorical-aesthetic* movement, one that aimed fundamentally to change people's minds through art. In Gates's blurb above, he notably celebrates writing of the movement for having "moved us toward new understandings of Black identity," focusing in on Black Arts writer-activists' work to persuade their primary audiences about the beauty and power of their Blackness. One artifact that demonstrates this is poet Haki Madhubuti's (then known as Don L. Lee) introduction to *Black*

Back: Back Black, a 1973 volume of poetry by fellow Black Arts poet Sarah Webster Fabio. Madhubuti boldly predicts that copies of Fabio's book will sell because of the significance of her poetry to the lives of Black people. But if they don't, he adds, they'll send them out for free: "Copies sold is not important; message received is" (Lee, "Introduction" iv). Madhubuti's statement here points to Black Arts poets' central rhetorical mission: create an art fired in the crucible of Black folk culture that would forge a new Black consciousness in their audiences, an attitude of self-love that would stir them to participation in a revolution for Black self-determination. Baraka's own reflections in 2013 on the goals of the Black Arts Movement show that these sentiments get to the heart of what Black Arts activists had hoped to achieve. Recalling in his review of *Angles of Ascent* the 1967 Black Writers' Conference at Fisk University—the conference to which he had been invited by then-Fisk student Nikki Giovanni and that served as the catalyst for Pulitzer Prize–winning poet Gwendolyn Brooks's legendary "conversion" to Blackness—Baraka remembers, "We said the art we wanted to create should be identifiably, culturally Black—like Duke Ellington's or Billie Holiday's. We wanted it to be a mass art, not hidden away on university campuses. We wanted an art that could function in the ghettos where we lived. And we wanted an art that would help liberate Black people" ("Post-Racial Anthology?" 167).

As I will show, Black Arts as a rhetorical movement succeeded in reaching these goals to a great degree. A rhetorical analysis of the movement, something hitherto not undertaken by scholars and critics, adds significant denotational boundaries to these broad concerns with its success and failure. The success of the movement that I historicize and analyze here, then, depends less on a concern with the literature's decontextualized aesthetic merit than on an understanding of the authors' ability to persuade, inspire, and motivate their primary audience specifically through artistic modes. In what specific ways did the Black Arts Movement achieve or strive to achieve its revolutionary goals by deploying rhetorical poetics—in what forms, to what audiences, and to what effect? In what ways can the movement be considered to have had *delayed success*, rhetorical, cultural, or political influence that became apparent only after the movement's period of greatest activity had ended?

The answers to these questions generate a litany of powerful Black Arts successes: Black Arts writers brought literary work to the people; established a broad and invigorated readership; artistically deployed the poetic and rhetorical tropes unique to that readership's speech community; used their works to encourage people to love themselves, see their own beauty, and be proud of their heritage and their cultural heroes; and encouraged people to work for the weakening or destruction of deeply rooted and institutionalized injustices. While intimately connected to practical political aims that would benefit the collective, these accomplishments significantly helped strengthen the subjectivities and selfhoods of individual members of their audience as well—an outcome that even the writers of Norton's blurb for *Angles of Ascent* above, who praise "poets [who] bear witness to the interior landscape of their own individual selves," would consider decidedly literary. So while detractors of the Black Arts Movement deem it a failure in that the inherently political art was neither "art for art's sake" nor an entirely successful tool in service of Black Power movements' broader political goals, the activists of the Black Arts Movement did succeed largely in winning the rhetorical struggle for *Black consciousness*. Although its legacies are more cultural than political, the Black Arts Movement has had far-reaching influence, particularly in developments in positive conceptions of Blackness, in the valorization of Black language practices and its subsequent effects on educational policy, in establishing a legacy of populist dissemination of African American vernacular culture through both writing and popular music, and in setting the groundwork for important considerations of the aesthetic intersections of race with gender and sexuality. These legacies stand as the movement's primary—and largely unacknowledged—successes, and they provide significant lessons for navigating our current political moment.

In the chapters that follow, I present rhetorical readings of the work of poets from the Black Arts Movement in order to demonstrate the various strands of rhetorical influence on the Black Arts project and the significant legacies these writers left behind. I have chosen to focus specifically on the work of Black Arts *poets* for several reasons. The majority of literary production during the movement took the form of poetry or drama—in part because these modes could be made accessible to audiences through both print and performance. Poetry in particular could reach perhaps the widest variety of audiences, including individuals who were not part of traditional or expected literary audiences. Poets could take advantage of the wide range of media available to Black Arts activists to disseminate their work: in addition to writing poetry for published books or chapbooks, poets could distribute their work as broadsides; record and distribute records of performative readings; and present their work live at schools, in community gathering places, and on street corners, free from the production constraints that might limit performances of dramatic works. As the product of the movement that most likely had the broadest reach, poetry works best as a means to discuss the rhetorical influence of BAM.

Specifically, I examine the work of Black Arts poets who proved influential during and after the movement in their incorporation of epideictic rhetoric (the rhetoric of praise and blame) in their poetry, in their valorization of Black vernacular forms, in their educational activism, and in their work to reach audiences through the range of media listed above. These authors, whom I call *poet-rhetors*, literary artists who used their acumen as rhetors to advocate publicly for the common good, include LeRoi Jones / Amiri Baraka, Gwendolyn Brooks, Margaret Burroughs, Mari Evans, Sarah Webster Fabio, Nikki Giovanni, Etheridge Knight, Ted Joans, the Last Poets, Don L. Lee / Haki Madhubuti, Kay Lindsey, Audre Lorde, Carolyn Rodgers, and Sonia Sanchez. To offer an alternative perspective to historicizations of the Black Arts Movement as uncomplicatedly misogynistic, I specifically emphasize the work of women writers and activists who subverted the movement's problematic ideological masculinism to achieve some of its most powerful rhetorical successes. An investigation of the rhetorical contributions of these writers allows us to deal realistically with the movement's problematic aspects while still devoting thoughtful scholarly attention to the successful legacy of the Black Arts Movement and the ways their work can continue to shape contemporary rhetorical activism.

Chapter 1, "'Art for All Our Sake': Frameworks for Assessing Black Arts Writers' Rhetorical Legacies," provides the context and rhetorical theories that serve as the groundwork for the analysis in the subsequent chapters. My framework for assessing the Black Arts Movement as a successful rhetorical-aesthetic movement, which I hope proves useful for scholars engaging in research on rhetorical poetics, depends on a broad cross-cultural conception of rhetorical influences. In particular, I work to establish what literary scholar Bernard W. Bell would call an African Americentric scope of theoretical foundations that meld African, European, and African American understandings of the power of the word. The full rhetorical reach of the Black Arts Movement comes through most clearly when we consider the movement's poet-rhetors as descendants of both traditional Western rhetoric and African rhetoric: as both citizen-orators and griots, as both *paideic* bards and wielders of the creative power of *nommo*—and as savvy wordsmiths who employ the rhetorical resources of their own era and immediate speech communities.

In chapter 2, "'Our Distaste for the Enemy, Our Love for Each Other': The Radical Rhetoric of Blame and Praise in Black Arts Movement Poetry," I argue that one of the movement's primary rhetorical goals was to expose and reject the mainstream ideals under which Black people had been dehumanized, dispossessed, defamed, and exploited as citizens of the United States. With regard to this goal, and with the ultimate hope of awakening and inculcating Black consciousness and self-love in their audiences, Black Arts poets used blame or *psogos* rhetoric to persuade Black audiences to abandon White values and instead adopt values articulated by a Black Power worldview. Writers worked to reinforce these new self-affirming values by engaging in rhetoric of praise, or *panegyric* rhetoric, through which they praised the heroism of Black radical activists.

In chapter 3, "'A Tradition of Beautiful Talk': The Black Arts Poet-Rhetor and the Black Is Beautiful Movement," I discuss the educative work of Black Arts poet-rhetors in aiming to teach their audiences that "Black Is Beautiful": to value both Black phenotypical physicality and, significantly, the aesthetic possibilities of Black language traditions. I argue that Black Arts poets most effectively accomplished this rhetorical task when Black aesthetics were not only the *theme* but the *form* of their work. This rhetorical effort produced a significant legacy by influencing scholars and activists to take the fight to recognize the aesthetic value of Black language into formal institutions of education.

Chapter 4, "'Most of My Heroes Don't Appear on No Stamps': Toasts, Hip-Hop, and the Black Pride Movement," is an investigation of the ways Black Arts poets advocated Black Pride, an appreciation of the complex culture and history of Black Americans as an African diasporic people, through the innovative reconstruction of heroes in the form of traditional *toast* narratives. Adding to the collective text of Black history by articulating defiant, mythical Black heroes through the toast, a verbal art form specific to Black speech communities, movement poets furthered their rhetorical advocacy of Black consciousness. The legacy of this work—of asserting the toast form as poetry and demonstrating the creation of defiant Black heroes to the public on a national scale—significantly influenced the development of hip-hop in the following decades.

In chapter 5, "'Woman Power / Is / Black Power / Is / Human Power': Resistance Rhetoric of Black Arts Women Poets," I affirm that, despite the vocal masculinist discourse present in some Black Arts poetry, women writers of the Black Arts Movement not only played a vital role in Black nationalist groups but also used their writing to advocate for more inclusive gender roles within these organizations. Specifically, the work of these women poets demonstrates their strategic use of two Black language practices: *signifyin* to argue against restrictive conceptions of femininity and homophobic prejudices, and *testifyin* to celebrate a range of representations of womanhood through a communal lyric voice.

The book's coda, "'A Language That We Been Speaking': Twenty-First-Century Echoes of the Black Arts Movement," suggests the implications of an alternative, positive understanding of the Black Arts rhetorical legacy in the era of Black Lives Matter.

CHAPTER 1

"Art for All Our Sake"

Frameworks for Assessing Black Arts Writers' Rhetorical Legacies

Haki Madhubuti's "A Poem to Complement Other Poems," which he published under his birth name, Don L. Lee, in *Don't Cry, Scream* in 1969, succinctly and profoundly captures the rhetorical mission of the Black Arts Movement. In line with the title's directive to use the poem as a resource to understand other poems, I read it as an *ars rhetorica*—an explanation of how poems of BAM were meant to reach and persuade their primary audience.

The poem begins by commanding the reader to "change," a word the speaker utters seventy-four times throughout the poem in various iterations. As if it were a musical composition, the poem opens by presenting change as its theme, and each subsequent set of lines is a witty variation, an example of or an argument for the kind of change the speaker is advocating. The word "change" appears both anaphorically at the beginning and as punctuation at the end of each of the speaker's riffs. The process of changing is one that the speaker promises will be "for the better" of the audience, one that will make them "into a realreal together thing." The speaker conceives of this audience, whom he addresses directly as "u," as full of potential, as "a match" the speaker "wd light . . . into something beautiful" (Lee, *Don't Cry, Scream* 36). But this faith in potential doesn't mean that the audience escapes critique. As the poem picks up speed, this refrain morphs from "change" to "change nigger" to "change. / know the realenemy" (36) to "change / yr/enemy," and it culminates pointedly in the energetic verbal jazz solo of the poem's final lines:

> know the realenemy. change. know the realenemy. change
>   yr/enemy change know the real
> change know the real enemy change, change, know the
>   realenemy, the realenemy, the real
> realenemy change you're the enemies/ change your change your
>   change your enemy change

> your enemy. know the realenemy, the world's enemy. know them
>   know them know them the
> realenemy change your enemy change your change change
>   change your enemy change change
> change change your change change change.
> your
> mind nigger. (38)

The speaker ultimately advocates for the audience to *change their minds*, to be persuaded by and to adopt a new worldview that activists of the era called "Black consciousness." The means by which the audience will become conscious is by "read[ing] a blackpoem" (37): "blackpoems / will change" (38), the speaker asserts confidently. The encounter with Black poetry, then, is the dynamic rhetorical process by which the ultimate change occurs: through the power of art, the "u"s of the poem will recognize that the "realenemy" is their own minds—a distorted consciousness that has internalized the White values that keep them from being fully empowered Black individuals. The "change change change" the poem calls for is the process by which the audience should cast off the "chain chain chain"s (echoing the chorus of Aretha Franklin's 1967 single "Chain of Fools") of ideological oppression that are the most powerful tool of anti-Black racist institutions. And the implication of this for Black Arts writers is that their primary work as revolutionary artists is *rhetorical* work—that they have to change minds first for any other political or social change to follow.

As this poem demonstrates, Black Arts Movement writers, aesthetic activists who considered their work the "spiritual sister" of the Black Power movement,[1] held poetics as the most powerful mode of persuasion. Poetry of the movement, as poet and literary scholar Cheryl Clarke notes in "*After Mecca*" (2005), served as "a principal instrument of political education about the new blackness" (2). This chapter introduces the ways in which Black Arts poets in particular were dynamic activists in Black Power's culturally nationalistic project to transform what they called assimilationist "Negroes" into self-determining "Black" citizens of the African diaspora. These writers' influence derived specifically from their role as what I call *poet-rhetors*, literary artists who used their acumen as rhetors to advocate publicly for the common good. The Black Arts poets' vocation was to educate the Black public through their commitment to direct action and the rhetorical power of their poetry, transforming the consciousness of their listeners and readers to be open to the political, cultural, and social possibilities of Black nationalism.

In order to do this, Black Arts poets conceived of themselves as educators of the citizenry of the ideal Black nation. They saw themselves as culture bearers and wielders of the word in the traditional West African sense, griots guarding the systematically silenced and denied history of African Americans. They crafted their works with performativity in mind to reach the broadest audience, deploying Black language traditions in ways that approximated the appeal of a musical performance. And they believed that the cultural work of aesthetic creation was not an end in itself, but a beginning, an act that would spark political and social revolution. What follows is an exploration of these contexts and ideologies that undergirded the fundamentally rhetorical mission of Black Arts Movement writers—the hows and whys of their work to change minds.

Black Consciousness and Literary Functionalism in the Black Arts Movement

The Black Arts Movement emerged in the mid-1960s as an aesthetic counterpart to the Black nationalist politics of Black Power. Believing, according to activist Kwame Ture (known as Stokely Carmichael before 1969), that African Americans were "dependent on, and at the discretion of, forces and institutions within the white society which have little interest in representing us honestly" (Carmichael 119), Black nationalists looked to create politically independent, self-determined communities of Black Americans, aiming to secure political efficacy, to make social changes for their own people, and to exist as independently as possible as a nation within a nation. Ture and Charles V. Hamilton define Black Power in 1967 as "a call for black people in this country to unite, to recognize their heritage, to build a sense of community. It is a call for black people to begin to define their own goals, to lead their own organizations and to support those organizations. It is a call to reject the racist institutions and values of this society" (44). Black nationalists saw this movement toward political and social independence as "the revolution."

The range of nationalist ideologies and practices that constituted Black Power politics can be found reflected in the diverse stances of politically engaged Black artists of the era, and some scholars have appropriately resisted monolithic representations of the politics of BAM. As literary historian James Smethurst astutely observes, "Black Arts poetics could be more accurately described as a series of debates linked to ideological and institutional conflict and conversation rather than a consistent practice" (*Black Arts Movement* 57).

Key to these conversations were several influential strains of Black nationalism that gained prominence in the mid-1960s as nonviolent civil rights protest methods experienced declining support: revolutionary nationalism, represented by the Revolutionary Action Movement (RAM) and the Black Panther Party for Self-Defense (BPP), which blended Black nationalism with Marxism-Leninism; conservative or millennial nationalism, represented by the Nation of Islam (NOI), which had developed a following in Black communities beginning in the 1930s and advocated strict racial separatism and predicted the imminent demise of the White race; and cultural nationalism, represented by the US Organization, a group of militant Pan-African cultural nationalists (whose acronym, which signifies "US" versus "THEM," was sometimes also explained to stand for "United Slaves") who aimed to unify Black people under their common culture.[2] At times, these ideological differences, along with less ideological struggles for power, contributed to violence among the cultural nationalist US and the revolutionary nationalist Black Panthers, such as the murder of the BPP's Alprentice "Bunchy" Carter and John Huggins and the wounding of US's Larry Watani-Stiner at UCLA in 1969 (Smethurst, *Black Arts Movement* 302). And while, as Smethurst points out, "these revolutionary nationalists and cultural nationalists emerged from largely the same political and cultural matrix" (249), they themselves often insisted on distinctions between their approaches to Black liberation.

One significant factor that distinguishes these versions of nationalism is their differing stances on Black cultural revolution as a factor in political and social change. While Marxist revolutionary nationalists believed that the change in cultural expression would follow the change in political and economic systems, cultural nationalists saw a renaissance of Black art as the precondition for political action.[3] On this point, cultural nationalist ideologies proved particularly influential to the advent of the Black Arts Movement. Certainly not all Black poets of the 1960s and 1970s—not even all overtly political Black poets of the era—would have called themselves cultural nationalists, and those who did voice Black Power politics often supported the efforts of several Black nationalist initiatives.[4] But Black artists of the era who openly identified with BAM coalesced ideologically around the movement's stated aim: to produce art that helped to form the revolution-primed community whose political eventuality was Black self-determination.

The legendary origin story of the Black Arts Movement credits writer and political activist Amiri Baraka (known as LeRoi Jones before 1967) for founding the movement. A Newark-born writer who left Howard in 1954, Baraka spent the late 1950s and the first half of the 1960s writing within the Beat movement in Greenwich Village. Galvanized by the assassination of Malcolm X in 1965, Baraka left the Greenwich Village scene for Harlem the following month, dedicated himself to Black cultural nationalism, and, with members of the nationalist-leaning Uptown Writers Movement, founded the Black Arts Repertory Theater/School (BART/S)—the event many mark as the Black Arts Movement's formal beginning (ya Salaam, *Magic of Juju* 29).[5]

While it is an oversimplification of the range of artistic and activist efforts across the country that contributed to BAM's flowering to point to Baraka as "the founder" and to BART/S as the definitive beginning, Baraka deserves acknowledgment as the one who named the movement and as perhaps its most prominent proponent and spokesperson (ya Salaam, *Magic of Juju* 37). Both Larry Neal, a poet and one of the key theorists of BAM, and Askia Touré (born Roland Snellings), a poet, visual artist, and theorist of revolutionary nationalism, were highly influential in the blossoming of the early movement on the East Coast and contributed a range of experience in combining cultural and political approaches to revolution from their involvement in RAM and the Uptown Writers Movement.[6] And while BART/S served as an example of the significance of institution building to the Black Arts project, its flowering was short-lived, lasting less than a year, and it did not establish Harlem as the definitive center of the movement. Instead, as Smethurst, ya Salaam, and others have argued, the Black Arts Movement developed from local and regional grassroots activism across the country, with particularly vibrant activity in the San Francisco Bay Area, Chicago, Detroit, New York, Newark, and New Orleans, that coalesced into a national movement under the shared goal of supporting rich Black cultural production that would help lead to Black political self-determination (ya Salaam, *Magic of Juju* x–xi).[7]

Arguably the most influential figure in the development of the Black Arts Movement is Malcolm X, although he did not live to see the movement come to life. While histories of the movement often acknowledge Malcolm X's influence on Baraka and on the advent of the Black Arts Movement through the tragedy of his death, to acknowledge Malcolm X's relationship to BAM *only* in this way is to grossly understate his significance in the development of cultural nationalism after 1964. As Larry Neal articulates Malcolm X's ideological influence, "Malcolm covered everything—nationhood, manhood, the family, brotherhood, history, and the Third World revolution. Yet it always seemed to me that he was talking about a revolution of the psyche, about how we should see ourselves in the world" (13–14). Beyond his assassination as an impetus for many to radicalize in the direction of Black Power in the mid-1960s, Malcolm X provided the ideological basis for the flowering of Black cultural nationalist movements, which he articulated at the founding rally of the Organization of Afro-American Unity (OAAU) on June 28, 1964, just eight months before his murder. Malcolm X's aim for the OAAU, which he modeled after the Pan-African, anti-colonialist Organization of African Unity, was "to fight whoever gets in our way, to bring about the complete independence of people of African descent here in the Western Hemisphere, and first here in the United States, and bring about the freedom of these people by any means necessary." A central part of this work, he asserts, is a "cultural revolution" whose aim is "to unbrainwash an entire people." Black artists were to fuel this cultural revolution by creating works that would educate Black people about the richness of their heritage to encourage them to embrace a positive Black identity, one based on a diasporic, Pan-African conception of Blackness. The cognitive dissonance that Black audiences would experience when confronted aesthetically with the contrast between the greatness of the African past and the harsh realities of a present in White supremacist America would spur them to participate in political action. As Malcolm X puts it, "When you let the black man in America know where he once was and what he once had, why, he only needs to look at himself now to realize something criminal was done to him to bring him down to the low condition that he's in today. Once he realizes what was done, how it was done, where it was done, when it was done, and who did it, that knowledge in itself will usher in your action program. And it will be by any means necessary." Malcolm X's plan was to create a cultural center in Harlem to serve as the epicenter of the cultural revolution, a community organization "which will include people of all ages and will conduct workshops in all of the arts, such as film, creative writing, painting, theater, music, and the entire spectrum of Afro-American history" (Malcolm X, "Speech"). When Baraka founded BART/S after Malcolm X's assassination in 1965, it was an effort, as Baraka writes in "A Poem for Black Hearts" (1965), not only to "avenge ourselves for his death" (Jones, "A Poem" 58) but to build literally from Malcolm X's blueprint for the beginning of a cultural revolution in Black America. Baraka later said of the project, "We went up town to Harlem and opened a theater, and blew a billion words into the firmament like black prayers to force change. And some change came. Some still changing" (*Raise* 112).

The linguistic and aesthetic particularities of these "billion words" proved significant to the Black Arts Movement project at large: to usher in a revolution, not just any art would do. Throughout the hubs of movement activity that sprang up across the country in the decade following 1965, Black Arts activists saw art not only as a way to express support for nationalist politics but as the *primary* rhetorical agent of change for Black nationalist efforts. Along with the expectation that the expressive character of Black art deeply and evocatively represents the Black experience in America, art also had to adhere to a strict functionalism, with its most important quality its ability to reach and change Black audiences. Movement activists developed a theoretical framework for the ideal production of Black art, conceptualizing a "Black aesthetic" that forwarded a separate, unapologetically Black set of criteria for the creation and assessment of art by Black artists and about Black life. As Neal explains it in 1968, "A main tenet of Black Power is the necessity for black people to define the world in their own terms. The black artist has made the same point in the context of aesthetics" (62).

Baraka's dedication to the kind of cultural revolution that Malcolm X envisioned led him to advocate the theories of Maulana Ron Karenga (born Ron Everett), cultural nationalist activist, Afrocentric theorist, and cofounder of the US organization. In a provocative essay for the January 1968 issue of *Negro Digest*, Karenga asserts the need for a Black aesthetic that would provide the "criteria for judging the validity and/or the beauty of a work of art" ("Black Art" 5). Positing that all art should be judged on both its aesthetic and its social dimensions, Karenga argues that the social impact outweighs the aesthetic impact, "For art does not exist in the abstract just like freedom does not exist in the abstract" (8). Making plain his stance in the context of the mid-1960s, he asserts in no uncertain terms that "all art must reflect and support the Black Revolution, and any art that does not discuss and contribute to the revolution is invalid" (5).

Applying the work of Senegalese cultural theorist, poet, and politician Léopold Senghor, Karenga proposes that Black art adhere to three criteria that he sees as characteristic of all African art: that it be functional, collective, and committing or committed ("Black Art" 5–6). Writing off the idea of "art for art's sake" as a "false doctrine," he defines functional as useful, where the explicit use of Black art is to "expose the enemy, praise the people, and support the revolution"—or more colorfully, "If we must paint oranges and trees, let our guerillas be eating those oranges for strength and using those trees for cover" (6). This revolutionary function relates closely to the second criterion of collectivity: that art "move with the masses and be moved by the masses" (7). For art to be collective, "it must be from the people and must be returned to the people in a form more beautiful and colorful than it was in real life. For that is what art is: everyday life given more form and color" (6–7). This aesthetic representation of everyday life would cause individuals to recognize characteristics of their own lives and subsequently invest themselves in membership in the Black collective. But the relationship between artist and audience—and the learning experience catalyzed by the creation of art—is necessarily reciprocal: artists must conceive of their work both "as a means of educating the people, and being educated by them, so that it is a mutual exchange rather than a one-way communication" (7). The third criterion, commitment, follows from the belief that membership in the Black collective would lead to solidarity, and solidarity would lead to the desire to enact political revolution. According to Karenga, art "must commit us to revolution and change. It must commit to us a future that is ours" (9). Karenga resists the critique that abiding by the three criteria limits artistic freedom, insisting that this version of the Black aesthetic merely pushes artists away from creating individualistically (according to a doctrine of "'me' in spite of everyone") and instead encourages creating diversely by expressing personality in a way that acknowledges culture and context (from an understanding of "'me' in relation to everyone") (7). Baraka explains this version of artistic freedom in a 1968 interview for the *Guardian* as "the right to express those goals in any way your personality ... conceives of it" (qtd. in Sollors 190). For Karenga, Baraka, and other proponents of this kind of aesthetic functionalism, the stakes were high. Art was the match that would light a revolution for self-determination in Black America. What the Black Arts Movement asked of its artists, then, was a commitment to creating "art for all our sake" (Karenga, "Black Art" 6).

As the face of BAM, Baraka was influential in advocating for Karenga's theories as the basis for the aesthetics and politics of the movement. While Baraka and Madhubuti were strongly influenced by Karenga, as were to a degree fellow Black Arts writers Larry Neal, Sonia Sanchez, Askia Touré, and Kalamu ya Salaam, they still diverged from Karenga on significant issues—Baraka by valuing the continuum of African American cultural production instead of solely valuing a "prehistoric neo-African counterculture" (as represented by the celebration of Kwanzaa, which Karenga initiated) and Madhubuti by arguing for dynamic roles for women in the movement (Smethurst, *Black Arts Movement* 58). Indeed, activists propounded a number of different iterations of Black aesthetic theory, many of which, including Karenga's, appear in the 1971 volume *The Black Aesthetic*, edited by literary critic Addison Gayle. The collection compiles essays, both contemporary and historical, that offer perspectives on "the function of the black artist in the American society and of the necessity for new and different critical approaches to the artistic endeavors of black artists" (Gayle xxiii). While *The Black Aesthetic* aims to amplify a variety of voices in the critical conversation, Gayle notes two places of common ground among the theorists: the understanding, first, that "the black artist, due to his historical position in America at the present time, is engaged in a war with this nation that will determine the future of black art," and, second, that "unique art derived from unique cultural experiences mandates unique critical tools for evaluation" (xxiii). As an expression of both points, many theorists offer versions of the Black aesthetic that reject the values of the global "West," a term they use to refer to White culture writ large. Baraka predicts in 1964 that critics of a Black aesthetic would object to politically oriented art, noting wryly in "The Revolutionary Theatre" that "[m]ost white Western artists do not need to be 'political,' since usually, whether they know it or not, they are in complete sympathy with the most repressive social forces in the world today" (Jones, *Home* 214). Black aesthetic theorists observe instead that the Western aesthetic's "universal" standards are actually cultural—created by those within Western culture in line with their particular experiences and values.

The argument for creating separate values for Black art depended, then, on defining Black culture as existing generatively outside the bounds of Western culture, which has historically and systematically denied aesthetic representations of Black experience a claim to "universal" significance. In "Tripping with Black Writing," poet and Black Studies activist Sarah Webster Fabio's contribution to *The Black Aesthetic*, Fabio outlines the work of destroying the Western category of "universality," which she describes as a "simple-minded, fascist, pseudo-Europeanized mandate," "a funk issue in any aesthetic consideration. A hustle to make walleyed, white-eyed America the all-seeing Cyclops of our age." She praises the work of Black writers past and present for "[b]ringing black perspective, black aesthetic, black rhetoric, black language to add authenticity to the felt reality. Knowing America has no rhetoric matching its racist reality; no reality matching its 'universal' and 'democratic' idealistic state of existence" (180). As Fabio argues, Black writers must continue to innovate the Black tradition of "speaking in tongues" with their own linguistic and aesthetic forms of expression to articulate their experiences on their own terms and leave behind White aesthetic ideals that hypocritically purport to assess all art by European-skewed expectations (173, 178). Hoyt Fuller, writer and editor of *Negro Digest / Black World*, provides a poignant example in his essay "Towards a Black Aesthetic" (originally published in the *Critic* in 1968) of the racism wielded toward Black writers by critics who vaunt the "universal," pointing to a review by poet and critic Louis Simpson of Gwendolyn Brooks's *Selected Poems* that appeared in the *New York Herald Tribune Book Week* in October 1963. (Brooks, who in the late 1960s threw the full weight of her writing career into Black Arts Movement activism, was already a Pulitzer Prize-winning poet at the time of the review.) Simpson's review includes the statement, "I am not sure it is possible for a Negro to write well without making us aware he is a Negro. On the other hand, if being a Negro is the only subject, the writing is not important" (qtd. in Fuller 4). Fuller interpolates from Simpson's statement "the plain but unstated assumption ... that there are no 'universal values' and no 'universal implications' in Negro life" (5). In addition to pointing out the obvious racist assumptions at play in Simpson's assessment of Brooks's work, Fuller also problematizes White critics' presumption that Western aesthetic "universals" serve the needs of Black Americans. He remarks wryly, "The 'great bard of Avon' has only limited relevance to the revolutionary spirit raging in the ghetto. Which is not to say that the black revolutionaries reject the 'universal' statements inherent in Shakespeare's works; what they do reject, however, is the literary assumption that the style and language and the concerns of Shakespeare establish the appropriate limits and 'frame of reference' for black poetry and people" (8).

Addison Gayle goes further in "Cultural Strangulation: Black Literature and the White Aesthetic," his essay for the volume (originally published in *Negro Digest* in 1969), by arguing that the aesthetic values inherent in traditional Western works—the standards of beauty and morality that equate Whiteness with goodness and beauty and Blackness with evil and ugliness, beginning with the writings of Plato—alienate and disparage Black selfhood (42). To free themselves and their audiences from these damaging cultural connotations, Black writers need not only an appropriate "frame of reference" that fundamentally connects Black art to Black cultural life, but a new language of aesthetic value. According to Gayle, "[T]he extent of the cultural strangulation of Black literature by white critics has been the extent to which they have been allowed to define the terms in which the Black artist will deal with his own experience." He argues that the first step in this fight is to reframe Blackness as something inherently beautiful, not only capable of aesthetic merit but exemplary of it (44). As part of the Black Arts rhetorical project, these new values that would free Black people from "cultural strangulation" are the fruits of a revolution in both the existing aesthetic values and the broader social order.

In the introduction to *The Black Aesthetic*, Gayle is adamant that a Black aesthetic must be a theory that works in the world. Critiquing Aristotelian Criticism, Practical Criticism, Formalist Criticism, and New Criticism as theories that "[aim] to evaluate the work of art in terms of *its* beauty and not in terms of the transformation from ugliness to beauty that the work of art demands from its audience," Gayle insists instead that "a critical methodology has no relevance to the black community unless it aids men in becoming better than they are," a process that involves evaluating a work of art for how far it has gone "in transforming an American Negro into an African-American or black man" (xxii). The rhetorical impact of Black art, then, is fundamental to Black aesthetic theory, and those Black writers who committed themselves to aesthetic functionalism as part of the movement did so for the sake of the larger creative product of defining and shaping Black selfhood. Indeed, proponents of the Black aesthetic construed "Blackness" as a creative project in itself—perhaps the movement's most important rhetorical project. As Karenga put it in 1968, "[T]he battle we are waging now is the battle for the minds of Black people, and ... if we lose this battle, we cannot win the violent one" ("Black Art" 5). Movement theorists and artists saw Blackness as a consciousness one achieves—essentially by eradicating all connections to White culture and social expectations and by valuing instead the particularities of Black American culture and African diasporic heritage.

The concept of "Black consciousness" arose as a revision of the concept of "double consciousness," articulated by sociologist and intellectual W. E. B. Du Bois first in "Strivings of the Negro People" in 1897 and again influentially in *The Souls of Black Folk* in 1903. "The Negro," Du Bois argues, is "born with a veil, and gifted with second-sight in this American world,—a world which yields him no true self consciousness, but only lets him see himself through the revelation of the other world. It is a peculiar sensation, this double-consciousness, this sense of always looking at one's self through the eyes of others, of measuring one's soul by the tape of a world that looks on in amused contempt and pity" (214–15). Du Bois believes that this dual perception of self causes an individual to exist as two separate beings: "One ever feels his twoness—an American, a Negro; two souls, two thoughts, two unreconciled strivings; two warring ideals in one dark body, whose dogged strength alone keeps it from being torn asunder" (215). Black Arts activists sought to end the ongoing internal struggle caused by the conflict between Black experience and White ideals by helping their audience members to resolve their double consciousness into a single, unified Black consciousness—a process that would involve violence of its own. Larry Neal proclaims in his essay "And Shine Swam On" (1968), "[T]he first violence will be internal—the destruction of a weak spiritual self for a more perfect self. But it will be a necessary violence" (23). Art was to be the tool that facilitated this process, the knife that would be first a surgical implement and then a revolutionary weapon. Neal calls the process one of self-integration, asserting, "We must liberate ourselves, destroy the double consciousness. We must integrate with ourselves, understand that we have within us a great vision, revolutionary and spiritual in nature, understanding that the West is dying and offers little promise of rebirth" (21). The Black consciousness that results from this process is inherently creative and generative, leading not only to self-love but to love of community. The political eventuality, Black Arts writers hoped, was that an awareness of what it was to be Black in America would lead, as Malcolm X predicted, to active moves toward nationalistic collectivity. And Black Arts activists believed that art would serve as the rhetorical catalyst of this metamorphosis.

This call to consciousness necessarily involved definitions of Blackness that starkly rejected White values and behaviors. Writers advocated separation from Whiteness on two levels: first, through the identification of Whites and White ideas as oppressor and, second, through the identification of behaviors or beliefs within Black communities that some believed capitulated to White oppression. This second level of separating resulted in an intraracial taxonomizing, a hypothetical distancing of those who were "culturally White" from the conscious Black collective. In its most extreme manifestations in Black Arts Movement writing, critical depictions of White culture punctuated by derogatory epithets, sometimes specifically anti-Semitic, appear within imperative descriptions of explicit physical violence. This language of violence toward Whites appears alongside language of violence toward unenlightened, capitulating "Negroes," suggesting an equation of the two groups as common enemies of revolutionary consciousness. Additionally, in some iterations of Black nationalist ideology—specifically those that valued patriarchal heterosexual unions as the microcosm of the new Black community—enemy forces of the revolution include homosexuality (which some considered a specifically White pathology) and agency of women in roles outside of supporting the male "warriors" of nationalist movements. For this reason, some Black Arts writing is strewn with homophobic and misogynistic language as well. It is important to remember, however, that not all Black Arts writers adhered to strict, essentialist conceptions of Blackness and that some of those who did promote them did so strategically. Movement writers and activists believed that those capitulating to White culture continued to do so because of a lack of awareness of their oppression, acknowledging that the desire to adhere to White ideals resulted from entrapment in and oppression by institutions of White power—learned behavior resulting from centuries of inculcation in these values. For many, the call to rally around Black identity was not an expectation of uniformity but a rhetorical means by which to convince others to reject the values of the cult of Whiteness as an oppressive force that had long been used to stifle Black empowerment. This is not to excuse the egregious extremes of this rhetoric, but it is important to complicate the idea that all Black Arts or Black Power rhetoric earnestly advocated the extremes.

One set of strict identity categories that proved central to this rhetorical work, however, was the assertion of "Black" as the ideological opposite of "Negro"—a shift initiated by increased circulation in the late 1950s and early 1960s of the theology and rhetoric of NOI leader Elijah Muhammad, primarily through his then-spokesman Malcolm X (Sanchez, "Poet as Creator" 27). As activists increasingly self-identified as "Black," they referred to "culturally White" individuals disparagingly as "Negroes," making the term representative of the old, skewed consciousness of unrealized Black selfhood. Where support of nationalist politics indicated consciousness, adherence to belief in the efficacy of nonviolent protest, integration, and civil rights legislation indicated a "Negro" mentality—not merely because of the difference in political views but because the older set of beliefs indicated faith in and a seeming desire for White acceptance. Holding any social position or job seen as dependent upon Whites or White authority, such as bureaucrat, police officer, or White-popular entertainer, indicated "Negro" consciousness as well. Capitulation to White aesthetic standards, in terms of both body image and speech, stood as another defining characteristic—the valuing of straight hair, lighter skin, "White" ways of speaking. Coming to Black consciousness necessarily meant that valuing anything associated with White America equated to worshipping a false god, and identifying as "Negro" indicated a lack of self-knowledge and self-love as a person of African descent. As Malcolm X expresses the sentiment in 1964, "When you have no knowledge of your history, you're just another animal; in fact, you're a Negro; something that's nothing.... You are Negro because you don't know who you are, you don't know what you are, you don't know where you are, and you don't know how you got here. But as soon as you wake up and find out the positive answer to all these things, you cease being a Negro. You become somebody" ("Speech"). Black Arts Movement proponents followed the prescription Malcolm X gives here for the process of leaving behind "Negro" existence. The alternative to being a "Negro" is to become "Black" by gaining consciousness about the value of one's Africanness and to abandon any desire for or to be with Whiteness. The only kind of integration supported by Black Arts activists, then, is the tongue-in-cheek version Haki Madhubuti presents in his poem "The New Integrationist":

> I
> seek
> integration
> of
> negroes
> with
> black
> people (Lee, *Black Pride* 11)

Beyond rejecting Whiteness, full attainment of Black consciousness necessitated embracing a diasporic Pan-African identity. In Malcolm X's formulation, Africanness negates Negroness, even in the minds of White folks: "They don't call Africans Negroes. Why, I had a white man tell me the other day, 'He's not a Negro.' Here the man was black as night, and the white man told me, 'He's not a Negro, he's an African.' I said, 'Well, listen to him'" ("Speech"). In line with Malcolm X and inspired by the international political climate of the time, Black Arts activists, notably Baraka and Karenga, forwarded Pan-Africanist ideology aesthetically and politically. The leaders of BAM had watched the succession of revolutions beginning in the mid-1950s in which African countries threw off their imperialist colonizers: Sudan in 1956, Ghana in 1957, Nigeria and the Congo in 1960, Sierra Leone in 1961, Algeria in 1962, Kenya in 1963, Zambia in 1964, Gambia in 1965, and others continuing into the 1970s (Warren 21). Baraka asserted a connection to African sensibility as essential to the quest for national culture and consciousness, pointing to the struggle of those in the African revolutions as a model for the efficacy of nationalist revolutionary ideals. Baraka related the struggle of Black Americans against White Americans to that of Africans against their colonizers, calling upon Black people in the "colonies" of the urban ghettoes to throw off their White oppressors and declare themselves a unified cultural nation. Ideologically, the revalorization of African culture in place of Western culture represented to movement theorists a decolonization of the mind. Karenga believed that Black Americans, who had been exploited by American culture, should consider themselves a transnational African people, and their artistic work specifically and cultural productions more broadly should reflect this shift in cultural focus (Van Deburg 171–72).

Despite the call to identify with and support a geographically broad diasporic community, the movement's strict prescriptions for Black art and Black selfhood, specifically insofar as these prescriptions unflinchingly rejected White culture, led movement artists to relate antagonistically to past eras of Black American writing. Some writers rejected earlier work on the grounds that Black writers in previous eras capitulated to the demands of the Western aesthetic and, in doing so, subordinated themselves to White approval. Black Arts writers' rejection of the Western aesthetic turned them off from any writing that employed the high style and esotericism of traditional Western literary forms—what Neal calls "the dead forms taught most writers in white man's schools" (20)—especially because they were likely inaccessible to broad Black audiences. Baraka even places the term "literary" itself under fire, depicting "literary Negroes" as Western cultural dependents who vomit up lifeless White creations: the problem with "SoCalled 'Literary Negroes,'" he claims, is that "[t]here is still an entrail, an inside navel connection with the bodies of the dead. The dead white babies puked out in a slow trickle and researched and sprayed, for life, and stood up and made to curtsy, an agonizing computerized boogaloo going for straighten up and be intelligent" (Jones, *Home* 122).

The most vitriolic representations of "literary Negroes" from past eras were of the Harlem Renaissance or New Negro Movement of the 1920s and 1930s. While Black Arts writers did not reject artists of the era wholesale—and in particular praised aspects of the work of Langston Hughes, Sterling Brown, Claude McKay, and Zora Neale Hurston[8]—the Harlem Renaissance posed a problem for Black Arts activists in that the goals of their movement seemed cut from the same cloth as those of New Negro Movement activists, and the New Negro Movement seemingly failed to achieve significant political outcomes. As New Negro Renaissance theorist Alain Locke expresses the aims of the rebellious writers of his era in "Negro Youth Speaks" in 1925, "Our poets have now stopped speaking for the Negro—they speak as Negroes. Where they formerly spoke to others and tried to interpret, they now speak to their own and try to express" (48). Although their work was akin to the Black Arts Movement in ideology, many writers of the Harlem Renaissance received criticism from Black Arts activists for their failure to engage the Black public in their art. Haki Madhubuti charges in his essay for *The Black Aesthetic* that the production of art during the Harlem Renaissance operated at an elite level, generally for the patronage of uptown Whites. Most Black folks living in Harlem at the time, he asserts, did not know that a literary movement was taking place, quoting Langston Hughes as admitting, "The ordinary Negroes hadn't heard of the Negro Renaissance" (qtd. in "Toward a Definition" 223). Larry Neal reinforces this criticism in a 1968 essay, charging that "[t]he so-called Harlem Renaissance was, for the most part, a fantasy-era for most black writers and their white friends. For the people of the community, it never even existed. It was a thing apart" (17).

Black Arts writers proposed to correct the Harlem Renaissance's failure by connecting art to Black life in terms of both creation and distribution—a connection they accomplished most successfully through attention to the dynamics of Black vernacular language. Use of Black language practices contributed to the Black Arts Movement project on several levels. First, in employing communicative practices familiar to the audience they wished to reach, writers foregrounded the revolutionary project of the work; presenting their message in the insular language of the Black community indicated writers' desire to address their message specifically to Black audiences. Second, Black vernacular culture provided artists with aesthetic forms and expressive modes that existed self-sufficiently outside of the White aesthetic realm. As Madhubuti notes of Black Arts writers' embracing of the vernacular for this purpose, "The language of the new writers seems to move in one direction; that is to say that the poets of the sixties are actually defining and legitimating their own communicative medium.... It's the language of the street, charged so as to heighten the sensitivity level of the reader" (Lee, "Toward a Definition" 226). Third, although a portion of the movement's definition of Blackness relied on opposition to White culture and values, celebrating the use of the Black vernacular helped them to positively define Black selfhood through practices already integral to individual and community identities. To associate oneself with a type of English that is overtly culturally Black would mean asserting an identity for oneself within the Black community. The use of uniquely Black language practices would also indicate a refusal to accept as dominant or authoritative the language of the White oppressor. By consciously rejecting the social dominance of White language, Black Arts writers consciously refused domination by the White worldview. The purposeful use of Black vernacular language was part of the rhetorical process of decolonizing Black minds. Writers turned instead to "Black English" (as African American Vernacular English was termed by linguists and proponents in the 1970s) in their search for a distinctly Black aesthetic and communicative form.[9]

Additionally, for the purposes of the verbal artist, Black English was the Black cultural form that most closely approximated the cultural function of music. Many Black Arts writers, notably Baraka, Neal, and Touré, held music as the communicative ideal—the purest form of Black cultural expression. And poetry was the next best thing, or as poet and activist Keorapetse Kgositsile expresses this view, "poetry is music made less abstract" (241). According to Neal in "And Shine Swam On," "The key where black people have to go is in the music. Our music has always been the most dominant manifestation of what we are and feel, literature was just an afterthought, the step taken by the Negro bourgeoisie who desired acceptance on the white man's terms. And that is precisely why literature has failed. It was the case of one elite addressing another elite" (21). Beyond serving as a model for expressivity, music demonstrated that art could have an organic and functional role in the Black community. This functionality and accessibility were crucial for the rhetorical aim of raising revolutionary consciousness, and Black Arts writers believed that art that was integrated into the lifework of a people was more culturally and historically true to African sensibilities. Traditional African peoples, according to Neal, experienced art *as* art "merely incidentally, for it was essentially functional in its natural setting" (16). Kgositsile goes so far as to call art "meaningless" without functional integration into the lived experiences of a people: "Poetry, like any other 'art' form, is meaningless, that is, has no use—beauty and good, inseparable—unless it be a specific act actual as dance or childbirth, carved bleeding from history, our experience" (244).

The goal became, then, to reformulate literature as a cultural product akin to the musical ethos: to create a literature that could exist organically within the community, and that, like music, could be the source of "collective ritual" (Neal 22). For this to be possible, the poet would have to take on a central and vital community role, which was modeled for poets by musicians. Touré asserts in "Keep on Pushin': Rhythm & Blues as a Weapon" (1965) that "[o]ur main philosophical and cultural attitudes are displayed through our MUSIC, which serves as the ROOT of our culture; from which spring our art, poetry, literature, etc. Our creative artists—especially singers and musicians—function as PRIESTS, as PHILOSOPHERS of our captive nation; a holdover from our ancient past" (Snellings 87). Neal expresses a similar belief, pointing to blues musicians (though Black Arts writers would point to jazz and R & B musicians as well) as "the true heroes and poets of the community because they are able to reveal the essential essence of human experiences. In this sense they are as spiritually dedicated to their tasks as any minister or social revolutionary."[10]

Blues musicians communicate the people's suffering back to themselves, and their connections to the people's experiences have made them and their art integral to the community's functioning. As Neal argues in "The Ethos of the Blues" (1971), "The singer is aware that his audience has been through the same changes as he has. His task is to express through his craft their suffering and his. Everything and everyone who he has encountered on his journey of the soul is mirrored in his art. He is appreciated as a meaningful member of the community to the degree to which he expresses the conscious and unconscious spirit of that community. Therefore, the blues singer should not be viewed apart from the community ethos that produced him" (115). Poets and their art, according to Black Arts theorists, should function within the community in the same way: as Neal argues in "I Sing of Shine," "Black literature must become an integral part of the community's life-style" (20). What has kept this from happening, Neal concludes, is that Black poets, influenced by White European ideals, have placed too much value on print as a marker of aesthetic value. He asserts, "[W]e have been tied to the texts, like most white poets. The text could be destroyed and no one would be hurt in the least by it. The key is in the music" (21). Many Black Arts writers embraced poetry, which is both inherently performative and easily distributable, as the genre through which they could free themselves from the necessity of publication and make conscious art exist centrally in Black people's daily lives.

With this goal in mind, the transition from Black music to Black English was not a difficult one. If music itself could not be translated, the language of musicians provided a significant source for *Black semantics*—the totality of idioms, terms, and expressions that are commonly used by Black Americans (Smitherman, *Talkin and Testifyin* 42–43). Music also related intimately to the structure and performative nature of many of what Geneva Smitherman, an influential sociolinguist who worked to codify the linguistic and rhetorical features of Black English in the 1970s, called the *modes of discourse* within Black English. Smitherman identifies two distinct groups in relation to language within African American culture. One group, significantly smaller than the other, consisted of the educated, literate Black elite. The other group consisted of the "Black masses," which related to language through folk-oral traditions. According to Smitherman, the Black experience of the educated group tended to be expressed in Standard American English (SAE) (the English codified in grammar books as "proper" English), while the language of Africanized-English speakers retained certain types of speech acts derived from African oral culture (*Talkin and Testifyin* 103). These formulaically structured speech acts, which took the form of verbal strategies, rhetorical devices, and expressive rituals, constituted the Black English modes of discourse. For movement writers, the strong oral inclination of these verbal art forms approximated the performative aspects of music. According to Neal, "We can learn more about what poetry is by listening to the cadences in Malcolm's speeches than from most of Western poetics. Listen to James Brown scream. Ask yourself, then: Have you ever heard a Negro poet sing like that?" (20–21). Artists who took on this mission valued above all what Cheryl Clarke describes as "the ultra-public role, the rambunctious orality, and the communal commitments of the poetry" (3). Because much of Black English, especially its modes of discourse, derives from the depth and character in oral culture, Black Arts Movement writers created work meant not only to be published but to be performed. The natural performability of Black English fit well into BAM's ideology of accessibility. Although music stood as the purest form of Black communication for some Black Arts theorists, Black English could approximate the musical ethos if performed—or conveyed on paper to resemble the language of performance. The emphasis on performance was not merely an ideological concern but a practical one. The linguistic and cultural inclusiveness of the writers' message would have no bearing if the information did not reach the Black public. With regard to written work specifically, Black English served as a communicative compromise between being true to the ideal of performance and the need to use publication of written texts as a resource to reach broader audiences.

Irrespective of the linguistic attributes of the writing, writers of the movement knew that mainstream publishers of the time would not value work inspired by and intended for Black readers—and that a significant portion of Black America was thoroughly uninterested in or unaware of literary books produced by White-owned publishing houses. Haki Madhubuti hyperbolically expresses this concern in a 1969 article for the *Black Scholar*, boldly asserting, "We as black poets and writers are aware of the fact that the masses (and I do not use the word lightly for I am part of the masses) of black people *do not read books*" (Lee, "Directions for Black Writers" 55). In line with their rhetorical mission to broadly spread the message of Black consciousness and nationalist politics to the Black public, Black Arts activists worked to disseminate their writing instead through a variety of independently produced and more accessible media. Modes of publication included chapbooks, produced inexpensively through Black-owned independent presses and by self-distribution; broadsides; leftist and movement-affiliated journals and magazines;

records; and live performances in Black communities and at universities.[11] This energetic effort to reach Black audiences by any means necessary demonstrates the vital rhetorical function of Black Arts writing: writers were fundamentally concerned not just with the creation but with the distribution of the work in such a way that it would have a palpable social impact.

And despite Madhubuti's concern above, the readerly culture of the "Black masses," which Black Arts writers cultivated thoughtfully and strategically, made the Black Arts Movement possible. Nationally distributed magazines and journals brought both the creative work and the ideological debates of the movement to broad audiences in Black communities, reaching beyond the upper- and middle-class elite in a way that was unprecedented in previous eras of Black literary activism. New York–based leftist journals *Freedomways* and *Liberator* published early work by Black Arts writers, but by the latter half of the 1960s a number of journals emerged that were specifically dedicated to publishing Black literary, scholarly, and political writing, including *Black Dialogue* (literature), *Soulbook* (politics and poetry), the *Journal of Black Poetry* (poetry), and the *Black Scholar* (Black Studies scholarship) (ya Salaam, "Black Arts Movement"). The most important periodical by far, however, was the Chicago-based and nationally distributed monthly magazine *Negro Digest*, which was renamed *Black World* in 1970. Launched in 1942 by the Johnson Publishing Company (which would become the largest Black-owned publishing company in the world) as a *Reader's Digest* for Black audiences, *Negro Digest / Black World* was a vital resource for the movement because of its established national readership and existing infrastructure for popular distribution.[12] Edited by well-connected and respected intellectual, writer, and activist Hoyt Fuller, *Negro Digest / Black World* published literary work by both emerging and established Black writers as well as criticism, political and literary theory, and a column by Fuller called "Perspectives" that announced conferences, publications, and significant events in the literary world (ya Salaam, "Black Arts Movement").[13] When Johnson Publishing shut down the magazine in 1976, reportedly over controversy about the magazine's publication of pro-Palestinian pieces, the Black Arts Movement suffered a major blow. With a readership that Fuller estimated at 180,000 in 1971 (Smethurst, *Black Arts Movement* 408), *Negro Digest / Black World* was arguably the primary vehicle by which print work of the movement reached broad audiences across Black communities.

In addition, two independent Black presses founded during the movement, Dudley Randall's Broadside Press in Detroit and Haki Madhubuti's Third World Press in Chicago, proved pivotal to poets of the movement in particular in making their books, chapbooks, broadsides, and recordings affordable for and accessible to Black readers. Beginning with publishing a broadside of his poem "Ballad of Birmingham" from his home office in 1965, Dudley Randall grew Broadside Press into the movement's central publishing house for both established and emerging Black poets, producing the work of more than four hundred poets in the over one hundred titles that made up the press's catalogue by 1975—an effort that earned Randall the honorific "the father of the black poetry movement" from *Black Enterprise* in 1978 (ya Salaam, "Black Arts Movement"; "Dudley Randall"). Beyond poetry, the press also published the Broadside Critics series for works of literary criticism and the Broadside Voices series for recorded performances by poets of the movement ("Dudley Randall"). Broadside Press is still in existence, having evolved in a number of ways since 1965—most recently by merging with poet Naomi Long Madgett's Lotus Press in 2015 to become Broadside Lotus Press. Similarly, Third World Press, which Haki Madhubuti founded in 1967 with support from fellow Chicago poets Johari Amini and Carolyn Rodgers, had humble beginnings but grew into an institution vital to the Black Arts Movement and one that would outlast the movement's flourishing. The press's first publications were produced in Madhubuti's basement apartment on a used mimeograph machine and funded by an honorarium Madhubuti had received from a poetry reading ("About Third World Press Foundation"), but its catalogue grew significantly to include literature across genres (including children's literature) and texts representing a broad range of Black Studies disciplines, aiming to put relevant, consciousness-raising books into the hands of those members of the masses who Madhubuti doubted had read books before. As a testament to its significance, Third World Press has published continuously since its founding, giving it the record for longevity among Black publishing houses in America.

Broadside Press and Third World Press were indispensable resources for the Black Arts Movement because of writers' insistence on publishing their work with independent Black presses instead of allowing White-controlled presses to continue to be gatekeepers of and profit from their creative work. For example, Gwendolyn Brooks notably severed her existing relationship with the mainstream Harper publishing house to publish with Broadside Press (and later Third World Press) when she joined the Black Arts Movement in the late 1960s. And the productions of Broadside Press and Third World Press did not conform to mainstream press limitations of how poetry should be published. As literary scholar Margo Natalie Crawford observes, BAM artists worked purposefully to counter the privileged nature of traditional texts and to offer alternative avenues into aesthetic literacies that would be more accessible to Black audiences at large. This significantly included mixed-media works (such as broadsides and books composed specifically as handbooks and children's books) that incorporated images and representations of orality alongside conventional written text—an innovation that Crawford reads as a way to make "the black book a type of counterpublic" catered specifically to Black readers (82–83).

Black Arts poets also significantly did not insist on printed versions of their works. Amiri Baraka's influential poem "Black Art," for example, which many read as an *ars poetica* for the movement, first appeared not in print but as a recording on free jazz musician Sunny Murray's 1965 album, *Sonny's Time Now*.[14] Poets throughout the movement, including Amiri Baraka, Sonia Sanchez, Nikki Giovanni, Haki Madhubuti, Jayne Cortez, and Sarah Webster Fabio, released records of their poems, and some poets, notably Gil Scott-Heron, the Last Poets, and the Watts Prophets, used records as their primary publishing medium. BART/S literally took poetry to the streets, performing ostentatiously on the streets of Harlem for anyone who would listen. Aiming to get the message to the people by any means necessary—but to maximize the power of the aesthetic in particular to persuade any and every Black person about the need for a revolution—the poets took on a mission to meet people where they were and hoped that the people would be convinced to meet them on the front lines.

An African Americentric Rhetorical Framework for Assessing Black Arts Poetics

The texts that Black Arts writers produced within this rich context tell the full story of the movement's rhetorical mission. And delving into the texts as a means of assessing the movement's rhetorical impact requires understanding the influences from American, African, and European rhetorical traditions that informed their interventions. In crafting a framework to evaluate the rhetorical work of Black Arts writers, I have assembled what literary scholar Bernard W. Bell would call an "African Americentric" set of rhetorical theories. Bell describes African Americentric approaches to texts as follows: "While implicitly acknowledging the complex interrelationship of chromosomes, color, ethnicity, class, gender, geography, age, culture, sexuality, consciousness, commitment, conscience, and choice in identity formations, African Americentrism names the specific historical and national grounding in the United States of

[a] dual mode of epistemological, ontological, and cultural inquiry in a particular language and worldview" (*Contemporary* 31). In performing an African Americentric rhetorical analysis of the Black Arts Movement, then, I privilege the rhetorical practices specific to Black American culture—the practices, as noted above, that Geneva Smitherman calls Black English "modes of discourse." In addition, I acknowledge the influence of rhetorical concepts and practices with origins in African and European cultures on the practice of African American rhetoric. My rationale here is that, as African American culture has both African and European roots that inform its specifically American practices and innovations, it is important to recognize rhetorical resources from African and European strains of ancestry that have residual presence in African American rhetorical traditions. As playwright and literary scholar Paul Carter Harrison describes it, "Wherever black people live in the world, and whatever the form of their oppression, many aspects of the Mother will be continued in secular rituals which designate man as a force among other forces. Life is experienced as a matrix of forces which, in the linear sense, is never static; it is dynamic and shaped by the interaction of many modes" (xv). I do not intend here to construct any historical causal relationships between the traditional and ancient European and African rhetorical practices I reference and African American rhetorical practice. Instead, similar to the way Maulana Karenga characterizes his Afrocentric rhetorical scholarship, I look to "identify shared insights and orientations in a larger . . . tradition of communicative practice and to recover and employ these classical . . . understandings to expand the range of useful concepts in defining and explicating communicative practice in general and the African American rhetorical project in particular" ("Nommo" 4). Specifically, I consider the reach of the Black Arts Movement's rhetorical influence through the lens of African American, African, and European rhetorical practices that (1) consider poetic works powerful vehicles for persuasion, (2) emphasize the mission of the rhetor to work for the good of the collective, and (3) call upon poets and rhetors to serve as educators of the public.

In her foundational work on African American language and rhetoric, *Talkin and Testifyin: The Language of Black America* (1977), Geneva Smitherman identifies four modes of discourse within Black language culture that I argue Black Arts writers used as resources in the rhetorical mission described above. Smitherman names these oral art forms as *call-response, tonal semantics, signification,* and *narrative sequencing*. Although I define these modes only briefly here, I offer detailed explanations and examples of them in rhetorical readings of Black Arts Movement poetry throughout the subsequent chapters of this book. The first mode of discourse, *call-response*, is an intricate form of communication built upon spontaneous verbal and nonverbal interactions between speaker and listeners; after each "call" or statement, the speaker expects a spontaneous response. This communicative form, which employs repetition and improvisation akin to musical antiphonal performances, depends on the speaker's engagement of a community of cocreators to participate in the speech act as communal ritual (104). The second mode, *tonal semantics*, conveys meaning in Black English discourse through the use of vocal rhythm and inflections in tone that imaginatively communicate attitude toward subject and audience, giving speech a "songified" or "musical" quality (134). The variations in tonal semantics often take the form of alliterative word play, repetition, rhyme, and intonational shaping. Listening to a speech act that artfully employs tonal semantics, a speaker of Black English may find it nearly impossible to separate the strictly abstract meaning of the word from the sociocultural implications of the fluctuation in tone (136). A listener not intimately attuned to Black English would not comprehend the full meaning of the statement, but a Black English speaker with a history of immersion in the cultural tradition would understand the statement in its subtlety and feel a resulting inclusion in the Black collective.

The third and fourth modes of discourse play a prominent role in the rhetoric of Black Arts poetry that I will discuss, and for that reason I will present them in somewhat more depth. *Signifyin*, a practice that takes place both in structured performative oral encounters and in everyday exchanges, serves as a way for a speaker to show verbal prowess by engaging in wordplay, demonstrating cleverness through metaphorical or rhetorical indirection.[15] The ability to signify implies the ability to "rap," or to dexterously wield the vernacular. The speaker must not only have control over language but also use that control to create a semantic surprise. Signifyin does not constitute a speech act on its own but is used as a rhetorical strategy within other speech acts. In formal rituals of verbal competition, speakers signify on each other in an attempt to wryly insult their opponents; when used by a singular speaker to express emotion or integrated into everyday dialogue, signifyin helps to drive home a point. Signifyin broadly involves the following characteristics: indirection (or circumlocution); metaphorical-imagistic language that roots its images in the everyday; humor, irony, puns; rhythmic fluency and sound; and the introduction of the semantically or logically unexpected (Smitherman, *Talkin and Testifyin* 121). In terms of audience, the speaker addresses signifyin only to individuals present in the situation or context, emphasizing interaction over insult. Further, the practice interestingly works as a tool to strengthen community solidarity. Because signifyin thrives on indirect insults, it allows speakers to make or listeners to take criticism without bringing it to the level of confrontation. As such, the practice serves as a tool for speakers to demonstrate their linguistic prowess and at the same time provide suggestions or corrections to members of the community without compromising speakers' and listeners' sense of shared belonging to that community.

The fourth mode of discourse, *narrative sequencing*, describes particular traditions of storytelling within Black English speech culture. Black Arts writers made particular use of two kinds of storytelling that aided in goals of consciousness raising and solidarity. *Testifyin* involves enacting a type of narrative sequencing that Smitherman defines as "a ritualized form of black communication in which the speaker gives verbal witness to the efficacy, truth, and power of some experience in which all blacks have shared" (58). While traditionally testifyin is used by preachers and in spiritual contexts, speakers employ it in secular contexts as well. A nonlinear, lyrical-leaning narrative, testifyin presents "a dramatic narration and communal reenactment of one's feelings and experiences" (150). This generally involves an intense use of tonal semantics to convey meaning beyond the referential significance of a word alone, often indicating an intensifying of spirit or emotion. When individuals testify before a group, they reaffirm their humanity, ridding themselves of feelings of isolation and articulating for themselves an identity within the group or community.

The *toast*, the second type of narrative sequencing significant to the work of this book, takes this community identification one step further. The toast is a type of performative, poetic narrative sequencing in which the speaker crafts a heroic epic in order to establish status or to articulate resistance to something oppressive. Toasts originated as creative retellings of well-known stories from the folk and oral traditions, such as "Shine," "Dolemite," "Stagger Lee," and "The Signifyin Monkey," in which the speaker uses signifyin and other techniques of verbal artistry to project the prowess of the hero of the tale. Modern toasts, although still concerned with relating the exploits of a hero, allow the speaker to invent heroes beyond those in the traditional tales, providing a forum for self-aggrandizement. While men in urban settings commonly practiced the toast as a pastime as a way to vaunt sexuality, fighting ability, defiance, and "general badness," women toast as well (Smitherman, *Talkin and Testifyin* 157). According to Smitherman, "The toast-teller projects himself (or herself, but usually himself) as a powerful, all-knowing, omnipotent hero, able to overcome all odds" (*Talkin That Talk* 275). The speech act focuses on aggrandizing the speaker's selfhood through a narrative-based exhibition of verbal artistry. Smitherman observes that by projecting personal heroism, "the toast-teller personifies the self-empowerment dreams of his Black audience and symbolizes for them triumph and accomplishment against the odds" (276). Toast tellers, then, signify constructively, for their own sake as well as for the sake of their listening communities.

Scholars of African American rhetoric connect the community-oriented nature of these Black rhetorical practices with practices from African rhetorical traditions. Rhetorical and literary scholar Keith Gilyard characterizes African American rhetoric as language that is used for both *persuasive* and *associative* ends in Black discourses, describing these discourses as "the major means by which people of African descent in the American colonies and subsequent republic have asserted their collective humanity in the face of an enduring White supremacy and tried to persuade, cajole, and gain acceptance for ideas relative to Black survival and Black liberation" ("Introduction" 1). In a similar vein, rhetorical scholar Elaine Richardson argues that vernacular linguistic and rhetorical practices by African Americans should be understood as "African American survival culture" (33). The character of African American rhetoric as aiming for the uplift—or in cases of extreme oppression, survival—of Black Americans as a people resonates with the central functions of African rhetorical practices. Karenga describes broad traditions of African rhetoric as follows:

> To engage in rhetoric as an African is to enter an ancient and ongoing tradition of communicative practice, a practice that reaffirms not only the creative power of the word but also rootedness in a world historical community and culture, which provides the framework for self-understanding and self-assertion in the world. It is a tradition that from its inception has been concerned with building community, reaffirming human dignity, and enhancing the life of the people. It has expanded in more recent times to include vital contributions to the struggles for liberation in the political, economic, and cultural senses as a rhetoric of resistance. ("Nommo" 5)

In relating these traditions to the specific work of Black Arts writers, I draw upon two specific aspects of African rhetorical traditions: the concept of *nommo* and the figure of the *griot*.

According to Nigerian novelist and literary scholar Isidore Okpewho, a service provided by oral literature in many traditional African societies was "to give the society—whether isolated groups within it or the citizenry as a whole—a collective sense of who they are and help them define or comprehend the world at large in terms both familiar and positive to them" (110). These significant themes appear not only in histories of the function of traditional African oral literature but also in formulations of African American rhetoric that draw upon practices recovered from the ancient Egyptians. In connecting African American rhetorical practices with traditions of ancient Egyptian rhetoric, Karenga characterizes African rhetoric overall as rhetoric of community, resistance, affirmation, and possibility ("Nommo" 5–6). These functional aspects of rhetoric depend on the idea of *nommo*, the word, a concept from the creation narrative of the Dogon people of Mali that many cultural nationalists in the 1960s rediscovered and followed as a guiding rhetorical principle. Karenga defines nommo as follows: "According to the Dogon sage Ogotommêli, the Creator, Amma, sends nommo, the word (in the collective sense of speech), to complete the spiritual and material reorganization of the world and to assist humans in the forward movement in history and society. It is through the word, Ogotommêli tells us, that weaving, forging, cultivating, building family and community, and making the world good are made possible" (8). Demonstrating Black Arts writers' recovery and understanding of nommo in his 1970 work on Black theater, Paul Carter Harrison offers a characterization similar to that of the Dogon creation myth about the respect Black artists should have for the power of the word—but with the linguistic flair of a Black Power activist: "The Nigguh reveals to us the power of the *word*, that Nommo force which manipulates all forms of raw life and conjures images that not only represent his biological place in Time and Space, but his spiritual existence as well. Nobody uses the *word* like nigguhs do" (xiv). References to nommo appear commonly in Black Arts texts, and one notable use of the term was as the name of the journal of the influential Organization of Black American Culture (OBAC) Writers' Workshop in Chicago. Black Arts activists believed that through harnessing the word's sacred and infinite power to create for the good of the community and the world, they could bring their audiences to proud, conscious Black selfhood and aim them collectively toward political change.

In traditional West African cultures—the cultures to which most enslaved Africans brought to North America belonged—the word was wielded by *griots* and *griottes*: storytellers, praise singers, culture bearers, and keepers of history.[16] African and French literature scholar Thomas A. Hale describes the vital role griots play not only as keepers of history but as their community's most respected rhetors who shape cultural values and influence cultural practices: "If history constitutes a rethinking of the significance of events and the people involved in them, then griots and griottes are the producers of this kind of thought in the societies in which they live.... They redescribe events in a fluid, situationally specific synthesis of past and present values.... The words of this rethinking of the past prompt and shape action by these listeners in the near or distant future" (420). This influence stems from the multifaceted roles griots play in their communities. As Hale puts it, "Griots operate at the center of society, linking ruler and subject, past and future, while serving many roles: genealogist, historian, adviser, spokesperson, diplomat, mediator, interpreter, translator, musician, composer, teacher, exhorter, warrior, witness" (420). Similarly, Black Arts poet Sonia Sanchez specifically describes her own mission as writer in the context of the African tradition of poets as "synonymous" with "the priest and the prophet," public figures who in some societies have been able to "create, preserve or destroy social values"—and may even have "infinite powers to interpret life"—*if* they are able to achieve social visibility ("Poet as Creator" 20). According to poet and scholar Lorenzo Thomas, this was precisely the aim of artists of the Black Arts Movement. He defines "the aesthetic goal of Black Arts music and poetry" as "an attempt to recreate in modern modes the ancestral role of the African griots who are poets, musicians, and dancers whose songs record genealogies and the cosmologies of societies" (316). Thomas points to Askia Touré's poem "Transcendental Vision: Indigo" as an aesthetic articulation of this aim:

> And
>   there
>   are
>   Whirlwinds embodied
> in
>   the
>   minds of
> Visionary griots/singing:
>   Tomorrow!
>   Tomorrow!) Language of
> transcendental passion-flame
>   (spirit-tongue. Surreal
>   Saint-

> inflected solo) motivating warrior
> generations
> venerating liberation
> in
> primary language of
> forever. (Touré 55)

The poem celebrates "visionary griots" who follow in the traditions of the ancestral "Saints" to move current and future "warrior / generations" to embrace freedom. And the message in which they "venerate liberation" is the word, nommo—the "primary language of / forever" that has always made and will always make the world. Through the lens of these traditions, Black Arts poets served rhetorically as griots and guardians of the word, bearers and sharers of cultural history that worked to shape listeners' conceptions of that history for what they believe is the political good of the community.

These African rhetorical traditions resonate strongly with two conceptions from ancient Western rhetoric, *paideia* and the *citizen-orator*, both of which, I argue, also present poetics as a powerful public rhetorical tool. According to the work of classical scholar Werner Jaeger, the ancient Greek practice of paideia was the education of the individual to be the ideal member of the community. Education involved not only sharing cultural practices but shaping the character of each individual to best be a member of society as a whole. And the best vehicle for inculcating individuals into these cultural values and ideals was poetic works. Jaeger writes, "The ancients were persuaded that education and culture are not a formal art or an abstract theory, distinct from the objective historical structure of a nation's spiritual life. They held them to be embodied in literature, which is the real expression of all higher culture" (v). This educational mission was the responsibility of both the poet and the legislator, wielders of the word, for "the only genuine forces which could form the soul were words and sounds" (xxvii). An application of the concept of paideia can be mapped clearly onto the rhetorical mission of Black Arts poets. To the extent that Black Arts writers practiced a form of paideia, they applied a method of inculcating an ideal collective identity into individuals through the performance of literature.[17] Like ancient Greek educators, Black Arts activists wanted their literature to inspire a nationalistic consciousness in Black Americans to bring them together as a community, both through an understanding of their common history and through their shared responses to the circumstances of the present, and the eventuality of this educative process would be the community's liberation from the shackles of institutionalized racism. For Sonia Sanchez, like Askia Touré in his characterization of the blues musician (and ideal poet) as priest-philosopher above, the "poet-priest" is historically one who does the paideic work of educating the people about their cultural values: "The priest as poet devoted him/herself to developing symbols of collective experience into teaching tools that inculcated the social values and wisdom of the culture and conveyed the nature of being and the interrelationship between man, God and the universe" ("Poet as Creator" 21). Similarly, Keorapetse Kgositsile asserts that it is the responsibility of the poet to teach the people how they can best serve their communities—or, in paideic terms, be ideal citizens within those communities. The work of the poet, Kgositsile argues, "is education because in any culture education serves to prepare people to be clear about their roles, to tap their potential so that their lives can be meaningful; so that they can better consolidate their resources and be productive in, and useful to, their communities" (239). In this way, Black Arts rhetorical practice demonstrates a reappropriated practice of paideia that uses literature as the persuasive vehicle of a counter-hegemonic discourse to educate individuals about their ideal collective identity.

To the extent that Black Arts poets practiced an African American version of paideia—one particularly inflected by the tenets of Black Power—I argue that they played the roles both of griots, as described above, and of *citizen-orators*, rhetor figures that appear in the rhetorical theory of ancient Greek rhetorician Isocrates. Isocrates's concept of rhetorical education centers on the idea of creating citizen-orators, whose role is to use oratory to lead citizens to the best political decisions for the polis. The citizen-orator uses logical and beautiful oratory to formulate sound judgments regarding deliberative issues of the state. According to rhetorical scholar Phillip Sipiora, Isocrates theorized that "[i]f these 'public citizens' are of sufficient number and take it upon themselves to dedicate themselves to deliberative activity within the *polis*, the state has the potential to rescue itself from present evils and head off future dangers" (13). Isocrates's rhetorical version of paideia depends on a deft understanding of *kairos*, rhetorical timeliness, by citizen-orators; he expects them to be individuals who "manage well the circumstances which they encounter day by day, and who possess a judgment which is accurate in meeting occasions as they arise and rarely miss the expedient course of action." This eloquent, kairos-savvy rhetoric would lead the community to agreement around appropriate *doxa*, beliefs or judgments about the best course of action for the community based on an assessment of practical wisdom (Poulakos 45, 54). The role of Black Arts poets simulates that of ancient citizen-orators, then, in the fundamental commitment of the poet to use well-crafted, kairic oratory and writing for the public's political well-being. The essential citizen-orator work of Black Arts poets is to bring their audience to Black consciousness so that they are prepared to make decisions about—and be part of—the revolution.

Enacting their paideic mission as hybrid griots and citizen-orators, these Black Arts *poet-rhetors*, as I refer to them throughout this book, significantly practiced *epideictic* rhetoric, the Aristotelian term for the rhetoric of praise and blame, to influence the values of their audiences. The epideictic task for Black Arts activists was to problematize and rearrange what the Black public understood as praiseworthy or blameworthy cultural values, specifically by aggressively rejecting those values rooted in a White-dominant worldview. This required incorporating a prevalent rhetoric of blame in their writing that indicted the existing order's ideals, followed by a rhetoric of praise that offered readers alternative values that would serve as the basis of a revolutionized political system. The writers' use of epideictic rhetoric constituted the main rhetorical strategy by which they carried out their paideic mission to reeducate the Black public—a tool they could wield pointedly to change the personal and social consciousness of their hearers. Strongly influenced by cultural nationalism, Black Arts writers believed that the revolution in values was the first step in leading their audience to belief in the rightness of the revolution and, ultimately, to their participation in it. It makes sense, then, that they rooted their rhetorical work in the species of rhetoric concerned with defining cultural values. But it was revolutionary that they staked a claim to epideictic rhetoric as the province of radical forces in society, and their work provides an important example of the strategic use of epideixis for subsequent radical social movements, particularly those that rely on art as a vehicle for their revolutionary message. Kgositsile's characterization of "applied poetry" as a weapon of the Black Arts Movement captures how epideictic rhetoric can be an invaluable revolutionary rhetorical strategy: "[T]he poet does not have explosives for the physical destruction of the West in general, and America in particular. Not yet. Thus, the immediate resort for the Black poet is applied poetry. He uses his sensibility as ammunition. Brotherly love. Virtue. Construction which, by definition, embraces and transcends the necessary destruction. Restoration of human and humane values for the salvation of man. NOW" (237). The poet begins the revolution with words as ammunition, breaking down old values and building up new ones that strengthen and invigorate those who will join the fight.

Taken together, these rhetorical theories and definitions form a toolkit for performing a *reception history* to assess the Black Arts Movement's rhetorical reach. Following historian Harold Marcuse's definition, reception histories are concerned with "the history of the meanings that have been imputed to historical events" by the range of groups who vest importance in those events, including participants, observers, and scholars and others who look to make sense of the historical events in retrospect. Marcuse identifies two aspects of this kind of investigation: first, assessing "the ways a person or event *was portrayed* (by the 'multipliers' and makers of public opinion)," and second, determining and theorizing "the ways those portrayals were *perceived* (by the populace at large)." The goal of performing a reception history is to make particular historical events meaningful for the present, to glean lessons that can inform the choices of contemporary culture. Rhetorical scholar Steven Mailloux portrays reception histories as inherently rhetorical inquiries, in which rhetoric is defined as "the study of textual effects, of their production and reception" (xii). In particular, a reception history uses a rhetorical approach "focusing on the historical effects of texts for specific reading communities" and likely incorporates one or several specific "cultural rhetorics," the "political effectivity of trope and argument in culture" (xii). In the case of BAM, the facets of this definition map clearly onto the work that writers openly promised to do: to affect the specific reading communities of Black America by employing the cultural rhetoric of texts crafted with the Black aesthetic as guiding principle, resulting in a high degree of political effectivity in support of a Black nationalist revolution. How the movement was portrayed subsequent to its years of most fervent activity does not fully capture its cultural impact, despite the breadth and importance of cultural legacies that are rarely noted as having been influenced by the movement's work.

With these sociohistorical and cultural contexts and rhetorical frameworks in mind, I develop throughout the chapters that follow a reception history of the Black Arts Movement—one that ultimately complicates the dominant Black Arts critical history of the movement as a failure by making a case for the *delayed* success of the movement, a success defined by movement activists' achievement of a wide range of rhetorical goals that left significant American cultural legacies. Much like the opening to this chapter, the remainder of this book delves deeply into the poetry of the Black Arts Movement to demonstrate how its poets deployed these rhetorical strategies to give their art the power to become what they dreamed it would be in the early days of the movement: "art for all our sake."

CHAPTER 2

"Our Distaste for the Enemy, Our Love for Each Other"

The Radical Rhetoric of Blame and Praise in Black Arts Movement Poetry

One of the primary tensions that governed the Black Arts Movement was the pull between what could be done with words and what needed to be done with physical, perhaps violent, resistance. Critics of Black Power and Black Arts, as noted in the introduction, often argue that Black nationalist movements of the era and their aesthetic counterpart failed because the radicals' activism did not ultimately culminate in a full realization of their political goals. Black Arts writers themselves engaged this concern as self-critique. Even at the height of the Black Power Movement, many writers expressed anxiety about whether the poetic message would actualize in revolutionary political change. Poet Nikki Giovanni expresses this concern about political impotence in her poem "For Saundra." After trying alternately throughout the piece to write a poem that rhymes, a "tree poem," and a "sky poem" but being thwarted by the starkness of her observations, the speaker wonders at the appropriateness of the poetic project in the face of revolutionary need:

> maybe I shouldn't write
> at all
> but clean my gun
> and check my kerosene supply
>
> perhaps these are not poetic
> times
> at all (*Black Feeling* 90)

In "Two Poems," poet Haki Madhubuti (formerly Don L. Lee) seems to lose faith entirely in the cultural nationalist project of creating conscious Black literature as the first step in sparking the revolution:

> i ain't seen no poems stop a .38,
> i ain't seen no stanza brake a honkie's head,

> i ain't seen no metaphors stop a tank,
> i ain't seen no words kill
> & if the word is mightier than the sword
> pushkin wouldn't be fertilizing russian soil/
> & until my similes can protect me from a night stick
> i guess i'll keep my razor
> & buy me some more bullets (Lee, *Black Pride* 14)

These writers' concerns speak to the role rhetoric plays in political and social movements as the *antistrophos*, the conjugate or counterpart, to physical violence. As rhetorical theorists Chaim Perelman and Lucie Olbrechts-Tyteca discuss in *The New Rhetoric* (1969), "[A]ll argumentation can be considered as a substitute for physical force which would aim at obtaining the same kind of results by compulsion" (54). If coercion begins specifically when persuasion fails, the fact that much of the Black Arts Movement was more talk than physical confrontation speaks to the rhetorical strength of the movement.

In his programmatic essay "Black Art: A Rhythmic Reality of Revolution" (1968), cultural nationalist theorist and activist Maulana Karenga sums up the rhetorical aims of Black Arts Movement literary writing as follows: "Let our art remind us of our distaste for the enemy, our love for each other, and our commitment to the revolutionary struggle that will be fought with the rhythmic reality of a permanent revolution" (9). In this chapter, I argue that Black Arts poetry may be best understood as epideictic rhetoric, specifically as rhetoric of both praise *and* blame. My argument expands on critical discussions of epideictic rhetoric in positing (1) that blame rhetoric especially serves the needs of marginalized radical groups as a vehicle to argue against dominant ideologies and (2) that this function as a rhetorical resource for radical groups demonstrates that epideictic rhetoric is not, as some have argued, inherently conservative. In the case of BAM, writers sought first to establish in their primary audience a "distaste for the enemy," using blame or *psogos* rhetoric to indict the White ruling class for injustices against Black America and to undermine the values that have prescribed or forgiven these injustices. Writers then sought to establish in the audience a "love for each other," using praise or *panegyric* rhetoric to establish pro-Black attitudes and heroes to replace those of the mainstream. Black Arts poet-rhetors ultimately aimed to inspire in their primary audience a "commitment to the revolutionary struggle," which involved in most cases willingness to spread the cultural nationalist message. A Black Arts advocate also had to be willing to "keep my razor / & buy me some more bullets," prepared for the possibility that rhetorical victories have their limits.

In what follows, I discuss the radical and revolutionary possibilities of epideictic rhetoric writ large as well as the ways poetic writing can be read as epideixis. I then present specific strategies used by Black nationalist rhetors with respect to their primary and secondary audiences and link them to practices of rhetorical praise and blame. In the second half of the chapter, I apply these frameworks to analyze influential Black Arts poems and conclude by suggesting implications of this discussion.

The Radical Possibilities of Epideictic Rhetoric

Recent scholarship on epideictic rhetoric has worked to complicate the assumption, strongly ingrained by the work of Chaim Perelman and Lucie Olbrechts-Tyteca, that epideictic oratory has an overwhelmingly conservative social and political function. Positing epideictic rhetoric as the foundation of the values that govern all other rhetorical deliberations, Perelman and Olbrechts-Tyteca assert that epideictic rhetoric is a tool only of powerful social groups to "defend the traditional and accepted values, those which are the object of education, not the new and revolutionary values which stir up controversy and polemics" (51). Since the 1990s, however, a strain of work by scholars such as Gerard Hauser, Nicole Loraux, John Poulakos, and Takis Poulakos has persuasively countered this argument, acknowledging that epideictic rhetoric certainly *may* reinscribe existing values but also may express dissenting voices. According to Hauser, the thrust of this scholarship emphasizes that, beyond mere commemoration, "the occasion for praising or blaming significant public acts and actors also afforded the opportunity to address fundamental values and beliefs that made collective political action within the democracy more than a theoretical possibility" (5). Hauser argues that the qualities praised as "noble" in an epideictic address are those that benefit the community, though what benefits the community is not necessarily maintenance and memorialization of existing values and practices. Epideictic rhetors may argue that change is good.

While this scholarship reconsiders the genre of epideictic rhetoric by complicating its characterization as a resource primarily supporting conservative impulses, it has left relatively unchallenged the assumption that epideixis is largely a rhetoric of praise. Rhetorical scholar Clarke Rountree notes the lack of oratorical examples of speeches of blame (psogos) contemporary to Aristotle's writing of *On Rhetoric* and suggests that one reason psogos oratory may not have been prevalent in Aristotle's time is that the theater provided a safer and freer venue for public blaming.¹ In other words, thinly veiled poetic critiques were not legal grounds for slander charges the way public speeches were. I suggest another reason that scholars have found few examples of ancient psogos speeches is that the rhetoric of blame becomes prominent in a culture's epideictic manifestations specifically during instances of political upheaval by a nondominant social group. Classical scholars generally note Aristotle's concern with Athens's democratic politics as an undercurrent of the *Rhetoric* and attribute Aristotle's willingness to concede the need for an art reliant on the inexactitude of *phronesis*, or practical wisdom, as a strategy to deal with what he considered imperfect political realities. Distrusting democracy's corruption in empowering non-noble citizens, Aristotle supports political reform that reinscribes traditional, hierarchical notions of nobility and virtue. Given this political inclination, it makes sense that the *Rhetoric* emphasizes and considers in detail the praise genres of epideictic rhetoric. To concede partially to Perelman and Olbrechts-Tyteca, traditional praise rhetoric does tend to have a conservative pull, one that reinforces foundational cultural values as the structures that undergird social stability. Additionally, there is certainly a place for psogos rhetoric in conservative politics; conservatives can use those whose actions or values deviate from the culture's master narratives as examples of the danger of straying from existing mores. But conservative epideixis primarily serves to reinforce established values by praising their enactment. An overabundance of blame rhetoric would highlight actions and beliefs that run counter to the status quo, drawing significant attention to alternative political and social possibilities.

Emphasizing alternative behaviors and belief systems has tended historically to better serve the rhetorical needs of radical movements. For a cadre of marginal radicals to gain converts from the ruling class or from those conceding to the power of the ruling class, rhetoric of blame plays a vital role in destabilizing the values that justify the existing political order. The epideictic task for radicals is to problematize and rearrange what the public understands as points of core epideictic *topoi*, "virtue and vice and honorable and shameful" (Aristotle, *Rhetoric* 1.9.1). This requires a prevalent rhetoric of blame that indicts the existing order's ideals (or hypocrisy in relation to those ideals as evinced by the oppression of the group the radicals represent) accompanied or followed by a rhetoric of praise that seeks to inscribe alternative values that will serve as the basis of a revolutionized political system. The kairos for radical marginalized groups' use of epideictic rhetoric hinges on the imperative of imminent political action. Epideictic rhetoric, which, according to Aristotle's formulation, focuses on the present, provides radicals with a vehicle through which to recruit comrades by changing the personal and social consciousness of their audience. Epideictic rhetoric's usefulness as an educative tool allows for this kind of conversion—particularly through psogos's function in providing alternatives to established values. For radical marginalized groups, psogos rhetoric enacts the kind of learning in which "it becomes clearer [to the listener] that he learned something different from what he believed, and his mind seems to say, 'How true, and I was wrong'" (Aristotle, *Rhetoric* 3.11.6). After their audience has experienced this conversion of consciousness, radical rhetors can introduce and reinforce an alternative value system through praise—one they hope will eventually lead their audience to action. In this way, the epideictic rhetorical act branches into the two other species of rhetoric. Although grounded in the immediacy of the present, epideictic rhetoric can effectively blame only by employing or alluding to forensic considerations, establishing with veracity that particular injustices have taken place in the past. In calling the listener to subscribe to new values and, even further, to act on those new values, epideictic rhetoric alludes to or employs deliberative rhetoric, hoping ultimately to affect and effect future actions. Epideixis, then, serves as the fundamental—and perhaps all-encompassing—rhetorical tool for those wishing to counter the status quo.

Instances of epideictic rhetoric from the margins tend to blur the generic lines between the rhetorical and the poetic. This assertion takes on several long-standing distinctions between rhetoric and poetics, many of which stem from incorrect or incomplete readings of Aristotle's work. First is the assumption that rhetoric and poetics are entirely separate modes of communication, which includes a dictum that poetic work cannot function rhetorically.[2] Second is the long-standing categorization of epideictic works not as a species of rhetoric at all but "merely" as a branch of literature (Perelman and Olbrechts-Tyteca 48–49). Third is the tradition that narrative and not lyric is the appropriate expressive mode for epideictic arguments.

Classical rhetorical scholar Jeffrey Walker's scholarship has offered significant arguments against all of these divisions and provides solid groundwork for an investigation of poetry as a significant source of epideictic rhetoric from radical marginalized groups. Specifically in terms of poetry as a valid form of epideictic rhetoric, Walker argues that classical epideictic was first expressed in the work of lyric poets in the tradition of Pindar and that epideixis "is philosophically, rhetorically, and formally prior to pragmatic discourse." He states that this is especially true in oral cultures, and the emergence and establishment of literacy "will tend to confuse the relationship" between epideictic rhetoric and lyrical form ("Aristotle's Lyric" 9). Further, he asserts that the critical elevation of narrative over lyric as the appropriate genre for epideictic expression stems from a misreading of portions of Aristotle's *Poetics* in which Aristotle was "evading, or minimizing . . . , the Platonic critique of poetry" (10). Lyric, incorrectly considered a less-sophisticated vehicle for epideictic speech or writing, instead is a medium that maximizes epideixis's rhetorical possibilities: "What the lyric of this paradigm offers to its audiences is epideictic argument intending praise, evaluation, and the creation of belief, argument in which the overt, rational persuasion of logos is 'lifted high' . . . by the graceful eloquence of lyric measure." Walker insists that epideictic lyric should not be construed only as occasional rhetoric but, in line with the assertions of scholars noted in the introduction to this chapter, should be defined as "argument directed toward the establishment, reconfirmation, or revision of general values and beliefs" (7). This framework makes space for scholars to consider the manifestations of epideictic rhetoric from marginalized groups across limiting genre and discourse divides—a consideration that will show the significance of poetry as a vehicle for epideictic strikes against dominant values.

Much of the work of the Black Arts Movement has been critically undervalued or dismissed in the decades following its flourishing—interestingly through arguments parallel to those that, according to Jeffrey Walker, demoted ancient epideictic lyric: "[T]he rhetoric of epideictic song employed by ancient lyric falls to the lowest status possible. Such a poetry now appears as little more than versified opinion, the discourse of a merely social and thus profane identity, and indeed a minor discourse aiming at no more than beautification of the cell-walls of a quotidian belief within the prison-house of public language" ("Aristotle's Lyric" 16). A consideration of the primary role of epideictic rhetoric in Black Arts poetry not only validates the possibilities of epideictic rhetoric as radical rhetorical practice but also offers a lens through which to reevaluate BAM's political, social, and aesthetic influence.

Black Arts Rhetoric and Its Audiences

Understanding the central role of epideictic rhetoric in the Black Arts Movement and other radical movements from the margins requires an understanding that Black Arts works were meant to have specific primary *and* secondary audiences: Black Arts rhetoric was meant to be *heard* by Black audiences and *overheard* by White audiences. The movement's primary rhetorical goal was to do violence to the insidious, hypocritical ideals under which Black people had been repressed. With regard to this goal, and the ultimate hope of bringing the listener to Black consciousness, self-love, and unity with others, the movement's psogos rhetoric depicted a poetic violence that exceeded much of the actual violence Black Power activists carried out in the physical world. Further, activists *benefited* from White audiences overhearing violent psogos rhetoric because it established a basis for political ultimatums: "If argument fails," they could suggest, "we, unlike our nonviolent Civil Rights predecessors, can and will use force for revolutionary ends." Again, according to Perelman and Olbrechts-Tyteca, "Recourse to argumentation assumes the establishment of a community of minds which, while it lasts, excludes the use of violence" (55). To the extent that their opponents heard of and feared the possibility of violence, they might be willing to deal rhetorically with demands of radical activists. In the case of the Black Arts Movement, the extreme violence prevalent in their psogos rhetoric may have taken the place of the enactment of physical violence in pursuit of Black Power imperatives.[3]

Afrocentric theorist and rhetorical scholar Molefi Kete Asante's (born Arthur L. Smith) work in *Rhetoric of Black Revolution* (1969) provides an important framework for understanding the way revolutionists, and specifically Black nationalists, address rhetoric toward their primary and secondary audiences. Asante argues that every revolution has rhetoric that attempts to justify the claims and legitimize the aspirations of the revolutionists. This rhetoric is meant to be at the same time *unifying* and *aggressive*: inspiring members of the primary audience to unify strategically around a commonality—here around Black identity—and aggressively assuming an offensive (instead of defensive) stance against the status quo. Aggressive rhetoric proves particularly beneficial for revolutionaries from nondominant groups because it keeps the opponent off-balance; the powerful opponents worry about defending themselves against the charges of the aggressor instead of mounting their own attacks. Asante sums up the Black nationalist rhetorical strategy as follows: "Anything that facilitates black unity is good; anything that indicts white America is good" (6). This tactic certainly involves some sacrifices. Forming a coalition around something as unwieldy as "Black identity" necessarily involves Black Arts activists calling for *strategic essentialism* from Black audiences that allows Black Arts poetry to function as both aesthetic and political. A term coined by feminist and postcolonial theorist Gayatri Chakravorty Spivak in 1984, strategic essentialism suggests that for the purposes of social change a broad coalition may be built around a common category of identity to support a struggle for the rights of those who share that identity (Gross 175–87). Cultural theorist Stuart Hall describes strategic essentialism in relation to Black liberation as follows: "[I]t may be necessary to momentarily abandon the multiplicity of cultural identities for more simple ones around which political lines have been drawn. You need all the folks together, under one hat, carrying one banner, saying we are for this, for the purpose of this fight, we are all the same, just black and just here" (qtd. in Bell, *Contemporary* 50). Asante underscores the strategic nature of Black nationalist coalition building by noting that Black audiences, though considered here as one unit, were highly diverse: urban and rural, religious and secular, of generations with conflicting ideals and values, and of a range of educational backgrounds. Black Power activists called for this sacrifice of the rich multiplicity of Black identities as a temporary alliance that would serve, as Hall suggests, specific and mutually beneficial political purposes. Unified under a banner of prescribed Blackness, movement activists could form a larger and more powerful political constituency.

In an inversion of Asante's theory, however, literary scholar Philip Brian Harper confusingly argues that Black Arts poems at large only ostensibly address Black readers as their primary audience. The poetry, Harper argues, "achieves its maximum impact in a context in which it is understood as being *heard* directly by whites and *over*heard by blacks" (247). He bases this argument on the intraracial divisiveness present in much of the movement's poetic rhetoric—rhetoric addressed to a specifically defined Black audience for the purpose of constructing a nationalistic subjectivity. According to Harper, this intraracial division, promoted for the sake of constructing the nationalist Black self, undermines the ability of Black Arts poets to project inclusiveness. Harper argues that the absence of a sense of collectivity affects readings of the poems' intended audience. The reader of Black Arts poetry, he states, posits a Black primary audience by conflating audience and addressee. With a White primary audience, poets directly affront Whites as enemies, and this affront allows an "overhearing" Black audience to see the poet as exemplary of the ideal Black selfhood. Harper further asserts that the use of violent rhetoric supports his claim about poetic audience: "The positing of this violent rhetoric as performative language predicates the status of Black Arts Poetry as being *heard* by whites and *over*heard by blacks. For if, in the performative logic of the Black Arts work, to be heard is to annihilate those persons who affect one's oppression, to be *over*heard is to impress upon one's peers just how righteous, how fearsome, how potently nationalistic one is, in contradiction to those very peers who are figured as the direct addressee of the Black Arts work" (254). This argument denies that the rhetoric of violence has a literal significance and posits it as placebo politics—a stand-in for the articulation of political direction—which (primarily) attacks White people and (secondarily) impresses Black peers.

I see two fundamental problems with Harper's argument. First, he assumes that White audiences had much more access to the corpus of Black Arts poetry than they did or, probably, even desired to have. Some Black Arts publications and recordings were made nationally available, but Black Arts writers focused the majority of their activity and the distribution of their work specifically in the Black communities in their hubs of regional and local activity. While it is likely these activists expected to be overheard by Whites, especially given the degree to which federal agencies conducted surveillance of Black nationalist groups, locating Black Arts activism centrally in Black communities would have been an extremely inefficient way of reaching a primary White audience.

Second, Harper bases his understanding of the audiences of Black Arts texts on a misunderstanding of the cultural nationalist project. As cultural nationalists, many poets of the movement believed that the cultural revolution—the battle for Black minds, as Maulana Karenga would put it—had to precede any kind of armed conflict or specifically articulated political action. Cultural nationalists, most visibly represented by members and supporters of Karenga's US organization such as Black Arts Movement leader Amiri Baraka (formerly LeRoi Jones), viewed Black people in America as a cultural nation that needed to unify under Black consciousness as a prerequisite to fighting the battle for Black self-determination. As Keorapetse Kgositsile describes this explicitly rhetorical work, the poet "has no explanations to make to the white world. His dialogue is strictly with black people. If he incites, excites, instructs or entertains, he does so to and for black people" (242). While Harper's argument interprets the focus on subjectivity as an end in itself, BAM artists saw the creation of liberated Black subjectivity—of the bringing of individuals to consciousness—as a precondition for the call to nationhood. Conscious minds would open the audience up to revolutionary ideas—ideas they could not accept or enact while influenced by the ideologies of White culture. The focus on selfhood, then, does not preclude the movement's collective goals, but forwards them. The primacy of this goal to create a liberated subjectivity necessitates that Black people be the primary audience of the poetry.

Given this understanding of the Black Arts Movement's audiences and the political and rhetorical potential of their poetry, it is important to link Asante's *aggressive* and *unifying* descriptors above to the praise and blame functions of epideixis. To the extent that Black nationalist poet-rhetors practiced *aggressive* rhetoric, they *blamed* past and present generations of White, mainstream America for social, political, and personal injustices. They often accompanied these charges with or couched them entirely in images of violence, suggesting that the extent of wrongdoing toward Black people merited violent retribution. In addition to blaming White actions and values for oppressing Black communities and individuals, poet-rhetors sought to *unify* the primary audience by *praising* the beauty of Blackness and the depth of Black experience in America, sometimes by articulating the stories of individual hero figures. These rhetorical moves should not be considered entirely discrete; for example, identifying a common enemy to a diverse group can give them cause to unify. But the praise and blame registers of epideictic rhetoric help to explain both the destructive and the constructive rhetorical tasks of Black Arts writers as radical activists.

Asante further identifies four specific rhetorical strategies that he argues are central to revolutionary rhetoric, two of which I classify as strategies of psogos and two of which I consider strategies of panegyric. The first of the psogos strategies, *vilification*, involves degrading an opponent's self, action, or ideas. The blame is directed to one well-known person whose shaming will prove specifically meaningful to the audience. The second, *objectification*, involves directing the grievances of one group toward another collective body. The rhetor often leaves ill-defined the group being objectified. In the case of Black nationalist rhetoric, this would include general indictments of White people at large, often through racial epithets and at times through anti-Semitic language. Asante links *objectification* directly to blame: "[B]lame is apparently the overriding element in the dynamics of objectification" (31). The two panegyric strategies are *mythication* and *legitimation*. A rhetor practices *mythication* by employing language that suggests the sanction of supra-rational forces (i.e., God or other powerful ethos figures) on the actions of the revolutionary group and the primary audience at large (34). *Legitimation* involves seeking to explain, vindicate, or justify through rational or emotional appeals the work of the activists involved in the movement (40). This praise work incorporates the range of rhetorical appeals in an effort to establish a new set of values in place of the ruling-class values indicted by the psogos rhetoric.

Mythication and legitimation also resonate with Aristotle's discussion of the specifically panegyric strategy of *amplification*. In the *Rhetoric*, Aristotle describes amplification as a rhetorical move directly linked to the demonstration of praise, particularly in establishing superiority of actions or ideals relative to what is honorable in a particular value system: "Amplification, with good reason, falls among forms of praise; for it aims to show superiority, and superiority is one of the forms of the honorable. Thus, even if there is no comparison with the famous, one should compare [the person praised] with the many, since superiority [even over them] seems to denote excellence" (1.9.39). Aristotle alludes to the relativity, and thus potential mutability, of value systems in his recommendations that the speaker be aware of the values of the epideictic audience: "Consider also the audience before whom the praise [is spoken]; for, as Socrates used to say, it is not difficult to praise Athenians in Athens" (1.9.30).[4] The role of the epideictic rhetor, then—and specifically here the revolutionary rhetor—is to portray actions or attributes that otherwise may be considered historically neutral and, through amplification, to use them to reinforce or challenge a particular audience's system of values: "Amplification is most at home in those [speeches] that are epideictic; for these take up actions that are agreed upon, so that what remains is to clothe the actions with greatness and beauty" (1.9.40).

Asante's formulations of revolutionary rhetoric, which elucidate the usefulness to the marginalized radical rhetor of both arms of epideictic rhetoric, map neatly onto declarations from Black Arts activists about their rhetorical goals. In his 1964 essay "The Revolutionary Theatre," Baraka relates the goal of African American cultural unity to the belief that well-composed art expands the minds of its audience. Art that clearly depicts Black life, he argues, can awaken individuals to the reality of their social situation and surroundings. The first step is to bring individuals to "consciousness" about the value of the Black self—a rhetorical process that involves both freeing the individual from the strictures of dominant White values and replacing them with a new racial consciousness. Baraka points to the development of affirmed Black selves as the first "change" that revolutionary art enacts: "The Revolutionary Theatre should force change; it should be change. (All their faces turned into the lights and you work on them black nigger magic, and cleanse them at having seen the ugliness. And if the beautiful see themselves, they will love themselves)" (Jones, *Home* 210). The metaphors in this passage elucidate Baraka's vision of the activist roles of artist and audience in the Black Arts project. The audience members, "all their faces turned into the lights," are primed to receive the revolutionary message. The artist presents them with what Baraka calls "black nigger magic"—defiantly deploying terms that connote evil, inferiority, and primitiveness in traditional Western anti-Black rhetoric and subverting their negative meaning to counter the distorted representation of Black life and culture. This kind of aesthetic and linguistic reappropriation represents the constructive epideictic mission of the Black Arts Movement. Challenging the aesthetic values of White middle-class culture, movement artists sought to dissociate "ugliness" (as Baraka notes it above) from "Blackness" and worked instead to valorize Blackness—in its personal and cultural manifestations—as an aesthetic ideal. According to Baraka's formulation, artists must represent Black culture in such a way that people realize the beauty of their Black identity: "[I]f the beautiful see themselves, they will love themselves."

Using epideictic rhetoric to set and reinforce a system of values that would eventually lead audiences to action, BAM artists pushed for Black racial and cultural consciousness as part of Black Power's advocacy of Black collectivity. The representation of Black life in the radical new art had to reveal to Black audiences the richness of their culture and, at the same time, appall them by the oppressiveness of the conditions in which they lived. Baraka argued that a renewed sense of selfhood and a critical view of social conditions would lead individuals to support the revolutionary politics of cultural nationalism. He asserts, "What we show must cause the blood to rush, so that pre-revolutionary temperaments will be bathed in this blood, and it will cause their deepest souls to move, and they will find themselves tensed and clenched, even ready to die, at what the soul has been taught" (Baraka, *Raise* 213). Art was meant to work rhetorically for revolutionary politics by laying the groundwork in the mind of the audience ("pre-revolutionary temperament") for support of Black nationalism. Enraged by anti-Black racial exploitation, attuned to the value of African American culture, and freshly proud of Black identity, audiences would turn to Black Power activism in order to enact change.

Baraka offers a hyperbolic depiction of the direct action the Black artist must perform to create this revolutionary mentality in the observer: "We will scream and cry, murder, run through the streets in agony, if it means some soul will be moved, moved to actual life understanding of what the world is, and what it ought to be" (Baraka, *Raise* 213). This early formulation of the movement's aesthetic directive foreshadowed the psogos rhetoric that figured prominently in much of its theoretical and creative work. Although Black Arts writers aimed ultimately toward the constructive goal of Black self-creation, much Black Arts poetry enacts verbal violence on White middle-class American culture and Western aesthetics. Insofar as Black Arts writers literarily "scream, cry, murder, and run through the streets," they perform a notably violent rhetoric of blame that sets the groundwork for the constructive end of "moving souls" to "life understanding." At the same time, however, they characterize Blackness positively—praising new self-reliant Black values and heroes connected to a resilient and resolute culture that sanctions art forms that exist independent of White knowledge or control.

The Violence of Psogos

With these frameworks in mind, I present readings of two oft-cited Black Arts poems that demonstrate the core function of blame rhetoric to the movement's project: Amiri Baraka's "Black Art" and Nikki Giovanni's "The True Import of Present Dialogue: Black vs. Negro." I have chosen these particular poems not only because of their notoriety but also because they point directly to some of the most problematic aspects of Black Arts rhetoric. One of the most anthologized poems from the movement,[5] Baraka's "Black Art" draws attention from critics as an example of the movement's controversial excesses: anti-Semitism, misogyny, homophobia, prescribed notions of Blackness, and explicit calls for racial violence. The poem is notable particularly because it voices from the perspectives of one of the movement's most vocal leaders a definition and directive about what constitutes "Black poetry." Giovanni's "The True Import of Present Dialogue: Black vs. Negro" interestingly is *not* often anthologized, but it receives significant critical attention as one of the most vocally and blatantly violent poems the movement produced.[6] Both poems serve as rich examples for exploring the nature and function of blame rhetoric in Black Arts poetry, specifically as it employs the language of violence in a dual effort to unify Black people and terrify White listeners.

"Black Art" stands as one of the Black Arts Movement's boldest and most provocative instances of rhetorical blame. The opening of the poem makes a direct metaphoric and imagistic connection between poetry and life, challenging the modernist axiom voiced poetically by Archibald MacLeish that "A poem should not mean / But be." The poem's speaker boldly asserts in the opening lines that poems prove worthwhile only if they display life as concretely as the tactile:

> Poems are bullshit unless they are
> teeth or trees or lemons piled
> on a step.

While tactility serves as the minimum requirement for a meaningful poem, ideal Black Arts poems use words to create their own life, their own vitality and corporeality:

> ... We want live
> words of the hip world live flesh &
> coursing blood. Hearts Brains
> Souls splintering fire. (Jones and Neal 302)

The connection on which Baraka's speaker insists between life and poetry relates to the poem's role as *ars poetica* of the Black Arts project (the title, "Black Art," directs the reader to this). According to Baraka, poetry that conveys the truth of Black life would allow for the development of Black consciousness by removing White influence from one's experience. An understanding of this truth itself would begin the process of collectivization, drawing conscious individuals together through their mutual relationship to cultural experience. Baraka asserts in his 1965 programmatic "State/meant," "The Black Artist must draw out of his soul the correct image of the world. He must use this image to band his brothers and sisters together in common understanding of the nature of the world (and the nature of America) and the nature of the human soul" (Baraka, *Raise* 251).

Instead of primarily depicting Black life through this poem, however, Baraka uses it as a manifesto, spending much of the work enacting verbal violence toward both Black and White enemies. Depictions of violence toward "niggers" who capitulate to White culture appear against images of violence directed toward epithetically represented Whites, pointing to both Whites and to certain Black ideas as anti-Black-nationalist forces or actions that must be eliminated:

> ... We want poems
> like fists beating niggers out of Jocks
> or dagger poems in the slimy bellies
> of the owner-jews.[7] (Jones and Neal 302)

Movement writers and proponents saw the valuing or acceptance of "cultural Whiteness," behaviors, attitudes, and aesthetics that they described as indicative of still being "Negro" and not yet "Black" (including support for the political goals and methods of integrationists), as detrimental to the push for Black collectivity. But they also viewed it as correctable, believing that those capitulating to White culture continued to do so because of a lack of awareness of their oppression. One's desire to adhere to "Negro" ideals was unnatural, resulting not from the autonomous Black mind but from a view of the world filtered through a lens of White domination. Movement writers saw "Negro" beliefs and tendencies as learned behavior and believed that coming to "Blackness" resulted in a reclamation and affirmation—if not full re-creation—of the self once the individual was unfettered from White control, a process that would likely involve at least internal violence.

Baraka applies this invective most extensively to White and Black leaders in "Black Art," undermining the authority of known enemies—the police—as well as that of former sympathizers or representatives of civil rights causes—liberals and "negroleaders." This comes through in the poem most strikingly in the image of the leader engaged in fellatio as a form of "negotiation":

> There's a negroleader pinned to
> a barstool in Sardi's eyeballs melting
> in hot flame Another negroleader
> on the steps of the white house one
> kneeling between the sheriff's thighs
> negotiating coolly for his people. (Jones and Neal 302)

The juxtaposition of these powerless leaders with the known terror of the police represents them as having the same specious authority to protect and improve Black life. Ideological blame proves crucial here: the speaker's violent depiction of leaders cautions the reader against trusting them and, as the poem proceeds, encourages the reader to trust only in Black self-reliance and revolution. Specifically, this enactment of literary violence on alluded-to authority figures is what Asante calls rhetorical vilification, the burning in verbal effigy of a leader whose ideals or actions are partly to blame for the group's oppression. Although the speaker does not overtly name the leaders he vilifies here, referring only obliquely to "the Liberal Spokesman for the jews" or "Another negroleader / on the steps of the white house," his pointing to individuals compels the reader to fill in the names of the blameworthy. A "negroleader" whom a reader had seen or could imagine walking the steps of the White House would likely be a prominent Civil Rights Movement figure, someone who would have made coalitions with White liberals for the sake of making integrationist inroads. The poem uses violence against these individuals as its primary method of asserting blameworthiness. The speaker lists no charges against them; the closest he comes to a critique is stating the complicity of White and Negro leaders and alluding to their ineffectuality. The imagistic power of the violence the poem describes itself contains the indictment: the speaker of the poem asserts that these leaders deserve violence, so they must be blameworthy. This broad-stroke vilification serves as an aggressive rhetorical technique to put the old option for political and social justice on the offensive and to underscore the need for the new generation of revolutionaries to separate themselves ideologically—to get out of the blast radius of the violence these leaders are calling upon themselves.

Baraka's call in the poem for a stark separation from integrationist politics and policies is not limited to his vilification of the movement's leaders. In fact, the poem uses rhetorical objectification to criticize not only the social mixing of races but also the aesthetic valuing of physical or cultural "mixedness" that tends toward the glorification of Whiteness. In offering criticism of integrationist behaviors within the community, Baraka evokes images of mulattos to represent intraracial betrayal and self-indulgent capitulation to White values, calling for

> Black poems to
> smear on girdlemamma mulatto bitches
> whose brains are red jelly stuck
> between 'lizabeth taylor's toes. Stinking
> Whores! (Jones and Neal 302)

In this passage, the disgusting images of racially mixed women's brains between Elizabeth Taylor's toes and of the body distortion of the girdle subvert the idealization of White standards of beauty. The smearing of the "Black poem"—this time not the taunting blackface of minstrelsy but a sign of restatement of ideals from within—on the faces of the mulattos, who would presumably have light skin, serves as a corrective measure, pointing the reader toward the priority of Black racial association and the reassertion of Black identity. Although "mulattos" here are objectified, they are not subjected to the intense violent acts depicted elsewhere in the poem. Instead, the implication is that those within the Black community can be rehabilitated by adopting Black identity that exists separate from mixedness and integration.[8]

The violence of blame the poem enacts on the "white," the "negro," and the "mulatto" suggests that the ideal alternative to these value systems and behaviors would come from separatism of a unified Black community. Critics of the Black Arts Movement appropriately point out, however, that the language of blame in some movement writings disrupts the possibility of seamless unification by excluding women and LGBTQ people from equal treatment or even recognition. For example, in "Black Art," Baraka's speaker gives the tactility of the poem a particularly male sexual bent, saying that the ideal Black poems he calls for "wd shoot / come at you." He further denigrates the women that he depicts as "girdlemamma mulatto bitches" by calling them "stinking whores." This language reflects the general tendency of some Black Arts writers to express empowerment in, at best, masculinist terms and, at worst, misogynistic and homophobic terms.[9] Poet and scholar Harryette Mullen connects the masculine bias to some movement writers' contention that attention to gender equality would weaken the solidarity of the Black struggle. She notes this sensitivity particularly in relation to women poets' "exposing to public scrutiny" the problem of sexual violence within Black homes and communities. Of the homophobic language, Mullen notes, "[h]omosexuality was frequently deplored in Black Arts writing as a pathology of European origin, and even as a form of genocide" (56). Given this mindset, denigration of homosexuality serves as another way for movement writers to separate themselves from White (European) culture at large, though projecting homosexuality as a specifically European form of "degeneracy" is an unsubstantiated and absurd stance.[10] As I discuss more fully in chapter 5, both women and queer writers fought to have strong voices in the Black Arts Movement, and these writers play out their complicated relationship to these problematic tropes through a variety of methods of poetic resistance.

In addition to prescribed ideas about gender and sexuality, anti-Semitic language appears in the poems of Black Arts writers as one of their most prevalent intolerances. Baraka's poem places "dagger poems in the slimy bellies / of the owner-jews," "crack[s] / steel knuckles in a jewlady's mouth," and mocks "the Liberal / Spokesman for the jews" as he "clutch[es] his throat / & puke[s] himself into eternity" (Jones and Neal 302).[11] This anti-Jewish sentiment was not limited to or new in Black Arts Movement writings. In a 1967 piece for the *New York Times Magazine* titled "Negroes Are Anti-Semitic Because They're Anti-White," writer and intellectual James Baldwin attempts to explicate Black anti-Semitism as resulting initially from Black-Jewish urban economic interaction. Recounting his own experience growing up in Harlem, Baldwin notes that the exploitation many urban Blacks experienced at the hands of local business owners, many of whom were Jewish, caused an associational and experiential animosity toward Jews: "Not all of these white people were cruel—on the contrary, I remember some who were certainly as thoughtful as the bleak circumstances allowed—but all of them were exploiting us, and that is why we hated them" (426). Baldwin's reference here to the specifically Jewish shop owners in his neighborhood as "these white people" indicates his understanding that Jewish Americans did not exist separately from the category of Whites. This assumption is reasonable; like members of other European ethnic groups that immigrated to the United State in large numbers during the late nineteenth and early twentieth centuries, many Jewish Americans worked to be considered racially White. Baldwin further expresses, however, that Jews exacerbate Blacks' animosity toward them by claiming special status as belonging to a people who have suffered. Baldwin claims that Jewish American suffering cannot be compared to the suffering of African Americans because Jewish oppression occurred primarily in a European—not an American—context, and their struggle, unlike the Black struggle, is exalted as heroic by American Whites: "The Jew's suffering is recognized as part of the moral history of the world and the Jew is recognized as a contributor to the world's history: this is not true for blacks. . . . The Jew is a white man, and when white men rise up against oppression, they are heroes: when black men rise, they have reverted to their native savagery" (428). According to Baldwin, this conception of Jews as people who benefit from White identity but who claim distinction from White oppressive behaviors accounts for overt expressions of anti-Semitism from Blacks. Jews are seen—from experience by those in urban ghettos—as just as exploitative as other Whites and are singled out because they claim special circumstances that mitigate the exploitative behavior. Speaking generally of a Jewish American individual, Baldwin states, "He has absolutely no relevance in this [American] context as a Jew. His only relevance is that he is white and values his color and uses it. He is singled out by Negroes not because he acts differently from other white men, but because he doesn't" (431).

Baldwin's explanation resonates with the appearance of anti-Semitic language in Black Arts poetry on several levels. Movement poets refer to Jews as a synecdochic representation of White culture at large. Consider the following passage from "Black Art":

> We want "poems that kill."
> Assassin poems, Poems that shoot
> guns. Poems that wrestle cops into alleys
> and take their weapons leaving them dead
> with tongues pulled out and sent to Ireland. Knockoff
> poems for dope selling wops or slick halfwhite
> politicians Airplane poems, rrrrrrrrrrrrrrr
> rrrrrrrrrrrrrrr . . . tuhtuhtuhtuhtuhtuhtuhtuh
> . . . rrrrrrrrrrrrrrr . . . Setting fire and death to
> whities ass. Look at the Liberal
> Spokesman for the jews clutch his throat
> & puke himself into eternity . . . rrrrrrrr

The call for the "Liberal / Spokesman for the jews" to "clutch his throat / & puke himself into eternity" and the provocation of the audience to place "dagger poems in the slimy bellies / of the owner-jews" (Jones and Neal 302) (a line from later in the poem) appear as parallel acts to having "tongues pulled out and sent to Ireland," making "Knockoff / poems for dope selling wops," and "Setting fire and death to / whities ass," all meant to indict various arms of White culture instead of Jews in particular. Movement poets' depiction of Jews as an outstanding symbol of White culture and oppression may draw from the anger Baldwin describes at the hypocrisy some saw in some Jewish Americans' denial of their privileged status as Whites. However, the movement's focus on reflecting the actuality of Black life—a dedication to Karenga's call for poetic "functionality"—may prove a stronger impulse in this representation. Baraka's reference to the "owner-jews" may have been an attempt to represent the actuality of the White presence in Black urban neighborhoods—to call to mind the Jewish landlord, the grocer, the pawnbroker whom Baldwin recalls from the Harlem neighborhood of his youth. Baraka's anti-Semitism may have been for him just another vivid connection to black life, another tactile image, another set of teeth or trees or lemons piled on a step. Specifically to make sense of the appearance of anti-Semitism in Baraka's writing, one should note that the connection the Black Arts poet was encouraged to make to Black life would not necessarily reflect his unique individual experience but should resonate with the common experiences of Black folks at large—should prove, in Karenga's terms, not only "functional" but "collective." Baraka himself was married to a Jewish woman, Hettie Cohen, with whom he had two children, while living in Greenwich Village—and also, for that matter, had been with male lovers (Baraka, *Autobiography* 149, 166). To the extent that Baraka chooses to overwrite his intimate experience with a Jewish individual by using generalizing and stigmatizing rhetoric in his poetry, one assumes that he sees himself as capturing a "truth" in broader Black culture or is perhaps testifying to the extent of his own conversion.

Though the hatred and prejudice inherent in the movement's anti-Semitic language are undeniable, an exploration of issues of audience reveals an embedded critique as well. A broad White audience would interpret the disparaging references to Jews as an assault not on Whites at large but on the Jewish minority in particular, taking the specificity of the attack as a purposeful distinction from other Whites. Unaware of the dynamics of Black urban life, White audiences would see the anti-Semitism as directed at Jews in an unqualified way. (The closest thing to Baldwin's explanation put forth in the poems above is Baraka's epithet "owner," which itself plays into stereotypes of Jews circulated by Whites as well.) A Black audience may have a fuller understanding of the broader meaning of the anti-Semitic language as Baldwin implies it, as the references to Jews may recall for them specific individuals who had exploited them economically in urban neighborhoods, as well as serving more generally as deep-set reminders of White oppression. To a Black audience, the derogatory references to Jews take on meaning that is at once more personal and broader than anti-Semitism in the "usual" sense. The hatred conveyed here is for individual exploiters, and this hatred extends to Jewish Americans insofar as they represent White culture at large. This disparity of reception, including the understandable offense on the part of the Jewish audience and others, may be an extreme result of what Baraka saw as the Black Arts project. In his "State/meant," he asserts, "The Black Artist's role in America is to aid in the destruction of America as he knows it. His role is to report and reflect so precisely that nature of society, and of himself in that society, that other men will be moved by the exactness of his rendering and, if they are black men, grow strong through this moving, having seen their own strength, and weakness; and if they are white men, tremble, curse, and go mad, because they will be drenched with the filth of their evil" (Jones, *Home* 251). As Asante argues, the rhetorical moves of Black revolutionaries were meant to terrify Whites and unify Blacks, and the vagueness and misunderstanding about who may be the target of violence is part of the terror (9). The extreme objectification of Whites at large through the primary vehicle of anti-Semitic language underscores that some Black Arts poetry was meant to be heard by both a primary Black audience and a secondary White audience. This aggressive rhetoric of blame confuses and frightens the White audience because they seem to hear the rhetoric by chance. The rhetor, however, is not unaware he is being overheard.

Significantly, in "Black Art" the poem itself serves as the subject, as the actor, in the violence it depicts. The speaker incites the addressee *to create poems* that kill and stab and pull out tongues (an act powerful in its implications in destroying Whites' power of expression). The speaker's climactic call for the poem to enact this violence indicates that the process, for the Black audience, has creative ends:

> Put it on him, poem. Strip him naked
> to the world! . . .
> . . . .
> Clean out the world for virtue and love

By giving the violence a purpose, Baraka evokes a sense of revolutionary struggle, of strife for the sake of a better world. By insisting on the poem as actor, Baraka calls for a revolution of expression. The poem's invocation asks his addressee not only to receive the poem but to take ownership in it and in the poetic project at large. The speaker invites readers grammatically through the inclusive "we," which appears throughout the poem and climaxes in these ending lines:

> We want a black poem. And a
> Black World.
> Let the world be a Black Poem
> And Let All Black People Speak This Poem
> Silently
> or LOUD

Baraka gives the addressee ownership in the poetic project by passing on the responsibility to recreate—or even cocreate—the poem: "Let All Black People Speak This Poem / Silently / or LOUD." The speaker gives the Black audience a choice about how to engage with the poem, although the capitalization of "LOUD" and its placement as the last word in the poem suggest that the audience is called to performance. Those who progress from "silent" to "loud" will have risen to the Black Arts call to develop confident Black selfhood that leads to revolutionary involvement. Poetic potential is equated here with both the capacity to love—tying it to one of the fundamental experiences of life—and the ability to fight, to wage war, implying that both poetic expression and revolutionary conflict are as essential to human generativity as loving and making love:

> ... Let Black People understand
> that they are the lovers and the sons
> of lovers and warriors and sons
> of warriors Are poems & poets &
> all the loveliness here in the world (Jones and Neal 302)

The work serves not only as an *ars poetica* but as a call for Black poets, by expressing violence toward the ruling class of Whites (instead of calling directly for its enactment), to engender a selfhood free from oppression and that has risen to a creative and expressive consciousness. It is significant that the poem progresses from rhetorical blame that calls for violence to end in a moment of praise and celebration of Black culture as Baraka envisions it— and that all of the accompanying destruction and recreation happens within literary acts. *Poems* destroy the impediments to Black selfhood so that the individual can create the new world order. And as long as the opponent fears the possibility of violence and is willing to negotiate, the battle remains rhetorical.

The title of Nikki Giovanni's "The True Import of Present Dialogue: Black vs. Negro" directs readers to the debate that gained fervency in the mid-1960s about whether "Black" should be adopted as the preferred term of racial identity over the standing term "Negro." Black nationalists challenged the "dominant position," as social data researcher Tom W. Smith describes it, that "Negro" had held since the 1950s as the preferred term of racial identity on the grounds of its deemed historical and ideological connection to "the remnants of slavery and racial serfdom" as a term that had been "imposed on Blacks by Whites, as denoting subservience, complacency, and Uncle Tomism" (499). "Black," a term that had gained social capital among nationalists from its positive public use by leaders like Malcolm X and Elijah Muhammad, gained further currency in the summer of 1966 when Student Nonviolent Coordinating Committee (SNCC) chairman Stokely Carmichael (later known as Kwame Ture) declared "Black Power" as a rallying cry for Black freedom fighters disenchanted with the nonviolent civil rights struggle. In ideological contrast to "Negro," "Black," according to Smith's description of its social reception, "was promoted as standing for racial pride, militancy, power, and rejection of the status quo" (499)—a marker both of forward-looking and empowered racial identity and of support for more radical approaches to liberation. As Malcolm X distinguishes the terms and their politics in "Message to the Grassroots" (1963), "What is the difference between a black revolution and a Negro revolution? . . . These Negroes aren't asking for no nation. They're trying to crawl back on the plantation" ("Message").

Although Black Power activists insisted on the importance to the struggle of this new marker of racial identity, many Whites and some Blacks, particularly elders, remained reluctant to adopt the new term because they failed to see the meaningfulness of the change, were uncomfortable with the cultural or political connotations of "Black," or had invested in a previous struggle to circulate the capitalized "Negro" as a term of respect (Smitherman, *Talkin and Testifyin* 35; T. W. Smith 503).[12] Giovanni uses the first line of the poem to address the strain of intraracial reluctance in the debate, contrasting the formal headline-like speech of the title with the brusque and pejorative first line, "Nigger." By using this single word as the opening line of the poem, Giovanni briefly answers the indirect question posed in the title about the "true import of present dialogue"—pointing out the reductive possibilities of a word so closely related to "Negro" that many White Southern speakers of the time used the two almost interchangeably. Although the title may attract a reader interested in engaging in the debate intellectually, the first line reduces the potential reader's intellect and complexities to the strictures of a hateful epithet. The word "Nigger" has the power to shut down debate and the possibilities of rhetoric. If this potent word remains a commonly circulating term for racial identification, the results, the poem goes on to suggest, may be violent.

After affronting the reader with the address in the first line, Giovanni establishes an opposition between the Black addressee of the poem and Whites through a series of invocations to violence. This opposition to Whites starts out in general terms—"Can a nigger kill a honkie / Can a nigger kill the Man"—and moves to calls for more explicit acts of violence:

> Nigger
> Can you kill
> Can you kill
> Can a nigger kill
> Can a nigger kill a honkie
> Can a nigger kill the Man
> Can you kill nigger
> Huh? nigger can you
> kill
> Do you know how to draw blood
> Can you poison
> Can you stab-a-jew
> Can you kill huh? nigger
> Can you kill
> Can you run a protestant down with your
> '68 El Dorado
> (that's all they're good for anyway)
> Can you kill
> Can you piss on a blond head
> Can you cut it off
> Can you kill (*Black Feeling* 19–20)

Although Giovanni grammatically constructs the calls to violence as questions, she does not punctuate them, giving them a more imperative, almost taunting tone. The speaker of the poem presents the proposed violent acts wryly, inserting a joke in the middle of graphic suggestions of ways to kill.

Our Distaste for the Enemy   65

These challenges to kill Whites, littered with generalizing epithets, immediately establish Whites as the foe of the poem's addressee. Like the strategy Baraka employs in "Black Art," Giovanni establishes the broad category of the collective White enemy by referring to the subject of violence interchangeably as "jew," "protestant," and "blond." Giovanni stacks these descriptors as a way of performing rhetorical objectification on a broad scale—one that would appropriately terrify a White secondary audience overhearing the poem: *all* White people are the enemy, and they all deserve to *die*. The poem implies to the primary Black audience that one should be able to kill Whites as a matter of course, and the violence, presumed in the subtext of the poem to be retaliation against anti-Black racism or oppression, would be justified. The message here is that no matter what White person hurt you—Jewish, Protestant, blond person, or White man at large—that person is a blameworthy member of the enemy contingent and deserves violent retribution.

The poem offers a specific reason to blame the enemy: Giovanni's speaker indicts the irony and hypocrisy of the U.S. government in sending Black soldiers abroad to fight for, ostensibly, the tenets of democracy while the promises of that democracy are consistently denied to them in their own country. "The True Import" is contemporary with the Vietnam War, which the poem mentions specifically: "We kill in Viet Nam / for them." The speaker also alludes to the history of problematic and ironic involvement of Black soldiers in international conflicts, including both world wars:

> A nigger can die
> We ain't got to prove we can die
> They sent us to kill
> Japan and Africa
> We policed europe

The speaker uses inclusive and exclusive pronouns specifically here to set up a group of insiders, Black Americans, both present and past, who have been exploited by a group of outsiders, the White ruling-class leaders of the United States, who have not only asked Black soldiers to defend rights they cannot exercise at home but also sent soldiers of color to kill other people of color around the world. Couching this reason for blame within the calls to kill reminds the reader of other instances, such as the Red Summer of 1919 and the Double-V era of World War II, in which anger at these ironies and injustices resulted in riots and protests. Having objectified Whites broadly on both personal and institutional scales, the speaker of the poem urges the addressees to use their lives for their own battles:

> We kill for UN & NATO & SEATO & US
> and everywhere for all alphabet but
> BLACK (*Black Feeling* 20)

The imperative here is to join the movement for a self-determined Black nation, one for whose ideals soldiers could give or take lives for causes that more directly serve their individual and collective interests.

In line with cultural nationalist ideology, however, this revolutionary struggle cannot be realized until individuals are brought to consciousness of their oppression and unified under the banner of Blackness. White people are not the only enemy here. The speaker juxtaposes the incantatory call to kill Whites with the idea of destroying the "nigger" as a version of the Black self. After lines of inciting violence toward White enemies, the speaker asks,

> Can you kill
> Can you kill a white man
> Can you kill the nigger
> in you
> Can you make your nigger mind
> Die (*Black Feeling* 20)

The progression of the lines indicates a parallel relationship between acts of violence toward Whites and acts of violence toward the "nigger" mentality. Juxtaposing the call to "kill the nigger in you" with the imperative to act out against the White foe, the speaker establishes the "nigger mind" as a second enemy that affronts the addressee to a degree comparable to Whites. In redirecting the call to violence from the external foe to the self, the speaker points to a need for self-change.

The poem's formal aspects emphasize its thematic push toward self-development. The incantatory and repetitive nature of the lines as well as the didactic tone set up the poem as a kind of secular sermon. The speaker directly addresses the audience and encircles, through creative indirection and the repetition of a provocative phrase, a theme of internal, if not spiritual, development. The interrogative grammar of many of the lines resonates with the calls a preacher would issue within the call-response dialogue of a sermon. Although Giovanni does not provide any of the addressee's responses, the poem's progression implies a succession of angry, secular "amens," rousing the addressee at the end of the poem to an inspired affirmation of the need for internal change. The grammatical structure of the calls to violence further points to Giovanni's poetic project here as creative. Although the calls to violence have a decidedly imperative tone, the poet significantly chooses not to form them syntactically as true commands. Though the poem both asks and insists "Can a nigger kill a honkie" and "Can you run a protestant down with your '68 El Dorado," these phrases call for a different kind of action than the same phrases put in imperative form: "Nigger, kill a honkie" and "Run a protestant down with your '68 El Dorado." Had the only goal of the poem been to incite violent retribution on White people, Giovanni could have relied on this more direct imperative form. Instead, Giovanni's phrasal structure, which serves as the backbone of the poem, emphasizes the *ability* to commit the act instead of directly advocating that the specific act be immediately committed: *can* you poison, *can* you stab, *do you know how to* draw blood. While the violent language vividly identifies the enemy to the poem's addressee, the syntax focuses meaning on the agency of the self in relation to this enemy, on creating a self-valuing Black consciousness that separates itself actively from White ways. Further, this focus on the ability to commit violence helps the poem brush up against, but not exceed, the limits to which revolutionary rhetoric looks to push its secondary audience. White listeners *should* be afraid here about the encouragement of violence as an appropriate means of retribution for racial injustices, but the language of the poem stops just shy of stating that the violence is imminent. This allows the negotiation to remain rhetorical; a radical group that voices a clear threat to a powerful enemy should fear that the enemy is no longer willing to keep the conflict in argumentative terms.

The succession of the last three lines of the poem delineates the process that moves from violence to self-realization. The first of these lines states, "Can we learn to kill WHITE for BLACK," drawing on the allusions to war and diplomatic alliances that appear throughout the poem to emphasize the idea of Black Americans as a political collective. As a nation in themselves, Black people should wage war on those who confront their ideals: White culture at large. The line that follows, "Learn to kill niggers," complicates this White-Black binary. In the syntax of the poem, the phrase appears as an appositive to the line above it—learning to "kill niggers" renames the struggle in learning to "kill WHITE for BLACK" and is synonymous with it. "Niggers" once again equates to the "WHITE," though the war one wages against "niggers" is an internal battle as opposed to external aggression against White foes. The last line of the poem, "Learn to be Black men," appears in the same appositive position as the line that precedes it:

> Can we learn to kill WHITE for BLACK
> Learn to kill niggers
> Learn to be Black men (*Black Feeling* 20)

"Killing niggers" is the same struggle as "becoming Black men," though the former draws on destructive action and the latter on creative action. The parallelism of the lines reads through as the progression from other-destruction to self-creation: destruction of the White enemy in the name of Black nationhood causes the rebirth of the repressed "nigger" as a fully conscious "Black" individual.

The struggle for Black selfhood significantly takes place in the poem as a battle of words. The "Negro/Black" argument has significant semantic implications for those concerned with developing Black consciousness. The battle for "Black" stood as a first step because of the cultural, historical, and value implications that accompany the use of particular terms by an insular group. Sociolinguist Geneva Smitherman states of the advocacy of "Black" by consciousness activists, "In a grand sweep to eradicate the old negative 'whiteness' from black minds, leaders ... deliberately chose a racial label that required blacks to purify themselves of white ideas and values, for to accept the 'black' of blackness amounted to the ultimate recognition that white skin and white values were no longer important." Favoring "Black" over "Negro" meant more than hoping to separate from the "nigger" epithet, though the close relationship in White mouths between "Negro" and the racist "nigger" underlies Giovanni's poem and the debate at large. Acceptance of the term "Black" as the racial identity marker of all shades of Americans of African descent would signify an implicit protest against a culture that consistently favored lighter-skinned individuals for jobs and set light skin up as the standard for beauty. By associating the collective with the darkest of skin tones, the term "Black" stood semantically against White social and aesthetic values. Smitherman explains,

> Given the conflictive dynamics of ... Black America, black, not Negro, becomes the appropriate antonym for white. *Black* calls to mind power, black magic, even evil, whereas, ironically, *Negro* suggests no such associations, especially to a generation of whites who had long since forgotten—if they ever knew—that *Negro* means black anyway. A black man, as opposed to a Negro man, is someone to be feared, reckoned with, and thus respected. (*Talkin and Testifyin* 41)

The term "Black," then, serves as its own aggressive and unifying rhetorical tool: those who adopt it have chosen to be within the struggle and are forces to be reckoned with. Giovanni's support for Black nationalist politics thwarts a reading of the violence in her poem as entirely figurative or rhetorical, but the call to violence here serves a subordinate role to the poem's advocacy of consciousness and self-realization. Like in other Black Arts poems that deftly incorporate psogos rhetoric, the verbal violence is deployed strategically as a weapon in a fundamental rhetorical battle for Black minds.

Rhetoric of Praise in the Black Arts Movement: Poems for Malcolm

Black Arts activists accompanied the calls for violence toward the ruling class in their rhetoric of blame with works that foregrounded praise for Black Power's alternative value systems. This impulse to praise, to establish new value structures to replace the excoriated values of the White power structure, is exemplified by the proliferation of "Malcolm poems" during the movement. Poems honoring Malcolm X were prevalent enough to constitute their own genre in the Black Arts corpus—a significance evinced by works like *For Malcolm: Poems on the Life and the Death of Malcolm X* (1967), a Broadside Press collection edited by poet and publisher Dudley Randall and poet and visual artist Margaret Burroughs entirely dedicated to mourning Malcolm and naming him as a galvanizing force of the Black Arts and Black Power movements. Most often elegies or encomia, Malcolm poems like those in the collection present Malcolm X as the martyred paragon of Black consciousness and Black Power politics.

The establishment of Malcolm X as the movement's patron and hero was both timely and purposeful. His assassination in 1965 sparked a change in the political atmosphere in the struggle for civil and human rights. Amiri Baraka points to Malcolm X's murder as the inspiration for his conversion from Greenwich Village Beat poet to Harlem Black cultural nationalist activist and founder of the Black Arts Repertory Theater/School (BART/S)—the moment many movement historians like to point to as the ceremonial beginning of BAM. More broadly, the assassination proved a last intolerable affront for the number of Civil Rights activists, particularly young members of organizations like SNCC, who were growing increasingly frustrated with nonviolent protest tactics. Several months before his death, Malcolm X declared at the June 1964 founding rally of the Organization of Afro-American Unity (OAAU) that the organization would, in stark contrast to the tenets of nonviolent Civil Rights Movement protest, "fight whoever gets in our way" in order to "bring about the freedom of these people [of African descent in the Western Hemisphere] by any means necessary." He further explicitly asserts "the Afro-American's right to self-defense" and the need for Black folks to collectivize and become an independent political entity, to "seek allies among people who look something like we do" ("Speech"). Malcolm's assassination motivated those who had lost patience with Civil Rights tactics to take up the battle where he left off—to serve as the avant-garde for the nationalist mission in the place of their martyred leader.

In retrospect, Malcolm seems a fitting patron for the Black Arts Movement in particular given the movement's mission and rhetorical strategies. First, in terms of the movement's primary goal of converting individuals from "Negro" politics and values to revolutionary Black consciousness, Malcolm's own public story of conversion—from pimp and hustler to Nation of Islam leader to post-Mecca OAAU activist—represented the generative possibilities of changing one's values and behaviors in deep and fundamental ways. In looking to convert their audiences, Black Arts writers were essentially suggesting that, like Malcolm, they complete their own pilgrimage, arriving finally at Black consciousness. Second, Malcolm's rhetorical savvy demonstrated the strategic use of the language of violence that movement writers would later incorporate into their literary work. As rhetorical scholar and poet Keith Gilyard has observed, Malcolm X's calls for freedom by any means necessary and affirmation of the right to self-defense resulted in very little actual violence—especially compared to the horrific persecution and retaliation from White leaders and individuals that nonviolent Civil Rights protesters heroically faced.[13] Malcolm's stance that violence toward Blacks should be responded to in kind was by no means a bluff; however, the rhetorical power of his public statement of this stance, a clear example of Asante's aggressive revolutionary rhetoric, may have contributed to the circumstances of a cold war in which activists could deploy language as their weapon of choice.

Given Malcolm's emotional and intellectual significance to those involved in the struggle, his elevation to martyr status within the Black Arts Movement makes sense as a way to establish and reinforce a new set of values. In poems of praise to Malcolm, the elegies most prominently employ tropes of Malcolm as martyr, often through Christ metaphors, praising him as the messiah who heralded the coming of the free Black nation. In "To Malcolm X," George Norman mourns, "You died like the Savior, who died on the cross, / a martyr, a prophet, your black brothers' loss" (Randall and Burroughs 23). Many writers go beyond metaphors of Malcolm as sacrificial lamb to emphasize his role as a specifically political martyr—a truly honorable alternative to leaders who are memorialized and mythologized in traditional American history. In "For Our American Cousins," Reginald Wilson analogizes Malcolm and Lincoln, referring to Malcolm's assassin, Talmadge Hayer, as "Wilkes Booth" (Randall and Burroughs 35). This comparison is freighted with an indictment of Lincoln; Wilson sets Lincoln, "The Great Emancipator" who initially freed only Confederate slaves as a wartime tactical move, against Malcolm, whose work and death were seen as part of a broad, radical, community-based movement for Black freedom. Margaret Burroughs places Malcolm, in "Brother Freedom," in the lineage of a new set of founding fathers—individuals who have led and died in radical revolts and movements for freedom throughout the history of the African diaspora:

> Immortal now, he sits in fine company
> With L'Overture and Joseph Cinque
> With Vesey, Turner and Prosser
> Lumumba and Evers and others. Brother Freedom. (Randall and
>   Burroughs 22)

In "For Malcolm," Joyce Whitsitt suggests through interrogative inflection that Malcolm was to be the American leader whose revolt would result in Black nationhood:

> Were you to be the leader
> Of a new flock from the dark skinned nation,
> The mastermind of precisioned flight
> Long grounded by fledglings
> Groveling in
> shadows of white fathers? (Randall and Burroughs 20)

Whitsitt, like many other Malcolm elegists, equates this leadership specifically with Malcolm's unapologetic achievement and demonstration of "elusive manhood"—a characterization that praises Malcolm for overcoming assaults on and fear of Black masculinity that have been part of Black-White relations since the institution of the slavocracy. Rhetorically, these common tropes within Malcolm poems demonstrate both mythication and amplification. Depicting Malcolm as a Christ figure strongly implies that God was on Malcolm's side—that his fight and sacrifice were unimpeachably just. Poets amplify Malcolm in a similar way by placing him in the company of known leaders and heroes—both those within and those without the accepted histories of the ruling class. The message here is that Malcolm deserves to be placed in the company of heroes—at least human if not divine.

In Black Arts elegies and encomia to Malcolm, writers testify to this superiority and virtuousness specifically on the grounds of his own rhetorical ability: Malcolm sets himself apart as a founding father by his ability to reorient his audience's values, to compel his listeners to abandon repressive, traditional White values and convert to the new Black consciousness. Margaret Walker demonstrates this type of amplification in "For Malcolm X," in which she aligns imagery of Malcolm as Christ-like martyr with a powerful appreciation of his rhetorical acumen:

> Our blood and water pour from your flowing wounds.
> You have cut open our breasts and dug scalpels in our brains.
> When and Where will another come to take your holy place? (Randall and Burroughs 32–33)

It is significant here that the rhetoric of praise *for* Malcolm depends on an already successful rhetoric of blame and praise performed *by* Malcolm: Malcolm established his virtue through his vocal denunciation of prevalent middle-class White American values and by elevating the selfhood and unity of his Black listeners. Consider the following poem, "My Ace of Spades," by Ted Joans:

> MALCOLM X SPOKE TO ME and sounded you
> Malcolm X said this to me & THEN TOLD you that!
> Malcolm X whispered in my ears but SCREAMED on you!
> Malcolm X praised me & thus condemned you
> Malcolm X smiled at me & sneered at you
> Malcolm X made me proud & so you got scared
> Malcolm X told me to HURRY & you began to worry
> Malcolm X sang to me but GROWLED AT YOU!!
> Malcolm X words freed me & they frightened you
> Malcolm X tol' it lak it DAMN SHO' IS!!
> Malcolm X said that everybody will be F R E E ! !
> Malcolm X told both of us the T R U T H . . . . . .
>   now didn't he? (5)

Joans interestingly conveys a clear understanding that Malcolm's Black nationalist rhetoric speaks simultaneously to two audiences: a primary Black audience (the poem's "me") and a secondary White audience (the poem's "you").

The anaphoric, parallel structure of the poem's lines presents iterations of Malcolm's ability to, respectively, unify and terrify these audiences: "Malcolm X made me proud & so you got scared"; "Malcolm X told me to HURRY & you began to worry"; "Malcolm X words freed me & they frightened you." The speaker even specifically describes these rhetorical actions as praise and blame: "Malcolm X praised me & thus condemned you." Further, Malcolm accomplishes his rhetorical successes by wielding the linguistic resources of both Standard American English and Black English. In addition to describing Malcolm's rhetorical acts as "praising" and "condemning," the speaker celebrates that Malcolm "sounded you," "TOLD you," "SCREAMED on you," and "tol' it lak it DAMN SHO' IS!!"—strategies of blaming and praising that draw specifically on insular Black rhetorical practices. As I will discuss in the next chapter, some of BAM's most important rhetorical successes happen through praising Black aesthetics and values in the voice of uniquely Black language. Malcolm, as an early and lasting hero of the Black Arts Movement, helped to inspire Black Arts writers to value Black English and its rhetorical possibilities.

Within the genre of praise poems to Malcolm, elegies to the leader memorialize him not only by relating his acts as a rhetorician but by perpetuation of his revolutionary message. In "Malcolm," Sonia Sanchez recalls him vibrantly as

> the sun that tagged
> the western sky and
> melted tiger-scholars
> while they searched for stripes

The speaker praises him as a skilled rhetor whose oratory trumped those whose formal education, but not rhetorical acumen, exceeded his own as an autodidact. She preserves his messages as follows:

> he said, fuck you, white
> man. we have been
> curled too long. nothing
> is sacred, not your
> white face nor any
> land that separates
> until some voices
> squat with spasms (38–39)

Her deeply mournful praise memorializes Malcolm's psogos of the sins of a White ruling class that thinks itself sacred to the exclusion of others, and she points to Malcolm's work to rebirth Black America as a self-determined nation—a process that, just like a literal birth, requires enduring the "spasms" of labor. Clarence Major's "Brother Malcolm: Waste Limit" honors Malcolm by reminding the reader of his definition of a "REAL REVOLUTION":

> He said A REAL REVOLUTION
> to change the structure
> of the society: money in the bank
> and not in the
> dresser drawer
> he meant
>   he also meant a lack of killing
> of the self
> which the peak of white society
> imposed on the bottom, the back porch
> of the empire.

Major here deftly enjambs lines to force the reader to dwell on words that signal the divergence of the new Black consciousness from old ways of thinking. His enjambment of "a lack of killing / of the self" juxtaposes Black Power ideology with what movement activists considered conciliatory and outmoded nonviolent protest tactics. He further compels the reader to pause at the line break in "the back porch / of the empire," aligning images of segregation and marginalized socioeconomic status with the vast American scale on which such oppression occurs. Major goes on to underscore Malcolm's message of "REAL REVOLUTION" as a reclamation of rhetorical power:

> No longer the white interpreter
> of things for the world
> of non-whites (Randall and Burroughs 8)

Praise rhetoric here and in the Malcolm poems at large does not serve, as it does when employed for conservative forces, as an impediment to action. In the case of the Malcolm poems, the writers argue that the best way to honor Malcolm's virtue and sacrifice is to act on the revolutionary principles he espoused. As Edward Spriggs writes in "For Brother Malcolm," the only true memorial for Malcolm is a dynamic memorial of action:

> there is no memorial site
> in harlem,
> save the one we are building
> in the street of
> our young minds

till our hands & eyes
have strength to mold
the concrete beneath our feet (Randall and Burroughs 73)

Conclusion

In this chapter I have argued that instances of violence in Black Arts Movement works can be read as having a specific and purposeful connection to the revolutionary rhetorical goals of the movement's activist writers. Specifically, poetic moments of explicit violence serve as psogos rhetoric that indicts actions and values of the ruling class. Black Arts writers employed the other arm of epideictic rhetoric through panegyric poetry that raised heroes like Malcolm X as exemplars of the alternative value system upon which the activists hoped to establish a Black nation. When writers performed this successfully within the hearing of both their primary and secondary audiences, they wielded epideictic rhetoric as the antistrophos to physical violence, unifying their primary constituency under the banner of Black identity and placing White opponents in a defensive position from which they would be more willing to negotiate with radical demands. As Haki Madhubuti observes at the beginning of the chapter, a poem may not be able to stop a bullet, but collective rhetorical action can accomplish things for radical movements that individual or even collective violence cannot.

In terms of the broader significance of this analysis for Rhetorical Studies, recognizing and validating the significance of psogos rhetoric can open rhetorical scholarship not only to a fuller understanding of the species of epideictic rhetoric but also to an appreciation of the rhetorical resources of radical movements from the margins. Epideictic rhetoric of blame can serve as a crucial tool for marginalized radicals to problematize and destabilize oppressive ruling-class values and beliefs—rhetorical moves that precede and are complemented by rhetoric of praise to instantiate new, revolutionary value systems. Moreover, the cultivation of psogos rhetoric by radical movements may allow for significant political shifts that rely not solely on violent action, but also on taking advantage of the dynamic capacities of rhetoric.

As a foundation for a rhetorical assessment of the Black Arts Movement, understanding the rhetorical significance of some of the most troubling aspects of Black Arts writing can, without apologizing for its limitations and prejudices, help move critical discussion toward the movement's more constructive accomplishments and legacies. In the next chapter, I will expand the discussion of the praise function of Black Arts poetry to examine ways that writers used tropes particular to Black English to argue for Black language and Black physicality as the new aesthetic ideal. Black Arts writers used praise rhetoric, as Baraka had predicted in 1964, for Black people to see themselves as beautiful and love themselves.

CHAPTER 3

"A Tradition of Beautiful Talk"

The Black Arts Poet-Rhetor and the Black Is Beautiful Movement

Although the public rallying cry to recognize that "Black Is Beautiful" achieved widespread popularity in the 1960s and 1970s, the sentiment certainly did not originate in the Black Power era. The common origin story attributes the first public statement of the concept, though not the pithy phrase itself, to Black abolitionist, physician, and Supreme Court litigator John Sweat Rock, who boldly affirmed the beauty of Black physicality in a speech at Boston's Faneuil Hall in March 1858. Likely in front of a mostly or all-White audience, Rock declares with honesty couched in wry humor, "When I contrast the fine tough muscular system, the beautiful, rich color, the full broad features, and the gracefully frizzled hair of the Negro, with the delicate physical organization, wan color, sharp features and lank hair of the Caucasian, I am inclined to believe that when the white man was created, nature was pretty well exhausted—but determined to keep up appearances, she pinched up his features, and did the best she could under the circumstances" (110). Records of the speech note that the audience laughed after this moment—perhaps because of the humorous picture he paints of Nature's making do with White folks' looks, but also likely because the assertion that Black phenotypical features could be more beautiful than White ones may have struck the audience as absurd. With roots in Western culture traceable back to ancient texts, standards of beauty and morality that equate Whiteness or lightness with goodness and beauty and Blackness or darkness with evil and ugliness stood as established pillars of Western aesthetics, both during Rock's time and at the beginning of the Black Power era over a century later.

Prior to the dynamic work of Black Power activists to actively reclaim and re-connote the term "Black," to describe someone as "black" was a significant insult because of its negative aesthetic connotations—indicating the opposite of Whiteness as the beauty ideal. Poet and activist Haki Madhubuti (born Don L. Lee) includes in his first published volume of poems, *Think Black!* (1967), a piece called "In a Period of Growth," in which his speaker describes what his pre-Black-consciousness response would have been to being called "black":

> like,
> if he had da called me
> black seven years ago,
> i wd've—
> > broke his right eye out,
> > jumped into his chest
> > talked about his mama,
> > lied on his sister
> > & dared him to say it again
>
> all in one breath—
> seven years ago. (Lee, *Think Black!* 19)

As the account in the poem demonstrates, calling someone "black" amounted to serious insult as late as the 1960s, provoking, as the speaker in the poem states with minimal hyperbole, both physical and cutting verbal retaliation. After Madhubuti's coming to Black consciousness, a process he describes in a subsequent poem (discussed below) as centrally involving his engagement with texts by politically aware Black writers—"pitchblack / paragraphs of / 'us, we, me, i' / awareness" (Lee, *Black Pride* 19)—his relationship to "Black" as a descriptor of selfhood has entirely reversed. The semantic significance of being "Black" shifts from being a detested insult to a chosen appellation that describes one's proud, affirmed racial identity—something, according to James Brown's funk anthem of the era, to "say loud." Given this context, the fight to assert the beauty of Blackness stands as one of the most daunting struggles and most significant rhetorical legacies of the Black Arts project.

Later in the speech noted above, John Sweat Rock astutely observes that standards of beauty are deeply socially contextualized. "When the avenues of wealth are opened to us, we will then become educated and wealthy," he predicts, ". . . and black will be a very pretty color." Rock further suggests that this aestheticizing will extend to Black language. Black social prestige, he asserts, "will make our jargon, wit—our words, oracles" (110). Rock's argument here interestingly predates the trajectory of Black empowerment promoted by revolutionary nationalists, most notably the Black Panthers, in the 1960s and 1970s. Advocating a Marxist program that posited that social change follows from primary changes in economic and political structures, the politics of revolutionary nationalists suggested that a revaluation of the aesthetics of Blackness would happen as a natural outcome of the revolution. Cultural nationalists, on the other hand, including many Black Arts activists, saw the trajectory toward empowerment beginning with a change in values that would then propel political and social changes. The impetus for revolutionary action, they believed, would be a rhetorical struggle for aesthetic values. Literary scholar and Black aesthetic theorist Addison Gayle predicted in 1969 that "[t]he acceptance of the phrase 'Black Is Beautiful' is the first step in the destruction of the old table of the laws and the construction of new ones" (44). In the Black aesthetic project, these "new laws" indicated a revolution in both aesthetic values and social order. The social order would begin with a new language of aesthetic value that elevated, if not privileged, physical, linguistic, and artistic aspects of Blackness.

Chicago poet, artist, and teacher Margaret Burroughs, an elder among the youthful Black Arts contingent in Chicago and founder of the Ebony Museum of Negro History and Art (later known as the renowned DuSable Museum of African American History), depicts the problem of re-aestheticizing Blackness in her poem "What Shall I Tell My Children Who Are Black?" Asking as the premise of the poem, "What shall I tell my children who are black / Of what it means to be a captive in this dark skin? / What shall I tell my dear one, fruit of my womb, / of how beautiful they are when everywhere they turn / they are faced with abhorrence of everything that is black?" Burroughs offers examples of the ways negative aesthetic connotations of Blackness saturate her and her children's world:

> The night is black and so is the boogyman.
> Villains are black with black hearts.
> A black cow gives no milk. A black hen lays no eggs.
> Storm clouds, black, black is evil
> and evil is black and devil's food is black...

She contrasts this with examples, specifically of the kinds of things children value, of how "white has been made to represent / all that is good and pure and fine and decent":

> ... clouds are white and dolls, and heaven
> surely is a white, white place with angels
> robed in white, and cotton candy and ice cream
> and milk and ruffled Sunday dresses
> and dream houses and long sleek cadillacs
> and Angel's food is white... all, all... white.

Most problematically, these color-specific connotations of aesthetic and moral value cause children to hate aspects of their own physicality—cause a child, the poem states, to "[come] home in tears because a playmate / Has called him black, big lipped, flatnosed and nappy headed." The solution, for Burroughs's speaker, is not only to assure her child that he is "no less beautiful and dear," but to use the art of story to excoriate the painful old aesthetic values and reinscribe the concept of Blackness as the beautiful. This is a paideic enterprise—a recasting of values that relies on literature as a rhetorical vehicle to convey cultural identity. Burroughs's speaker, the poet-rhetor,

> will lift up their heads in proud blackness
> with the story of their fathers and their father's fathers.
> And I shall take them into a way back time
> of kings and queens who ruled the Nile,
> and measured the stars and discovered the laws of mathematics.
> I will tell them of a black people upon whose backs have been built the wealth
>   of three continents.
> I will tell him this and more.
> And knowledge of his heritage shall be his weapon and his armor.

I argue that Black Arts poets most effectively accomplished this rhetorical task when Black aesthetics were not only the *theme* but the *form* of their work. In this chapter, I look specifically at the ways Black Arts poets served as educators of the Black public, rhetorical hybrids of African griots and European citizen-orators. These poet-rhetors aimed to teach their audience that "Black Is Beautiful," valuing both Black phenotypical physicality and, significantly, the aesthetic possibilities of Black language traditions. As I discuss in the poems below, Black Arts writers argued that Black Is Beautiful both as physicality and as artistic expression. Just as these activists asserted that being called "black, big lipped, flatnosed and nappy headed" should be understood as a compliment about one's beauty, so should the sophisticated use of Black English language and rhetorical modes be considered a compliment about one's literary acumen. Importantly, conveying these messages through the vehicle of Black English—educating people about the value of their culture in the insular language and rhetorical forms of that culture—allowed these poet-rhetors to have far-reaching and long-lasting influence.

In what follows, I present rhetorical readings of poems that demonstrate how Black Arts poets used the form as the message in articulating the aesthetics of Blackness. I then discuss the legacies of this rhetorical work, specifically in terms of the way that the work of Black Arts poets in the aestheticization of Black language influenced scholars and activists to take the fight for Black English further into formal institutions of education.

The Bad Rap of "Black Is Beautiful"

Sonia Sanchez, a poet, playwright, educator, and activist in the Black Arts scenes on both the East Coast and the West Coast, employs Black English grammar, lexicon, and modes of discourse as both means and message in her poetry. Born in Birmingham, Alabama, and raised and educated in New York, including political science studies at Hunter College and postgraduate work in poetry at New York University, Sanchez has for most of her career coupled being a writer with being an educator. In the mid-1960s, she moved to San Francisco to build a Black Studies program at San Francisco State University, the first such program in the United States, where, among other challenges, she was under investigation by the FBI for teaching W. E. B. Du Bois. One of her missions at San Francisco State during the early years of Black Studies was to persuade her students that Black English was a beautiful and nuanced vehicle for writing. As she recalls in an interview with H. Samy Alim,

> When my students began writing, they did so in their own language. I accepted it in class. I encouraged it. I saw that they were nervous about writing. It seemed to me that what was important was to get them to write down what they spoke. I told people to get tape recorders, have someone write down what they said. So when they brought their papers in, here was this magical writing with all this language. And it was like, Black English, you know. It had all the lyricism. It had all the beat. And I said, "Read it out loud." And they read it out loud. And they heard the music. They heard the beauty. ("Sounds" 92)

For Sanchez as a vocal poet-rhetor and educator, the advocacy of the Black Is Beautiful message relied integrally on expressing it through the aesthetics of Black language. She could articulate the beauty of Black people most profoundly and persuasively in a medium familiar and particular to herself and her audience.

The title poem of her 1970 volume, "we a baddDDD people," exemplifies her use of Black English's unique linguistic attributes and rhetorical resources to educate her audience about the beauty of Black bodies, Black style, Black culture, and Black language itself. Beginning with the title, the grammar of the poem indicates to the Black addressee that the poet intends the work as a celebration of collective selfhood. In Black English grammar, the use of the unconjugated form of the copula ("be," though occasionally regularized to "bees") as the verb for any particular subject indicates habitual action or condition. The poem begins with the statement "we bees real / bad" and continues to assert through the use of the habitual "be" a general, almost natural condition of Black collective "badness":

> i mean.
>   we bees real
> bad.
>   we gots bad songs
> sung on every station
> we gots some bad   N A T U R A L S
> on our heads
>   and brothers gots
> some bad loud (fo real)
>   dashiki threads
>   on them.
>   i mean when
> we dance   u know we be doooen it
>
>   when we talk
>   we be doooen it
>   when we rap
>   we be doooen it
>   and
> when we love. well. yeh. u be knowen
>   bout that too.   (uh-huh!) (*We a BaddDDD People* 52)

Sanchez spends much of the poem contextualizing and defining this excellence of character, thematically enforcing the culturally circulating premise that Black Is Beautiful—often using the grammar of the habitual "be" to generalize this excellence as a natural condition of existence. The final lines of the poem read

> we a BAAAADDD people
>   & every day
>   we be gitting
>   BAAAADDER (*We a BaddDDD People* 53)

This statement indicates that the condition of "badness" for Black folks habitually and continually progresses.

The full meaning of these statements to a Black audience depends upon reading the word "bad" in the context of Black semantics. When Standard English words receive a Black semantic gloss, their range of referents increases, often to the point of including the word's standard antonym in its list of referential possibilities. While most twenty-first-century Americans have already absorbed the dual Black semantic referents for "bad," sociolinguist Geneva Smitherman, writing in 1977, still notes a difference between White and insular Black connotations of the term: "Take the word *bad*. For blacks and whites, it suggests negativity, unpleasantness, distastefulness. For blacks only, it can also suggest something positive: good, extraordinary, beautiful" (*Talkin and Testifyin* 59). As a statement from a Black speaker to a Black reader, the poem's announcement that "we bees real bad" serves as an assertion of habitual excellence, of the natural beauty of the collective character. This meaning explains the speaker's use of "badder" in the poem's final line. "Badder," in this context, has a far different meaning than the implied Standard English replacement "worse," and the dominance of the Black vernacular grammar of "badder" here indicates a rebellion against the limiting rules of White expression. The White reader's colonizing rules of grammar and diction are unimportant here. The speaker instead asserts the beauty and excellence of Black culture most persuasively by voicing it in Black language.

This valorization of Black expression, both implicit and explicit in the poem, begins at the structural level. The title, "we a baddDDD people," directs the reader to Sanchez's use of Black English grammar through the "zero copula," the expression of indicative statements without a form of the verb "to be" (Smitherman, *Talkin and Testifyin* 5).[1] Disregarding the spelling conventions of Standard English throughout the poem, Sanchez forms words to reflect speaking conventions, later recognized by Black English linguists as norms of Black phonetics. For example, the spelling of words like "fo real" and "sistuhs" shows the tendency to leave off the final liquid (here "r"). Consider also the following passage:

and we be gitten into a
SPIRITUAL thing.
      like discipline
of the mind
soul. body.   no drinken cept to celebrate
our victories / births.
      no smoken.   no shooten
needles into our blk / veins
      full of potential blk/
gold cuz our
      high must come from

>   thinking working
>   planning fighting loving
>   our blk / selves
>   into nationhood. (*We a BaddDDD People* 53)

The frequent spelling of the gerund as ending with an "-en" suffix instead of an "-ing" suffix—as in "gitten," "drinken," "smoken," and "shooten"—shows the tendency to substitute the dental nasal "n" for the velar nasal "ng." The fact that Sanchez does not substitute this spelling consistently—choosing at times to use the Standard English spelling of the gerund ("thinking working / planning fighting loving")—subtly indicates Black English speakers' organically pluralistic relationship to English. Although Black English has distinct characteristics that differentiate it from Standard English, most speakers do not experience it within a linguistic vacuum. The characteristics of Black English themselves did not originate as codified rules but emerged descriptively in linguistic studies as general tendencies of Black speech.

In the same way that the phonetic and grammatical patterns of most White speakers vary unconsciously between Standard English and the tendencies of a particular regional dialect, the patterns of some Black speakers also vary unconsciously between Standard English and the Black English ethnolect. Sanchez obviously slants her spelling toward White conventions only with the term "knee/grow," which she uses to indict, alongside Whites and police, individuals clinging to a "Negro" mindset instead of embracing Black consciousness and Black nationalists politics:

>   we got some
>   BAADDD
>   thots and actions
>   like off those white mothafuckers
>   and rip it off if it ain't nailed
>   down and surround those wite/
>   knee / grow / pigs & don't let them
>   live to come back again into
>   our neighborhoods (we ain't
>   no museum for wite
>   queer/minds/dicks/to
>   fuck us up) (*We a BaddDDD People* 52)

The altered spelling both visually disconnects the word from associations with Black identity and jabs at the obtuse disconnect between spelling and performable speech in Standard English. Underscoring the role of Black Arts poet-rhetor as public performer and educator, Sanchez's attention to phonetics gives the poem the presence of actual speech and, accompanied by inclusively addressing the reader as "we," indicates a Black speaker addressing a Black audience.

The rhetorical mode of the poem serves as a powerful tool to communicate this message to Black speech community insiders. The speaker of the poem is *testifyin*—enacting a type of narrative sequencing, as noted in chapter 1, present in both sacred and secular contexts in which a speaker relates a powerful feeling or experience that resonates with the common experiences of those in the community. True to traditional oral testifyin that often involves the intense use of tonal semantics to convey emotion, Sanchez deploys tonal semantics orthographically in the poem by elongating vowels ("when we rap / we be doooen it"), using slash marks to indicate emphatic breaks ("wite / knee / grow / pigs"), and adding emphasis through capitalization ("we a BAAADDD people").

Sanchez builds the intensity of the poem with these devices to climax toward the end of the poem in a repeated phonetic cry of "aaa-ee-ooo-wah / wah":

> i mean.
>
>   when we spread ourselves thin over our
>   land and see our young / warriors /
>   sistuhs moven / runnen on blk /
>   hills of freedom.
>   we'll boo ga loo
> in love.
>   aaa-ee-ooo-wah / wah
>   aaa-ee-ooo-wah / wah
>   aaa-ee-ooo-wah / wah
>   aaa-ee-ooo-wah / wah
>
>   git em with yo bad self. don. rat now.
>   go on & do it. dudley. rat now. yeah.
>   run it on down. gwen. rat now. yeah. yeah.
>
>   aaa-e-ooooooo. w̄āh / w̄āh.
>   aaa-e-ooooooo. w̄āh / w̄āh. (*We a BaddDDD People* 53)

This cry indicates a fullness of celebration that defies the confines of words, bringing the reader fully into a sense of performative oral engagement. The speaker ends the poem while still at the height of tonal semantic use,

86 Chapter Three

talk-singing, and most likely engaging in clapping or stomping or some other kind of expressive action of the body indicated by the two underlined spaces "___ ___." This last stanza indicates as well the speaker's switch from caller of the testimony to respondent. The speaker gives the respondent a parenthetical voice earlier in the poem, interjecting "(fo real)," "(uh-huh!),", and perhaps even the longer parenthetical "museum" segment. In the last stanza, the speaker herself proclaims known response phrases: "git em with yo bad self," "rat now," "go on & do it," "yeah," "run it on down." She identifies the new callers as well—other poets and figures of the movement: "don," referring to Don L. Lee; "dudley" referring to Dudley Randall; and "gwen," referring to Gwendolyn Brooks, to whom Sanchez dedicates the poem. This change from caller to respondent locates both the speaker and the reader in an inclusive community of expression about the nature of Black culture, implicitly giving readers the opportunity to share in the celebration and definition of Blackness as beautiful through their own testimony.

Sanchez's rhetorical choice to testify and to call for testimony indicates that one of the poem's rhetorical aims is not only to educate the audience about the beauty of Blackness, but to persuade the audience members to proclaim the truth of this value themselves. According to Smitherman, testifyin by nature valorizes the self and invests the self in a community: through testifyin, "one's humanity is reaffirmed by the group and his or her sense of isolation diminished" (*Talkin and Testifyin* 134). The poem further suggests ways audience members can demonstrate their belief in these values, not only valorizing Black communicative modes as beautiful but also celebrating the natural attributes of Black bodies and the richness of Afrocentric culture. Sanchez opens the poem by evoking the popular appearance of the revolutionary: "we gots some bad NATURALS / on our heads / and brothers gots / some bad loud (fo real) / dashiki threads / on them." If the poem has successfully converted audience members to or deepened their affinity for the "BAADDD thots and actions" promoted by Black nationalist movements, these individuals can show their belief in the beauty of Blackness on their bodies. The conversion to Black consciousness, then, becomes performable not only for the Black Arts Movement's poet-rhetors but also for its army of cultural revolutionaries.

Sanchez's dedication of "we a baddDDD people" to Gwendolyn Brooks, whom she calls "a fo real bad one," may surprise readers who think of Brooks as a poet of the generation preceding the Black Arts Movement, an Afromodernist and Pulitzer Prize winner whose work had already been accepted by the White literary establishment by the 1950s. Brooks, renowned elder

Chicago poet, educator, and activist, is perhaps the most notable convert in the 1960s of established, senior writers to the Black Arts project. In *Report from Part One*, the first volume of her autobiography, she describes her famous conversion to Blackness, which was sparked by her experience with young writers at the 1967 Fisk University Writers' Conference in Nashville. She calls the conference her first experience with the "New Black"—particularly with youth energized by the Black Arts project and who considered established "Negro" writers complicit with White institutions:

> Coming from white white white South Dakota State College I arrived in Nashville, Tennessee, to give one more "reading." But blood-boiling surprise was in store for me. First, I was aware of a general energy, an electricity, in look, walk, speech, *gesture* of the young blackness I saw all about me. I had been loved at South Dakota State College. Here, I was coldly Respected.... All that day and night, Margaret Danner Cunningham—another Old Girl, another coldly Respected old Has-been—and an almost hysterical Gwendolyn B. walked about in amazement, listening, looking, learning. *What was going on*! (84–85)

Instead of taking offense to the younger generation's cold reception—especially compared to what she describes as their jubilation at the presence of Amiri Baraka—Brooks became captivated by the dynamic energy of the young writers. She states, "In 1967's Nashville, . . . I was in some inscrutable and uncomfortable wonderland. I didn't know what to make of what surrounded me, of what with hot sureness began almost immediately to invade me. *I* had never been, before, in the general presence of such insouciance, such live firmness, such confident vigor, such determination to mold or carve something DEFINITE" (85). The "something definite" these activists hoped to sculpt was a new image and understanding of Blackness, a new Black consciousness that would inspire individuals to political activism by affirming their beauty and the depth of Black culture. Brooks describes her own coming to Black consciousness humbly: "I—who have 'gone the gamut' from an almost angry rejection of my dark skin by some of my brainwashed brothers and sisters to a surprised queenhood in the new black sun—am qualified to enter at least the kindergarten of the new consciousness now. New consciousness and trudge-toward-progress" (86). Significantly, the early stages of this conversion for Brooks involved her revaluation of Black as beautiful in relation to perceptions of her own physicality—the move from "an almost angry rejection of my dark skin" to "a surprised queenhood in the new black sun"—and this change appears notably in her post-1967 work.

As a sign of her devotion to advocating the new Black consciousness, in the late sixties Brooks left major publisher Harper & Row, with whom she had been publishing since 1945, to contribute her work to Broadside Press, an independent Black press run by Detroit poet Dudley Randall. One reason for the "cold respect" Brooks received from young writers at the Fisk conference was their concern that her previous writing, with its development of European American forms and complex modernist imagery, had not been intended for Black audiences. For example, Haki Madhubuti, in the introduction to *Report from Part One*, states straightforwardly about her Pulitzer Prize–winning work, "*Annie Allen* (1949), important? Yes. Read by blacks? No" (Lee, "Gwendolyn Brooks" 17). Along with her move to Broadside, Brooks articulated a renewed dedication to making her work significant for and accessible to Black audiences: "My aim, in my next future, is to write poems that will somehow successfully 'call' (see Imamu Baraka's 'SOS') all black people: black people in taverns, black people in alleys, black people in gutters, schools, offices, factories, prisons, the consulate; I wish to reach black people in pulpits, black people in mines, on farms, on thrones; *Not* always to 'teach'—I shall wish often to entertain, to illumine."[2] Faithful to this aim as well as to her affirmation that "[m]y newish voice will not be an imitation of the contemporary young black voice, which I so admire, but an extending adaptation of today's Gwendolyn Brooks' voice" (*Report* 30), some of Brooks's post-1967 work builds on her established deep talent as a narrative poet—but now more closely aligned with Black vernacular narrative traditions.

Family Pictures (1970), one of the five poetry volumes Brooks published with Broadside Press between 1969 and 1975, includes "The Life of Lincoln West," a narrative poem in which Brooks explores through a young protagonist the possibilities of turning "black" as insult into "Black" as proud marker of identity. Here Brooks employs the long-standing tradition of narrative sequencing, rhetorical storytelling, to argue for the positive connotation and aestheticization of Blackness. In addition to recognizing the practice of narrative sequencing in distinct or ritualized storytelling traditions such as testifyin or the toast, Smitherman points to storytelling as a general register of Black communication. "Black English speakers," she states, "will render their general, abstract observations about love, life, people in the form of a concrete narrative. . . . The relating of events (real or hypothetical) becomes a black rhetorical strategy to explain a point, to persuade holders of opposing views to one's own point of view" (*Talkin and Testifyin* 147–48). In "The Life of Lincoln West," Brooks uses the narrative as a subtle argument for the beauty of Black features as markers of inherent Africanness—of adopting Black identity because of the deep beauty of African roots.

Brooks introduces Lincoln West ("Linc") as "Ugliest little boy / That everyone ever saw. That is what everyone said." This publicly acknowledged ugliness, which Brooks describes as the consensus among both the Black and White individuals Linc encounters, stems from their common dislike of Linc's pronounced phenotypically Black features:

> ... The pendulous lip, the
> branching ears, the eyes so wide and wild,
> the vague unvibrant brown of the skin,
> and, most disturbing, the great head. (*Family Pictures* 9)

Brooks contrasts Linc's "ugly" features with what the speaker describes as his "all pretty" White kindergarten teacher: "she was all pretty! all daintiness, / all tiny vanilla, with blue eyes and fluffy / sun-hair" (10). From the first introduction of Linc, though, the speaker describes his looks as more significant than their subjective "ugliness," suggesting instead that they are markers of a deep and valuable lineage: "These components of That Look bespoke / the sure fibre. The deep grain" (9).

The poem details a series of rejections and embarrassments that Linc experiences during his young life from most everyone he encounters—his parents, his teachers, strangers—all based on the fact that he has "That Look." These anecdotes build to a life-changing experience he has while at the movies with his mother when seven years old. A White man who sat down next to Linc in the theater whispers, within Linc's and his mother's earshot, to a companion,

> THERE! That's the kind I've been wanting
> to show you! One of the best
> examples of the specie. Not like
> those diluted Negroes you see so much of on
> the streets these days, but the
> real thing.
>
> Black, ugly, and odd. You
> can see the savagery. The blunt
> blankness. That is the real
> thing.

Linc's response to this assessment is surprising. While his mother, embarrassed and outraged, curses the man and pulls Linc out of the theater, Linc has what the speaker calls a "new idea":

> All the way home he was happy. Of course,
> he had not liked the word
> "ugly."
> But, after all, should he not
> be used to that by now? What had
> struck him, among words and meanings
> he could little understand, was the phrase
> "the real thing."
> He didn't know quite why,
> but he liked that.
> He liked that very much. (12)

Linc here chooses to own the White man's observation without accepting the accompanying connotation.

Instead, Linc finds meaning in the idea of himself as authentic, as not a "diluted Negro" but "one of the best / examples of the specie." While the White man, viewing Linc's phenotypically Black facial features through the lens of anti-Black racism, had seen them as exemplifying ugliness, oddity, savagery, and blankness, Linc chooses to believe instead that he is in earnest one of the best examples of humanity, taking the man's message and reinventing and adapting its connotation. After the incident, Linc comes to own the idea of being "the real thing" and makes it into a tool for survival:

> When he was hurt, too much
> stared at—
> too much
> left alone—he
> thought about that. He told himself
> "After all, I'm
> the real thing." (12–13)

This survival strategy of taking oppressive White language and meanings and reversing or revising them, flipping the script on them, has long been part of Black language practice, and Linc exemplifies how taking power over words can help one to resist the oppressive messages and practices of racist communities and individuals.

More specifically, Brooks uses Linc's narrative here to enact the process of an individual coming to Black consciousness—and in particular of an individual coming to love his physical Blackness in spite of all of his social encounters and lessons having taught him to despise his looks. Instead of being physically "diluted" by generations of mixture with Whites, Linc's body represents what the reader imagines is the "sure fibre" and "deep grain" of lineage that connects back to African ancestors. Brooks underscores the lesson with her protagonist's name: the young boy in the poem comes to love himself when he sees himself as a "link" to African authenticity for those in the Western arm of the African diaspora. Brooks ends the poem with a young Linc who believes in his worth despite his still having to suffer name-calling and loneliness. The lesson is not about changing others but about coming to self-love through Black consciousness—a self-love that recognizes African ancestry as beauty and richness. By conveying this subtle lesson through poetic story, Brooks, as an elder aiming to teach values, is performing the paideic act not only of the poet-rhetor but of the griot.

Like Brooks, Sarah Webster Fabio, an Oakland-based poet, performer, and professor, enacted a fundamental responsibility of the griot by making the passing down of Black language traditions central to her work. Fabio exemplifies the Black Arts poet-rhetor who worked to disseminate her message to the people by any means necessary. In 1973, she published an accumulation of her work in a seven-volume series of chapbooks called *Rainbow Signs*, which included *Together/To the Tune of Coltrane's Equinox, Boss Soul, Jujus & Jubilees, Soul Ain't Soul Is, My Own Thing, Jujus/Alchemy of the Blues*, and *Black Back: Back Black*. She also recorded a series of Folkways records in the early 1970s, in which she performed to instrumental accompaniment many of the poems distributed in print as part of her chapbook series and other publications. A professor during the height of the movement at Merritt College, a hotbed of Black Power activity, Fabio pioneered Black Studies programs both at Merritt and at the University of California, Berkeley, earning her the honorific "Mother of Black Studies" from fellow activists. For Fabio, the paideic Black Arts Movement mission was meant to be enacted in both informal and formal sites of education, and this conversion of her students and listeners to Black consciousness necessarily involved advocacy of Black Is Beautiful in both its physical and linguistic senses. For Black folks, engaging in "Black Talk," as she expresses in a poem of that name, constitutes "natural / acts / like / fondling, / sucking teeth / and teat, / feelings / passing / between / folk, / springing / like / mother's milk / from a / well of / being" (*Black Back* 18). Using and teaching the aesthetic value of Black language traditions equates to passing along the mother's milk of Black culture.

"Black Back," the title poem of her 1973 chapbook, employs the Black English mode of testifyin and poetic-performative uses of repetition, rhyme, and chiasmus as tonal semantics to argue for the empowering possibilities of conceiving of one's body and selfhood as "Black." True to the generic conventions of testifyin, Fabio's speaker shares in first-person her individual experiences, but these experiences ring true to the common experiences of her Black audience and affirm her connection with them as part of a Black collective. Further, the speaker's repetitive interjections of "Check it out" and "Dig" throughout the poem ("dig" and "check it out" both appear five times in the 115-word composition) mark the piece as a hybrid of the spoken and the written—or, more specifically, a written iteration of a fundamentally oral and performative rhetorical mode. The speaker addresses the poem, in colloquialisms that mark semantic emphasis in verbal exchange, directly to an audience of hip speech community insiders whom she hopes to persuade to "dig" her message. Additionally, Fabio deploys rhyme, repetition, and alliterative word play in the poem in a rhetorically effective use of tonal semantics. Smitherman argues that "[t]he key to understanding black tonal semantics is to recognize that the sound of what is being said is just as important as 'sense.' Both sound and sense are used to deliver the Word. . . . These songified patterns of speech reach down to the 'deep structure' of life, that common level of shared human experience which words alone cannot convey" (*Talkin and Testifyin* 135). Fabio's use of tonal semantics in the poem constitutes both part of the message and part of the rhetorical strategy to bring her listeners into Black selfhood.

The formal techniques in "Black Back" reflect both Fabio's poetic sensibility in a European American sense (she was trained formally as a writer at both Fisk University and San Francisco State College) and her deep respect for and advocacy of the aesthetics of Black English. In her foreword to *A Mirror: A Soul. A Two-Part Volume of Poems* (1969), she asserts that her poems are "bi-lingual, if not tri-lingual" because of her discrete and hybrid use of the "standardized English" of the "exiled European" in America as well as the "black mother tongue." In affirmation of Black English as a vital form of expression for many and as a significant formal aspect of her own writing, she states, "For that great bulk of American Blacks who are and have always been outside the pale of America, there is a black mother tongue, born out of necessity from a period where not only were their bodies shackled, their minds enslaved but their tongues were tied." This language, the vehicle that can best "approximate [one's] black experience in America," deserves respect as an aesthetically rich form of expression.

The recording of the poem "Black Back" on Fabio's album *Boss Soul* (1973) is prefaced by a statement about Black language: "Black talk has always taken words and images and broken or distorted them to present world view, to code a new language which would be foreign to those who control and repress. Double-talk with two levels of meaning." Fabio employs the layered semantics characteristic of Black language in the poem through the unadorned repetition of "back /Black, / Black / back," letting each word encompass a range of significations, all of which juxtapose the ideas of valorizing the phenotypically Black body and of simultaneously adopting a politically radical Black consciousness. In the opening lines, the speaker declares she is "Back / Home again," a homecoming she describes as "Black back / all the way / back. Black. Dig" (*Black Back* 4). "Black back" could describe the physical back of the body, a charged synecdochic representation of the Black self in the context of severe beatings and whippings that were part of the history of American slavery. The reference to "Black back / all the way / back. Black" could also refer to the speaker affirming Blackness as her identity and the long-standing identity of her ancestors. The speaker coming "back Black" suggests that she has redefined herself in the new Black consciousness—no longer "Negro," but Black in the sense of having affirmed selfhood, pride in African lineage, and support of the nationalist politics of self-determination. This recasted positive Black identity is not only something the speaker applies to her generation but also something she bestows on the generations before her: she's Black from *all* the way back. The "Dig" that caps these opening lines allows the reader or listener to pause to appreciate all of the layered meanings of these straightforwardly repeated words, to appreciate both their semantic glosses and the emphatic meanings Fabio creates by pairing these words through rhyme and alliteration.

The poem goes on to relate the speaker's celebration of her full physical self as Black:

Check it out.
Black from
the tips
of my
black kinks
to the
hard earth-caked
soles of my feet.
Dig.
To the
bruised
dark blood

of my being;
to the
core of
my black
soul,
dig. (*Black Back* 4–5)

In her imagery here, Fabio uses language that may conventionally have negative connotations but flips its meaning in order to celebrate beauty. The speaker describes her hair as "black kinks," which would not have been celebrated by previous generations who valued straight hair as a beauty standard. She describes the soles of her feet as "hard" and "earth-caked," perhaps a literal description, but also perhaps a celebration of the color and character of her feet that diverges from the ideal of lovely "ladylike" feet as delicate, soft, and protected from use by shoes. She describes her blood as "bruised," a figurative reference to the idea of even her blood as proudly blue-black, resilient from the suffering of generations. Fabio enacts in her physical descriptions the same kind of connotative inversion that Black Arts and Black Power activists were looking to accomplish by taking the term "Black" from insult to primary marker of identity, indicative of both beauty and heritage.

Fabio continues in the poem to praise the beauty of Blackness through language play. By playing with the pronoun "I," the speaker expands her proud Blackness to encompass not only her body but her mind, her God, and her ideals:

And the
black eye
of my
i-
magination,
to the
black
i-
mage of
my God,
to the
black
i-
dea
of beauty

> and wisdom
> flowing
> naturally
> from
> this
> black
> thing.
> Dig. (*Black Back* 5)

Continuing her technique from earlier in the poem, Fabio inverts the connotation of "black eye," referring not to the injured body but to a particularly Black perspective that inflects her "i- / magination," her individual creative self. The poem resonates here with the ideology behind the Black aesthetic—that there is a unique artistic point of view that can be expressed only from an author's lived experience as Black in America, from an aware, resolved double consciousness that speaks through art. "Black eye" quickly and playfully becomes "black / i" in the lines that follow. The speaker's subsequent repeated emphasis on "i" in "i- / mage" and "i- / dea," each time placing the first-person pronoun emphatically on its own line, underscores the poem's privileging of versions of the world that are filtered through the individual Black consciousness. The image of God, which so often as presented by American religious institutions does not look phenotypically Black, is instead a "black image" that the empowered speaker produces herself. The concepts of beauty and wisdom are also "black ideas" that "flow naturally" from the speaker's consciousness, from her "black thing." This realized Black selfhood, the self to which the speaker has come "back Black," becomes the source of her worldly and spiritual knowledge and her creative output. And the poem's repetition and wordplay direct the reader to this theme of primacy of the self.

The last thirteen lines of the poem turn from the speaker's personal testimony about coming to Black consciousness to a call to readers to affirm their own Black identities—to accept Black physicality ("Be Black / back") and to be converted to Black consciousness ("Be back / Black"):

> Be Black
> back
> Be back
> Black
> Check it out.
> Be back
> Black

> now
> Black
> back
> Now.
> Check it out.
> Dig. (*Black Back* 6)

At this point in the poem, semantics become secondary to the sound play. As a piece to be not only read but heard (recorded or live) by audiences, the poem's persuasiveness as a call to Black consciousness climaxes here in the emphatic use of rhyme and repetition, interspersed with commands to "be" Black "now." After having first demonstrated her ethos through her testimony, the speaker here shows her dexterity with language to relate to her audience even more closely. The message is a celebration of the beauty of Blackness in body, mind, and speech, and Fabio, to use Baraka's words, invites her audience to "come on in."

Black Arts poets were able to reach such broad audiences in advocating that Black Is Beautiful perhaps because many of their poems dealt self-consciously and honestly with the personal challenges the poets faced in looking to change their own self-conceptions. In "Naturally," poet Audre Lorde questions how the Black Is Beautiful fight might end up supporting exploitative economic and social institutions instead of resulting in the change cultural nationalists had hoped. The poem's speaker offers that "Since Naturally Black is Naturally Beautiful / I must be proud / And, naturally / Black and / Beautiful," although she describes herself as "a trifle / Yellow / And plain, though proud, / Before." And although the speaker has been with the program, she questions what impact her personal changes have made:

> Having spent the summer sunning
> And feeling naturally free
>   (if I die of skin cancer
>   oh well—one less
>   black and beautiful me)
> Yet no agency spends millions
> To prevent my summer tanning
> And who trembles nightly
> With the fear of their lily cities being swallowed
> By a summer ocean of naturally wooly hair?

What if, the speaker wonders, none of this is revolutionary after all? She closes the poem ironically, admitting that

> I've bought my can of
> Natural Hair Spray
> Made and marketed in Watts
> Still thinking more
> Proud and beautiful Black women
> Could better make and use
> Black bread (*New York* 35)

This poem asks honestly and critically how this speaker's demonstration of pride in Black physicality has resulted in changing her circumstances for the better, especially given that she was "proud before."

But individuals with the long-standing confidence of Lorde's speaker were likely the exception. For example, in Haki Madhubuti's "The Self-Hatred of Don L. Lee," the speaker confesses that he experiences a mixture of self-love and self-loathing on both sides of his conversion to Blackness. He writes that prior to his education about the depth and value of Black culture, a learning process he describes as "painfully / struggling / thru Du Bois, / Rogers, Locke, / Wright & others"—the "pitchblack / paragraphs of / 'us, we, me, i' / awareness" that "vanquished" his "blindness"—he valued the lightness of his skin because of the social privileges White people and institutions bestowed upon him because of it:

> i,
> at one time,
> loved
> my
> color—
> it
> opened sMall
> doors of tokenism
> &
> acceptance.
>
>   (doors called, "the only one" & "our negro")

After coming to value the beauty of Blackness, however, the speaker leaves behind the Whiteness-privileging colorism that motivated his earlier self-conception. But this also comes at a price: he now disdains his light-skinned physicality:

> i
> began
> to love
> only a
> part of
> me—
> my inner
> self which
> is all
> black—
> &
> developed a
> vehement
> hatred of
> my light
> brown
> outer. (Lee, *Black Pride* 19)

Certainly Black Arts poets, as rhetors looking to invert the aesthetic connotations of Blackness, did not intend to perpetuate the same kinds of hierarchies under which they had suffered. And Madhubuti, one of these poet-rhetors, presents a message here that political Blackness has nothing to do with one's "outer" self—being educated about the value of Black culture, specifically through its texts, gave the speaker an "inner / self which / is all / black" whose self-love comes from participation in Black collectivity instead of White-privileged exceptionalism. Madhubuti's honesty here about the complexity of waging a rhetorical war for values points to the ongoing struggle within and outside of Black communities for recognizing the beauty of Black bodies and the aesthetics of Black language and communicative forms. The work of Black Power and Black Arts activists opened up as never before standards of beauty in popular culture to take singular privilege away from light skin, straight hair, and slight bodies. Although these hierarchies are far from eradicated, this inclusive broadening of beauty standards marked a significant cultural shift. But the strides these activists made in cracking the foundations of White aesthetics can be traced through many facets of American culture. In particular, the valorization of Black language as art caused significant changes in literary theory and educational practice.

Vernacular Theory of African American Literature: The Legacy of Stephen Henderson

"Of course there is a 'Black poem,'" Sarah Webster Fabio asserts in an interview included in *Black Back: Back Black*:

> It is one that first of all comes from the culture and has a voice that is distinctive to the culture. This doesn't mean there will be any simplistic stereotype Black voice because ... Black voices vary greatly in their use of idiom, even in rhythm patterns. It all reflects where you came from two generations ago, and what routes you took through the Middle Passage, and things like that. But I think that rhythm, voice, use of idiom, similes and metaphors that come from folk tradition—these are all things you might look for in a "Black poem." (vi)

One of the most significant outcomes of the language arm of the Black Is Beautiful fight is the development during and subsequent to the Black Arts Movement of a vernacular theory of African American literature, a theory that asserts and explicates how "the vernacular informs and becomes the foundation for formal black literature" (Gates, *Signifying Monkey* xxii). For early advocates of vernacular theory as expressive of the Black aesthetic, it was possible to perceive Blackness as an inherent element of a text, and the inherent Blackness significantly contributed to the text's aesthetic value. Here, the insistence of Black Arts poet-rhetors that Black Is Beautiful helped to make inroads into the established literary canon for works that valorized Black English and its rhetorical modes.

To trace this influence, it is necessary to examine the foundational early articulation of this critical stance developed by Black Arts Movement scholar Stephen Henderson. "The Forms of Things Unknown," the provocative introduction to his 1973 anthology, *Understanding the New Black Poetry: Black Speech and Black Music as Poetic References*, both directly responds to poetic works of the Black Arts era—hence the promise of the anthology's title to explicate what the "New Black Poetry" is doing—and serves as a critical resource for major works in vernacular theory by Henry Louis Gates Jr., Houston Baker Jr., and Bernard W. Bell that would appear in the 1980s.[3] Henderson argues in his introduction that, in contrast to the tenets of the dominant Western aesthetic that privileged "universal" writing over writing that emphasized the particularities of the Black experience, the intrinsic Blackness of a literary work can be what makes it most aesthetically and rhetorically valuable. In doing so, he offers a framework to look at Black literature that includes particular formulations about what makes literature "Black." Starting from the premise that "Black poetry in the United States has been widely misunderstood, misinterpreted, and undervalued for a variety of reasons—aesthetic, cultural, and political" (3), Henderson advocates reading and interpreting Black poetry as organically tied to culturally specific traditions in music and language. Underlying this assertion is Henderson's controversial premise that there is a tangible Blackness present in certain American cultural productions and that palpable Blackness is beautiful—indicative of an invaluable type of American aesthetic production.

Henderson identifies and interrogates the following criteria:

Black poetry is chiefly:
1. Any poetry by any person or group of persons of known Black African ancestry, whether the poetry is designated Black or not.
2. Poetry which is somehow *structurally* Black, irrespective of authorship.
3. Poetry by any person or group of known Black African ancestry, which is *also identifiably* Black, in terms of structure, theme, or other characteristics.
4. Poetry by any identifiably Black person who can be classed as a "poet" by Black people. Judgment may or may not coincide with judgments of whites.
5. Poetry by any identifiably Black person whose ideological stance vis-à-vis the history and the aspirations of his people since slavery is adjudged by them to be "correct." (7)

Although, as Henderson himself notes, these criteria themselves rest on a number of debatable assumptions, Henderson's willingness to offer a formulation of what makes Black poetry *Black* gives readers and scholars a framework by which to approach Black poetry as a body of work. Further, of all types of literature, poetry, as "the most concentrated and the most allusive of the verbal arts," is best equipped to convey the essential Blackness Henderson contends exists in African American writing: "[I]f there is such a commodity as 'blackness' in literature (and I assume that there is), it should somehow be found in concentrated or in residual form in the poetry" (4).

Henderson presents a framework that is both literary and linguistic. He offers a three-part set of criteria to assess and understand Black poetry: theme, structure, and saturation:

(1) By *theme* I mean that which is being spoken of, whether by specific subject matter, the emotional response to it, or its intellectual formulation.

(2) By *structure* I mean chiefly some aspect of the poem such as diction, rhythm, figurative language, which goes into the total makeup. (At times, I use the word in an extended sense to include what is usually called genre.)

(3) By *saturation* I mean several things, chiefly the communication of "Blackness" and fidelity to the observed or intuited truth of the Black Experience in the United States. It follows that these categories should also be valid in any critical evaluation of the poem. (10)

Henderson argues that the characteristic theme of Black poetry is "Liberation," "the great overarching movement of consciousness for Black people" that encompasses freedom "from slavery, from segregation and degradation, from wishful 'integration' into the 'mainstream,' to the passionate denial of white middle-class values of the present and an attendant embrace of Africa and the Third World as alternative routes of development" (18). Liberation thematically manifests itself in Black poetry through both the historical and the mythical, and the works that relate it must do so in a manner that presents the range of beautiful and sordid aspects of the African American experience to the Black reader or listener in works that posit Black folks as the primary audience.

Poetic theme here relates closely to Henderson's discussion of "saturation," which he defines in part as "(a) the communication of Blackness in a given situation, and (b) a sense of fidelity to the observed and intuited truth of the Black Experience" (62). The most unwieldy and controversial of Henderson's categories, saturation depends on the reader's or listener's subjective perception that the work deals deeply and legitimately with the Black Experience, "even though there are no verbal or other clues to alert him" (62). Henderson glosses his concept of the Black Experience only in such broad strokes to say that it consists of a mutually shared set of experiences common to individuals who inhabit a Black identity. The audience's ability to judge saturation, then, is a matter of sensibility: "[O]ne may feel, for example, that a word, a phrase, a rhythm, is so *right*, so *Black*, that its employment illuminates the entire composition" (65). Henderson's assertion that saturation must be considered in understanding Black poetry is important rhetorically; New Critical dictates to the wind, a poem may never be considered in isolation but always in relation to the audience—and specifically an audience who has a claim to the Black Experience (62).

Henderson deals with the significance to Black aesthetics of Black English's insular rhetorical modes in his discussion of the inherently Black "forms" of

Black poetry. He defines literature as "the organization of experience into beautiful forms" but asserts that his definition should be considered only within culturally specific parameters: "[W]hat is meant by 'beautiful' and by 'forms' is to a significant degree dependent upon a people's way of life, their needs, their aspirations, their history—in short, their culture. Ultimately, the 'beautiful' is bound up with the truth of a people's history, *as they perceive it themselves*" (4). Significantly, the cultural parameters for aesthetic quality here are self-referential. Black writing should be assessed in terms of its insular aesthetic forms by those who know, use, and claim them primarily from lived cultural experience as Black Americans.

For Henderson, Black English is not limited by class parameters: "By Black speech I mean the speech of the majority of Black people in this country, and I do not exclude the speech of the so-called educated people" (31). Henderson believes that Black English has the communicative agility to represent all possible poetic meanings, although he also concedes that most Black poets tend to use the range of their bi- or multi-dialectalism: "[N]o one to my knowledge has demonstrated that the language of the streets *is not* capable of expressing all that a poet needs to say, especially if he is speaking *to* the people. Nor have I seen any contemporary Black poet restrict himself exclusively to the language of the streets" (32). The use of Black language in poetics is practical for directing one's work to Black audiences and, in doing so, is a fundamental characteristic of poetry's rhetorical power: "Poets use Black speech forms consciously because they know that Black people—the mass of us—do not talk like white people" (33). Henderson enumerates the following tropes as formally characteristic of Black language: virtuoso naming and enumerating, jazzy rhythmic effects, virtuoso free-rhyming, hyperbolic imagery, metaphysical imagery, understatement, compressed and cryptic imagery, and "worrying the line"—a technique that he describes as both an "elegant gesture" and an iconoclastically blunt form of truth telling (41). He also presents what he calls "mascon words," so named for their "*massive concentration of Black experiential energy which powerfully affects the meaning of Black speech*" (44), as a unique and essential element of the Black English lexicon. According to Henderson, the use of these tropes or linguistic innovations allows a reader to perceive a poem as "structurally Black" though no other indicators direct the reader toward the poem's relationship to Blackness.

Henderson identifies the call to collective ritual as a specific purpose of Black Arts era poetry: "[T]he tendency since the sixties has been mainly toward public statement, toward didacticism, toward collective ritual" (25–26).

This ritual is the process of revealing the "truth" of the Black experience—through theme and saturation, yes, but most importantly through the linguistic forms, the "tradition of beautiful talk": "For there is a tradition of beautiful talk with us—this tradition of saying things beautifully even if they are ugly things. We say them in a way which takes language down to the deepest common level of our experience while hinting still at things to come" (33). It is in this sense that Black Arts poet-rhetors, part griots and part citizen-orators, deploy in a distinctly African American way the tradition of nommo, of understanding the word as a life-giving and life-changing force with transformative political and spiritual power.

Critics of Henderson, such as scholars Henry Louis Gates Jr. and Keith Byerman, have alleged that Henderson's theory promotes a limiting or even damaging essentialism and rests on vague, tautological definitions. Gates and Byerman both critique the way Black aesthetic proponents like Henderson aim to supplant "Western" aesthetic values with a concept of "metaphysical blackness," a zero-sum exchange that merely replaces one essentialist notion with "another transcendent signified" (qtd. in Dubey 28–29). Gates is particularly critical of Henderson's work in his 1978 essay "Preface to Blackness: Text and Pretext," in which he quarrels with Henderson's parameters for identifying a Black text as circularly defined and relying not on formal or linguistic evidence but ascribing vague authority to Black critics' prerogatives: "Had Henderson elaborated on 'residual form' in literary language, measured formally, structurally, or linguistically, he would have revolutionized black literary criticism and brought it into the twentieth century. But his theory of poetry is based on three sometimes jumbled 'broad categories' that allow the *black* critic to define the 'norms' of 'blackness'" (247). Rejecting what he sees as the essentialism upon which Henderson's concept of saturation is based, Gates charges, "One imagines a daishiki-clad Dionysus weighing the saturated, mascon lines of Countee Cullen against those of Langston Hughes, as Paul Laurence Dunbar and Jean Toomer are silhouetted by the flames of Nigger Hell. The blacker the berry, the sweeter the juice" (249).

Other critics, however, while acknowledging the essentialist aspects of Henderson's theory, reasonably suggest that his conceptions work to establish a *strategic* essentialism that allows Black Arts poetry to function as both aesthetic and political. In *Black Women Novelists and the Nationalist Aesthetic* (1994), a work that both critiques the limitations of the Black Arts period and acknowledges how the movement set the stage for the flourishing of Black women novelists in the 1970s and 1980s, Madhu Dubey recognizes that the

"Will-to-Blackness" communicated in theories like Henderson's depends on essential notions of Blackness but also opens the door for political and rhetorical possibility: "The writing of black nationalists like . . . Stephen Henderson . . . bristles with a sense of the sheer possibility of blackness. The rhetorical energy of black nationalist discourse mobilizes the sign of blackness, opening it to a process of textual transfiguration. The essential blackness celebrated in these writings emerges, then, not so much as a settled, naturally given value but as a hard-won linguistic achievement, a testament of visionary political desire" (29).

Despite Gates's critique of Henderson's work as failing to rely more fully on linguistic evidence, Gates stands on Henderson's shoulders by looking to Black vernacular traditions to explain the "black difference" in literary works. In his well-known and deeply influential *The Signifying Monkey: A Theory of African-American Literary Criticism* (1988), Gates asserts, "Whatever is black about black American literature is to be found in [its] identifiable Signifyin(g) difference" (xxiv), the play of repetition and revision characteristic of the Black English rhetorical practice of signifyin, and he underscores that "a truly indigenous black literary criticism is to be found in the vernacular" (xxii). Similarly, in his important *Blues, Ideology, and Afro-American Literature* (1984), Houston Baker points to the blues as a Black vernacular practice that is a "matrix" of all Black cultural expression. Unlike Gates, though, Baker points distinctly to Henderson as an influence, calling Henderson "the spokesman par excellence for an entirely new object of literary-critical and literary-theoretical investigation" and attesting that his formulations in "Forms of Things Unknown" "mark a high point in the first generational shift in the recent criticism of Afro-American literature" (74). Baker states that Henderson's insights come from his careful observation of Black poetry of the 1960s and 1970s and his assessment that "the expressive modes of a black urban vernacular are dominant shaping influences in the work of Afro-American poets" and that these vernacular modes work in "reciprocity" with "self-conscious, literary expression" (80). In short, Baker attests, Henderson's work importantly foregrounds for subsequent vernacular theorists the idea that "*all* black poetic expression can be understood in terms of such a pattern" of the interplay between literary and vernacular traditions (81).

Bernard W. Bell's *The Folk Roots of Contemporary Afro-American Poetry*, published as part of Broadside Press's Critics Series in 1974, articulated contemporary to Henderson a similar understanding of Black language and music traditions as foundational to Black Arts poetry: "[C]ontemporary Afro-American poetry has its roots in the African slaves' lyrical affirmation of life.... And whatever is distinctly ethnic in the poetry of this generation of Black poets... is attributable to the creative forces of this heritage" (45–46). Bell later developed this critical stance in his first major work on the Afro-American novel, *The Afro-American Novel and Its Tradition* (1987), in which he "explain[s] the richness of the Afro-American novel as a hybrid narrative whose distinctive tradition and vitality are derived basically from the sedimented indigenous roots of black American folklore and literary genres of the Western world" (xii). Although Bell differs from Gates and Baker in choosing not just a single trope (such as signifyin or the blues) as the primary vernacular source of African American literature but instead providing a broad framework to include oratory, myth, legend, tale, and song (21), his work aligns with Baker and Gates in the tradition of Henderson by presenting a theory in which the vernacular tradition informs and provides a foundation for Black literature.

In the years subsequent to the Black Arts Movement's ebb, this kind of scholarship would significantly change the place of and understanding of Black literature in the academy. In fact, the influence of vernacular theory on the study of African American literature is a realization of the goals of Black Studies activists who insisted on works by Black writers as worthy of literary study and of the Black Arts scholars and writers who insisted on a Black aesthetic as the theoretical lens through which Black art should be understood. As Hoyt Fuller writes in "Towards a Black Aesthetic" in 1968, the development of an interpretive theory for Black art was a goal of the movement—one that evolved from Black America coming to consciousness of their beauty writ large:

> Across this country, young black men and women have been infected with a fever of affirmation. They are saying, "We are black and beautiful," and the ghetto is reacting with a liberating shock of realization.... They are rediscovering their heritage and their history, seeing it with newly focused eyes, struck with the wonder of that strength which has enabled them to endure and, in spirit, to defeat the power of prolonged and calculated oppression. After centuries of being told, in a million different ways, that they were not beautiful, and that whiteness of skin, straightness of hair, and aquilineness of features constituted the only measures of beauty, black people have revolted. (7–8)

As a direct result of the "Black Is Beautiful" fight, Fuller claims, "The young writers of the black ghetto have set out in search of a black aesthetic, a system of isolating and evaluating the artistic works of black people which reflect the special character and imperatives of black experience" (8). And this is precisely what Stephen Henderson and the influential vernacular theorists that he influenced accomplished. Addison Gayle, as noted in the beginning of this chapter, saw the first step in the cultural revolution as "[t]he acceptance of the phrase 'Black Is Beautiful,'" but he goes on to argue that "[t]his step must be followed by serious scholarship and hard work; and Black critics must dig beneath the phrase and unearth the treasure of beauty lying deep in the untoured regions of the Black experience—regions where others, due to historical conditioning and cultural deprivation, cannot go" ("Cultural Strangulation" 44–45). The work of Stephen Henderson, then, points to the branches of aesthetic theory that grew from the roots of BAM.

Black Language in the Schools: The Work of Geneva Smitherman

The legacies of Black Arts Movement poets can be seen not only in developments in academic theory but in more concrete interventions in educational institutions as well. During the movement and in the years following its flowering, many Black Arts poets took their work as educators from the page and the street into formal sites of education. Haki Madhubuti founded a network of independent schools in Chicago that employed a cultural nationalist-influenced Afrocentric curriculum. Sarah Webster Fabio taught at Oakland's Merritt College during the height of Black Panther activity and was at the center for the struggle for Black Studies there. Sonia Sanchez helped build the nation's first Black Studies program at San Francisco State University. And many Black Arts poets have continued their educative mission as faculty, speakers, and guest artists at schools and universities for decades. But beyond these individual interventions, the rhetorical influence of Black Arts poets' advocacy of the beauty and validity of Black expressive traditions broadly influenced educational policy in K–12 schools and in college composition classrooms through the scholarship and activism of linguists like Geneva Smitherman.

In tracing the legacy of Black Arts poets in Black English activism and educational reform, Geneva Smitherman deserves distinct attention for several reasons. First, although a number of linguists and scholars, including Claudia Mitchell-Kernan (whose important work preceded and influenced Smitherman's), were working to affirm Black English as a systematic and rule-governed language during this era, Smitherman's 1977 *Talkin and Testifyin* stood as a groundbreaking work identifying and explicating both the linguistic and rhetorical attributes of Black English. Second, Smitherman directly notes the influence on her work of the Black Power Movement and of Black

Arts Movement writing. She states in her 1985 afterword to a reprint edition of *Talkin and Testifyin*, "Although I grew up speaking Black English, I did not become conscious of the disparity between my native tongue and the language of America's majority culture until I was forced to take a speech class to qualify for a teaching certificate.... While that memory lingered throughout my years of teaching . . . , it was the clarion call of the Black Power Movement of the 1960s that propelled me to view my personal encounter with linguistic imperialism as a lesson in Black Life and, finally, to articulate that vision in *Talkin and Testifyin*" (242). She credits the work of Black Arts writers—poets especially, whose work she calls "the most important manifestation" of Black Arts writing—with the rhetorical power to make this kind of clarion call: "The creator of Black Arts Literature envisions himself as a Necromancer, a skillful manipulator of the Art of Black Magic, whose job it is to 'heal' Black folks through the evocative power of Art, and transform their suffering into constructive political action" ("Power of the Rap" 259). Third, Smitherman responded to the call to participate in constructive political action by making strides toward affirming the place of Black language in institutions of formal education both during and in the years following the height of BAM. Two of these victories in asserting the aesthetic and linguistic value of Black language, the Students' Right to Their Own Language declaration (1974) and the *King v. Ann Arbor* Supreme Court case (the Black English Case) of 1979, I will discuss below.

In *Talkin and Testifyin*, Smitherman points to two major forces that have generated concern over Black language in educational programs. The first is the Civil Rights and Black Power / Black Arts Movements of the 1950s through the 1970s. The second is what she calls "White America's attempt to deal with this newly released black energy by the implementation of poverty programs, educational and linguistic remediation projects, sociolinguistic research programs, and various other up-from-the-ghetto and 'Great Society' efforts" (2). Smitherman argues that this second factor emerged to exert cultural control over newly empowered Black Americans: "As we all know, these two forces have not acted in concert. While blacks were shouting 'I'm black and I'm proud,' Anglos were admonishing them to 'be like us' and enter the mainstream. While you had black orators, creative artists, and yes, even some scholars rappin in the Black Thang, educators (some of them black, to be sure) were preaching the Gospel that Black English speakers must learn to talk like White English speakers in order to 'make it'" (2). With the advent of compensatory education programs in the 1950s and 1960s, interest in Black English developed outside of academic linguistic and anthropological circles as well.

Beginning in 1959 when the first study working to change Black speech patterns was conducted,[4] educators began to develop and employ "deficit" and "difference" models of education to take into account the presence in schools of what they then identified as Black language (Smitherman, *Talkin and Testifyin* 201–2). Where deficit models clearly devalue Black English's linguistic power and relevance by asserting that Black English speakers use deficient or "broken" English, Smitherman argues that difference models, which recognize the legitimacy of nonstandard language forms in their contexts, similarly reinforce White middle-class language norms (203). Difference (or "bi-dialectal") theories operate under a kind of "separate but equal" ethos, which is complicated by the same issues that mar the concept when dealing with physical segregation: nonstandard forms are recognized as legitimate as long as they stay in their place (204), and bi-dialectal students need to master prestige language forms if they want to succeed in larger society (207). Smitherman takes umbrage at these kinds of assertions, however, because, as she notes, "[t]he history of black people has shown what continues to be true today: speaking White English is no guarantee to economic advancement. For educators, linguists, and anybody else to push that notion off on kids is to deal them a gross lie" (207). Instead of a difference or deficit theory of Black language, then, Smitherman proffers an inclusive pedagogy that allows for Black English to be integrated into and valorized in schools.

As a member of both the Executive Committee of the Conference on College Composition and Communication (CCCC) and of the CCCC committee appointed to draft a policy position on students' dialects in fall of 1971, Smitherman poised herself to advocate for the linguistic legitimacy and educational importance of Black English. Concerned that "[i]f the patriarchally-constituted social and economic structure would not accept non-mainstream speech varieties, then the argument for *difference* would simply become *deficiency* all over again" ("Students' Right" 21), Smitherman and her dialect committee members presented the following resolution to the CCCC Executive Committee in March 1972:

> We affirm the students' right to their own patterns and varieties of language—the dialects of their nurture or whatever dialects in which they find their own identity and style. Language scholars long ago denied that the myth of a standard American dialect has any validity. The claim that any one dialect is unacceptable amounts to an attempt of one social group to exert its dominance over another. Such a claim leads to false advice for speakers and writers, and immoral advice for humans. A nation proud of its diverse heritage and its cultural and

racial variety will preserve its heritage of dialects. We affirm strongly that teachers must have the experiences and training that will enable them to respect diversity and uphold the right of students to their own language. ("Students' Right")

Passed by the CCCC Executive Committee in November 1972 and made official policy of CCCC in April 1974, the Students' Right declaration marked official recognition by a national organization of writing and communication scholars (deeply influenced by the scholarship on Black English specifically) that language varieties like Black English should have a legitimate place in educational institutions. The organization further supported the passage of the resolution by devoting the full fall 1974 issue of its journal, *College Composition and Communication* (*CCC*), to research and resources that would support the implementation of Students' Right. Subsequently, the National Council of Teachers of English (NCTE), the umbrella organization of English teachers of which CCCCs is an independent but affiliated arm and whose membership consists of K-12 as well as college teachers, passed a similar though weakened version of the declaration in 1974. Although the NCTE version maintains an endorsement for the writing conventions of Standard "edited American English" and fails to commit significant resources to supporting the resolution's implementation (Smitherman, "Students' Right" 23), the passage of the Students' Right resolution in this large and influential organization marked an opening for significant change in educational policy. As of 1974, thousands of teachers were advised by their professional organizations to "promote classroom practices to expose students to the variety of dialects that occur in our multi-regional, multi-ethnic, and multi-cultural society, so that they too will understand the nature of American English and come to respect all its dialects" ("Students' Right").

This kind of policy requires that scholars, linguists, teachers, and educational advocates cultivate a deft understanding of the salient linguistic features of the range of linguistic codes that students bring to their classrooms. Smitherman's *Talkin and Testifyin* provides such a resource, in language accessible to teachers inside and outside of the academy, for the understanding of Black English. Smitherman expands on previous linguists' work by defining Black English as having two dimensions: language and style (3). "Language" here refers to sounds and grammatical structure. "Style," she states, "refers to the way speakers put sounds and grammatical structure together to communicate meaning in a larger context. Put another way, language is the words, style is what you do with the words" (16). Pointing to the way the language aspects of Black English reflect residual forms of African languages as well as to the way that the style of Black English evolved from strategies of survival and resistance during centuries of enslavement and institutionalized racism, Smitherman argues, "Black English, then, is a language mixture, adapted to the conditions of slavery and discrimination, a combination of language and style interwoven with and inextricable from Afro-American culture" (3). Her assertion that the Black idiom is used by 80 to 90 percent of Black Americans at least some of the time further supports the language's organic relationship to the culture and lives of African Americans (2).

Part of the impetus for pushing through the Students' Right resolution was Smitherman's conviction, partly from experience, that a teacher's misunderstanding of a student's spoken or written use of Black English could lead to their discouraging or disparaging valuable and complex literacy practices that originate in students' home language culture. One egregious such instance of institutional misunderstanding of—or, perhaps, disregard for—Black language practices led to the 1979 federal "Black English Case": *Martin Luther King Junior Elementary School Children v. Ann Arbor School District Board*. Distressed by school officials' labeling of their children as "slow," "educationally retarded," "learning disabled," and "handicapped" in regard to their language learning abilities and placing them in special education classes (Smitherman, "Introduction" 11, 13), parents of Black students at Ann Arbor's King Elementary filed a suit against the school board for failing to comply with the Equal Educational Opportunities Act of 1974. The law states that "[n]o state shall deny equal educational opportunity to an individual on account of his or her race, color, sex, or national origin, by . . . the failure by an educational agency to take appropriate action to overcome language barriers that impede equal participation by its students in its instructional programs" (qtd. in Smitherman, "Introduction" 17).

Judge Charles Joiner, who presided over the case, wrote in his 1979 *Memorandum and Order* that the litigation was "a straightforward effort to require the court to intervene on the children's behalf to require the defendant School District Board to take appropriate action to teach them to read in the standard English of the school, the commercial world, the arts, science and professions. This action is a cry for judicial help in opening the doors to the establishment. . . . [I]t is an action to keep another generation from becoming functionally illiterate" (qtd. in Smitherman, "Introduction" 11). Although the court found in favor of the children on July 12, 1979, the ruling only generally stated that the Ann Arbor School District had violated the children's right to equal educational opportunity based on failing to overcome language barriers. Black English per se was not indicated as the specific barrier between the children and the educators, so the ruling did not mandate a dual-language program that taught both varieties (Smitherman, "Introduction" 19). The case still stood, however, as a watershed moment for Black English educational activists and spawned a significant conference at Wayne State University in February 1980.[5] Smitherman herself served a pivotal role in the school children's success in the case. After a chance viewing of a television interview where Smitherman was discussing *Talkin and Testifyin,* Michigan Legal Services attorneys Kenneth Lewis and Gabe Kaimowitz brought in Smitherman as a consultant and chief witness to advocate that "schools must teach speakers of Black English literacy in the language of the school, the professions, and the marketplace, while simultaneously recognizing... the legitimacy of the language of Black America" (Smitherman, *Talkin and Testifyin* 243–44).

As the *King* case demonstrates, instituting change in schools takes not only the understanding of the language and style of Black English but the dedication of individuals to work to change the broader institution. As Smitherman argues in *Talkin and Testifyin,* "Notwithstanding all that has been said about the overwhelming power of the school as an *institutional* entity, I contend that it is still *individual* teachers in their *individual* settings that are the single most important factor in the educational process" (216). For Smitherman, the work boils down to a commitment to teach communicative competence—to speakers of Black English, Standard American English, and other language varieties alike—in hopes of preparing all students for life in a multilinguistic, transnational world. Communicative competence, the ability to communicate effectively (and, increasingly, in multimodal forms of literacy) (228), relies on students' rhetorical training in the use of all of the codes at their disposal. Smitherman asserts, "Communicative competence, in all the communication skills areas, has to do with linguistic and semantic appropriateness, and with the ability to employ rhetorical strategies to create a desired mood or effect in your audience and to move that audience in the direction you desire" (233). Cultivating this kind of classroom environment requires not only that teachers be familiar with students' nonstandard language varieties and respect them as legitimate forms of communication, but also that they allow these language varieties to be used liberally in classroom interactions, especially in the early grades when students are establishing crucial literacy foundations (221). Change for Smitherman, then, begins in the classroom, but teachers and activists must advocate for these kinds of approaches to become part of institutional policy. She reminds us, "[T]he real concern, and question, should be: How can I use what the kids *already* know to move them to what they *need* to know?" (219). And in those educational moments when Black English is understood by both students and educators to be not only legitimate but aesthetically rich language, the classroom has the potential to be a starting place for significant social change.

Although the trajectory of influence is not uncomplicated, the rhetorical work of Black Arts poets to affirm the aesthetics of Black language stands as one of the galvanizing forces of Smitherman's activism. In fact, Smitherman's early scholarship documents the influence specifically of Black Arts poetry on her groundbreaking sociolinguistic work on Black English. Her first journal publication in 1972, a piece for *English Journal* entitled "English Teacher, Why You Be Doing the Thangs You Don't Do?," uses a poem by Haki Madhubuti as inspiration to take to task correctionist English teachers who claim they are "readying Black students for the real world (read: white America)" by stigmatizing students' use of Black English and purging it from their writing.[6] She presents as an alternative an outline of a rich critical pedagogy that she calls a "Five-Point Program for teaching English in the inner city" (62), a play on the Black Panther Party's Ten-Point Program, which includes encouraging teachers to "combine language study with that of literature by letting your students dig on some of the new Black poetry, most of which is highly oral and written in the Black" (64). The Five-Point Program as a whole aims to strengthen the rhetorical acumen of students—what Smitherman describes as "survival strategies that extend far beyond the classroom":

> I am talking about the acquisition of those tools essential for thinking through a situation and making decisions. I am talking about telling it like it T. I. is so effectively and persuasively that your audience will move in whatever direction you desire. I am talking about teaching Black students that language can be/is power, that they can/must develop that power, and that ultimately in the struggle for Black liberation, the pen may be/is mightier than the Molotov cocktail. (65)

Stepping into this power for Smitherman involves education through Black Arts poetry, which exemplifies the ways Black English can be embraced and deployed powerfully as a rhetorical-aesthetic tool—or even a revolutionary weapon.

Smitherman further develops her stance on the significance of Black English as the medium of Black Arts poetry in "The Power of the Rap: The

Black Idiom and the New Black Poetry," a 1973 *Twentieth Century Literature* article that precedes the publication of *Talkin and Testifyin*. Published, along with the article above, while Smitherman was a member of the first generation of Afro-American Studies faculty at Harvard University, the article asserts that Black Arts poets are reshaping both the aesthetic and political American landscapes by valorizing Black linguistic and rhetorical practices in their work: "[T]he Black Poet of today is forging a new art form steeped in the uniqueness of Black Expressive Style. When used skillfully, . . . this Style becomes an excellent strategy to deliver a political message and to move Black folks to constructive political action. This, then, is 'The Power of the Rap'" (272). She specifically characterizes "the New Black Poetry" as "the most important manifestation" of Black Arts literature because of poetry's generic ability to incorporate the power of Black English not only structurally but performatively, exemplifying in its written form the systematic and rule-governed aspects of the language and the formal aspects of its modes of discourse, and expressing the power of its paralinguistic features when performed. Detailing in the article the ways that the New Black Poets have "capitalized on the Black Idiom for maximum power and poetic effect" (263), Smitherman uses examples from poems by Haki Madhubuti (whom she points to most prominently), Amiri Baraka, Sonia Sanchez, Etheridge Knight, and Nikki Giovanni, among others, to demonstrate aspects of Black English lexicon, syntax, phonology, and what she in this early scholarship calls "stylistic features" instead of the later term, "modes of discourse": "the Dozens, the Toast, Call-Response, Signification, Rhythmic Pattern [tonal semantics]" (266). Smitherman interprets Black language practices in the poems as a practical political "vehicle for the conveyance of Black Consciousness" (263) that is at the same time inherently aesthetic—while "Black Art, then, must of necessity, be functional and relevant to the lives and daily struggles of Black people," it still "must be *Art*" (259), and the poets' insistence on the beauty inherent in Black language makes it so.

As is clear from her early scholarship, Smitherman's powerful impact as a scholar, educator, and activist was significantly inflected by her experiences with the Black Arts Movement and its poetry. Inspired by the dynamism of the Black Power era and by her contact with confident Black Arts texts that asserted the beauty of Blackness both as the message and as the mode, Smitherman stands as one of the most significant educational advocates for social justice of the latter twentieth century, and the legacies of *Talkin and Testifyin*, Students' Right, and the *King* case continue, along with Smitherman's ongoing work, to evolve in the twenty-first century.

Conclusion

Certainly formulations of Black language and affirmations of Blackness as beautiful existed before the 1960s, and writers like Langston Hughes and Sterling Brown (although the exception rather than the rule) pointedly chose to use the Black vernacular and affirmations of Black aesthetics in their poetry to render Black life delicately and deeply. As early as 1922, the speaker of Hughes's poem "Negro" (the proem of *The Weary Blues*) declared, "I am . . . / Black as the night is black, / Black like the depths of my Africa" (Hughes 22). Also, forms of verbal artistry particular to Black English do not have to be academically recognized or linguistically codified to be valued by the Black community, which maintains and develops such practices in implicit acknowledgment of their cultural value. What Black Arts writers uniquely accomplished, however, was to combine assertions of the beauty of Black bodies and Black forms of expression as art with a populist methodology of distribution to their primary audiences. By aestheticizing Black language specifically through written work, Black Arts writers touched on the close associational relationship between literacy and freedom acknowledged in the Black public sphere since the time of Frederick Douglass—and affirmed the prediction of John Sweat Rock that when Black folks make social strides "black will be a very pretty color" and "our jargon, wit—our words, oracles" (110). Showing the people their verbal traditions as literary forms created the possibility of expanding the definition of literacy and of asserting Black speech traditions as distinct and worthwhile markers of affirmed Black selfhood. An understanding of the constructive project framed by the language of Black Arts poetry, which turned up the volume on Black vernacular expression more perhaps than any African American literary movement before or since, provides the basis for further discussion about the aesthetic and social—and, most broadly, rhetorical—legacies of BAM. Black Arts writers looked to develop conscious, affirmed Black selfhood in their audiences by grounding their works in ethos of collective ritual—the rebirth of foundational values through praise rhetoric voiced in spoken and written language insular to the Black community. Deploying poetry rhetorically in this way made the role of the Black Arts poet specifically educative, formally and informally, extending from the mirror to the corner and the barbershop to the local school and the ivy tower.

CHAPTER 4

"Most of My Heroes Don't Appear on No Stamps"

Toasts, Hip-Hop, and the Black Pride Movement

Many activists of the Black Arts Movement expressed clear views about what kinds of poets the revolution needed. For example, if Black Arts poet and critic Larry Neal had placed an ad in the Newark, Chicago, New Orleans, or San Francisco classifieds for poet-activists in 1967, it may have read like this:

> [T]he poet must become a performer, the way James Brown is a performer—loud, gaudy, and racy. He must take his work where his people are—Harlem, Watts, Philadelphia, Chicago, and the rural South. He must learn to embellish the context in which the work is executed; and where possible, link the work to all usable aspects of music. For the context of the work is as important as the work itself. Poets must learn to sing, dance and chant their works, tearing into the substance of their individual and collective experiences. We must make literature move people to a deeper understanding of what this thing is all about, be a kind of priest, a black magician, working juju with the word on the world. (22)

Implicit here is the idea that the revolutionary poet be able to wield the vernacular dexterously within the hearing of the Black public and with all the style and energy of the Godfather of Soul urging audiences to "Say It Loud: I'm Black and I'm Proud"—an ability that for Black Arts writers could yield powerful aesthetic, political, and rhetorical outcomes.

One thing these Black Arts poet-rhetors significantly accomplished in treading the line between the poetic and the musical was to bring Black oral folk traditions to the fore to enhance the articulation of Black nationalist movements' call for "Black Pride." Although the term "Black Pride," much like "Black Is Beautiful" in the previous chapter, should and does conjure a range of significations, I define it here as the affirmation that Black history and Black cultural heroes have distinct cultural capital, and that acknowledging the existence and value of Black history and Black heroes contributes to the development of affirmed Black consciousness. I argue that one distinct way Black Arts poets left a significant legacy as Black Pride advocates was in their employment and wide dissemination of *toasts*, performative poetic narratives in which speakers praise a hero, either a mythic figure or the self, whose defiance, omnipotence, and general *bad*ness allow them to overcome all odds.

In this chapter, I look at the ways Black Arts poet-rhetors incorporated the toast form in their works, both in celebrating the traditional stories and in innovating the form to articulate contemporary conscious Black heroes. I then extend this examination to discuss hip-hop music as a legacy of the Black Arts Movement. Although hip-hop began to develop as a cultural phenomenon after the most active years of the Black Arts and Black Power Movements had passed, hip-hop artists inherited Black Arts writers' mission to cultivate Black consciousness through affirmations of Black Pride delivered in the poetics of the Black vernacular. The braggadocio of the toast returns here, generally not to celebrate a third-person hero but to allow rappers to proclaim their own prowess—remixing the traditional themes of sexual virility and fighting ability, but basing hero status on assertions of virtuoso verbal artistry. Although hip-hop alone lacks the organization and purposive momentum of a "movement," it has the potential through its musical medium to argue powerfully for social change. Beyond the historical limitations of a particular political project, Black Arts poets have left a significant legacy in elevating the rhetorical power of African American expressive traditions, giving the hip-hop generation the tools to articulate their own heroes.

The Toast as Resistance Rhetoric

Toasts (as noted in chapter 1) are long-standing narrative epics from the Black oral tradition, stories like the Signifying Monkey, Stagger Lee, Shine, and Dolemite that relate the triumphs of larger-than-life heroes who defy social and moral limitations. Linguist John Rickford and his son, journalist Russell Rickford, characterize toasts as "often contain[ing] profanity, lawless capers, improbable sex romps, and exploits of heroes who ... fall into two main categories: tricksters and badmen" (82). A *trickster* dominates his opponent intellectually through the virtuosity and indirection of linguistic *signifyin* (whose specific relationship to the toast I discuss below); a *bad*man is a defiant, larger-than-life figure entirely unconstrained by physical limits or social mores. According to sociolinguist Geneva Smitherman, "Toasts let it all hang out. The hero is fearless, defiant, openly rebellious, and full of braggadocio about his masculinity, sexuality, fighting ability, and general badness.... [T]his epic folk style is a tribute—that is, a 'toast'—to this superbad, omnipotent black hustler, pimp, player, killer who is mean to the max" (*Talkin and Testifyin* 157). Consider the poem "I Sing of Shine," a version of the traditional Shine toast crafted by Black Arts poet Etheridge Knight and collected in Dudley Randall's 1971 anthology *The Black Poets*. The speaker introduces Shine, who worked on the infamous *Titanic*, as "the stoker who was hip / enough to flee the fucking ship / and let the white folks drown / with screams on their lips." The speaker demonstrates this by narrating three encounters Shine has with White folks who beg him to save them while he swims away from the *Titanic*. In the first, a millionaire offers Shine a million dollars to save him, but Shine tells him to save himself:

> ... the millionaire banker stood on the deck
> and pulled from his pocket a million dollar check
> saying Shine Shine save poor me
> and I'll give you all the money a black boy needs—
> ... Shine looked at the money and then at the sea
> and said jump in muthafucka and swim like me—

In the second encounter, a young White woman (the millionaire's daughter) offers herself to Shine sexually if he'll save her, but he rationally refuses:

> ... the banker's daughter ran naked on the deck
> with her pinktits trembling and her pants roun her neck
> screaming Shine Shine save poor me
> and I'll give you all the cunt a black boy needs—
> ... Shine said now cunt is good and that's no jive
> but you got to swim not fuck to stay alive— (209)

The third, a preacher, calls upon Shine to save him in the name of Christian morality, but Shine outright ignores this argument and retaliates when the preacher gets in his way:

> then Shine swam past a preacher afloat on a board
> crying save me nigger Shine in the name of the Lord—
> ... the preacher grabbed Shine's arm and broke his stroke—
> ... Shine pulled his shank and cut the preacher's throat— (209–10)

Demonstrating superhuman strength and endurance, Shine swims across the Atlantic and reaches the East Coast faster than the news of the *Titanic*'s sinking—and in plenty of time to celebrate his safe arrival:

> And when the news hit shore that the titanic had sunk
> Shine was up in Harlem damn near drunk—

and dancing in the streets.
yeah, damn near drunk and dancing in the streets. (210)

Shine's exploits in this tale exemplify the way toasts serve as resistance rhetoric. Shine acts in the interest of his own survival, and none of the lures or coercive forces the White characters offer derail him from his mission of self-preservation—not the promises of wealth or sex with a White woman, not the authority of the church or the expectation of deference to White folks in general. Shine's actions, and the direct truth telling that accompanies them, boldly contradict racist stereotypes of Black people, and of Black men in particular, broadly circulated by White culture: accusations of greediness, laziness, docility, and uncontrollable longing for White women. Further, Shine's physical power and linguistic cleverness both far outshine those of the White characters; not only does he easily survive the sinking of the *Titanic* while they perish, but he *tells* them about themselves before he swims away.

The linguistic virtuosity of the hero is a reflection of the expectations of the toast teller, and the teller's clever utilization of the formal aspects of the toast can contribute to the poignancy of the resistance narrative. The straightforward structuring of the story in rhymed couplets contrasts with the unapologetically raw language of the story, gesturing toward the superficiality of White expectations of propriety and order—expectations that, in "Shine," the White characters abandon when their lives are at stake. The form also sets the audience up to look for a semantic surprise at the end of each rhymed couplet as a demonstration of the speaker's wit, much in the same way an ironic revelation is expected in the last line of a twelve-bar blues stanza. The regularized structure of the poems' rhymed couplets provides counterpoint for the looseness of the toast's episodic narrative structure, allowing the speaker to engage the audience in the narrative through creative linguistic improvisations that use the rhyme scheme as a resource for semantic surprise. As folk poetry, toasts have traditionally been delivered in a communicative atmosphere that allows the toast teller to use profanity and sexual allusions to colorfully portray the prowess of the hero—or as Smitherman puts it, "Toasts are replete with funk in practically every rhymed couplet" (*Talkin and Testifyin* 157). And the speaker's comfort in and artful use of Black vernacular throughout the poem indicate whom the story is for as well: Black folks are welcomed in to appreciate the toast's irony, humor, and wry truth telling and the indefatigable *bad*ness of its hero, unconcerned about offending any White folks who happen to overhear.

In this way, toast tellers in the Black oral tradition portray heroes like Shine in epic proportions to serve as an antidote to the indignities and inhumane treatment suffered by many as a result of anti-Black racism. Among other forms of resistance, toast stories allow tellers and listeners to fight back with words, to offer a corrective to the blows dealt to the selfhood of Black folks by the narratives that enforce White power. Rickford and Rickford argue that this resistance rhetoric proves especially powerful for Black men: "For black men, who have been physically and psychologically castrated during their North American internment, assertions of manhood—of strength, potency, and bravado—must be larger than life. The badmen of toasts thus represent irreverent heroes of redemptive proportions" (84). The widespread circulation of these kinds of narratives, then, certainly served the rhetorical aims of the Black Arts Movement in underscoring messages of Black Pride. Lifted from the community loci of storytelling and oral tradition and distributed on a national scale through books and records, Black Arts poets' toasts offered loud and unmasked assertions of Black Pride through the unapologetic exploits of their heroes.

Significantly, though, Black Arts poets incorporated into their work not only traditional toast stories but a modernized version of the toast form in which speakers toast in first person, casting *themselves* as the larger-than-life heroes. Similar to traditional toasts in that they relate the *bad*ness of a defiant, sexually and physically powerful hero, these versions diverge by merging the hero and the toast teller. Instead of providing the audience with a historic or ahistorical figure as an example of defiance, the speakers themselves provide evidence of their own power and ability to resist. But true to traditional toasts, deft demonstrations of verbal artistry are key to these self-proclamations of heroism. Although at first blush it may seem counterintuitive, these epics of the *bad* self accomplish the rhetorical task of *community* empowerment. The toast heroes, as individuals standing before or living alongside the audience members, insist on empowerment as a living reality, challenging the listeners to define and verbalize their own power. In line with the nature of the toast in folk practice as emphasizing the need to resist White supremacy, Black Arts poets use first-person toasts in their works to reinforce values of pride associated with Black consciousness, creating heroes that epitomize the boldness and self-affirmation of conscious Black revolutionaries.

These boast versions of the toast rely stylistically on the Black verbal art form of *signifyin*. In its broadest sense, as discussed in chapter 1, signifyin is the demonstration of verbal skill and wit through wordplay that involves metaphorical or rhetorical indirection. According to linguist Claudia Mitchell-Kernan, signifyin has two modes: "Signifying can be a tactic employed in game activity—verbal dueling—which is engaged as an end in itself..., [but] also refers to a way of encoding messages or meanings in natural conversations which involves, in most cases, an element of indirection" ("Signifying and Marking" 165). This chapter deals specifically with the first mode incorporated in verbal dueling, while the next chapter deals specifically with signifyin as coded insult or correction relying on indirection. Rickford and Rickford describe this performative or competitive mode of signifyin as "ritualized wordplay, a highly stylized lying, joking, and carrying on with such virtuosity as to inject one's message with metaphor and eloquence while elevating one's social status and parodying one's interlocutors or their attitudes and behaviors" (81). Literary and hip-hop scholar Adam Bradley defines it succinctly as "a rhetorical practice that involves repetition and difference, besting and boasting" (181). The ability to signify implies the ability to *rap*, or to dexterously wield the vernacular, and the speaker not only must have control over language but must use that control to create the semantically unexpected.

In "Rap's Poem," a selection from the autobiography of H. Rap Brown (so named as a tribute to his verbal virtuosity) that Stephen Henderson includes in *Understanding the New Black Poetry*, Brown demonstrates the stylistic and rhetorical use of signifyin in his first-person toast. Brown offers the toast in response to a hypothetical verbal challenge: "A session would start maybe by a brother saying, 'Man, before you mess with me you'd rather run rabbits, eat shit, and bark at the moon.'" Brown responds with a verse replete with signifyin:

> Man, you must don't know who I am.
> I'm sweet peeter jeeter the womb beater
> The baby maker the cradle shaker
> The deerslayer the buckbinder the women finder
> Known from the Gold Coast to the rocky shores of Maine
> Rap is my name and love is my game.
> I'm the bed tucker the cock plucker the motherfucker
> The milkshaker the record breaker the population maker
> The gun slinger the baby bringer
> The hum-dinger the pussy ringer
> The man with the terrible middle finger.
> The hard hitter the bullshitter the polynussy getter
> The beast from the East the Judge the sludge
> The women's pet the men's fret and the punks' pin-up boy.
> They call me Rap the dicker the ass kicker

> The cherry picker the city slicker the titty licker
> And I ain't giving nothing but bubble gum and hard times and I'm fresh out of bubble gum. (Brown 27–28)

The language in the passage demonstrates a number of the characteristics that Smitherman describes as indicative of signifyin (see chapter 1), most prominently the use of everyday language to create rich, imagistic metaphors, whose semantic surprise is underscored by poetic attention to sound. Brown marks much of his signified language with intricate rhyme and assonance: "sweet peter jeeter the womb beater," and "the cherry picker the city slicker the titty licker." He varies from the rhymed couplet form in favor of double, triple, or even quadruple internal rhyme in a line, sometimes carrying the repeated sound through to the line below. Brown's verse, like much signifyin in this context, focuses on the permutations of language rather than on the weight of thematic content. This concentration on word play does not keep the speaker from emphasizing his theme through layers of metaphor and semantic surprise, asserting the *bad*ness of his sexual virility through terms that don't carry innuendoes in other contexts: "deerslayer," "bed tucker," "cock plucker," "milkshaker," "cherry picker." Brown's signifyin is at its height when he aligns all of these techniques—when the rhyme and assonance reinforce the unexpected, indirect meaning of his metaphorical language. By showing his verbal prowess in this way, Brown offers evidence for the *bad*ness he asserts; his deft linguistic play serves as evidence to reinforce his self-affirmations, and he earns the respect of his audience.

It is important to underscore the role toast narratives like those noted above played in the rhetorical fight for Black Pride. While a range of Black Power, Black Arts, and Black Studies activists worked to gain widespread acknowledgment for the existence and vital importance of the African diasporic history of Black Americans by recovering and celebrating historical figures, Black Arts writers insisted through their work on the acknowledgment of folk heroes, past and present, as part of this history. In his 1967 essay "And Shine Swam On," Larry Neal argues that the acknowledgment of Black history and its heroes plays a crucial role in the fight to raise Black consciousness: "There is a tension within black America. And it has its roots in the general history of the race. The manner in which we see this history determines how we act.... [T]he sense of how that history should be felt is what either unites or separates us." He goes on to assert that the history of Black folks is haunted by ghosts, both historical and mythical: "The ghosts of that tension are Nat Turner, Martin Delany, Booker T. Washington, Frederick Douglass, Malcolm

X, Garvey, Monroe Trotter, Du Bois, Fanon, and a whole panoply of mythical heroes from Brer Rabbit to Shine. These ghosts have left us with some very heavy questions about the realities of life for black people in America" (8). Neal points to Shine in particular as a figure whose exploits represent both the difficulties and victories of the historical Black struggle in America. For Neal, the story of Shine "is part of the private mythology of black America. Its symbolism is direct and profound. Shine is US" (7). The work of Black Arts writers, then, served to affirm the complexity of Black history by asserting traditional folk hero narratives as powerful poetic forms and rhetorical modes. As the aesthetic arm of Black Power, Black Arts writers not only elegized and praised heroes of Black history who had lived (as I discussed in chapter 2), but also brought the powerful, defiant heroes of myth to the center of the struggle for Black consciousness.

In her poem "blk/rhetoric," published in her 1970 volume *We a BaddDDD People*, Sonia Sanchez straightforwardly calls out Black Arts rhetors:

who's gonna make all
that beautiful blk/rhetoric
mean something.

In particular, she asks for activists to find and voice suitable heroes who will draw young people's attention away from the repressive behaviors and distractions that keep them from fully realized selfhood:

who's gonna give our young
blk people new heros
(instead of catch/phrases)
(instead of cad/ill/acs)
(instead of pimps)
(instead of white/whores)
(instead of drugs)
(instead of new/dances)
(instead of chit/ter/lings)
(instead of a 35¢ bottle of
                ripple)
(instead of quick/fucks
  in the hall/way of
          white/america's
              mind)
like. this. is an S.O.S.

>   me. calling. . . .
>   calling. . . .
>   some/one.
>   pleasereplysoon. (15–16)

I suggest here that some Black Arts poets rose to the occasion, using the rhetorical and poetic tools of Black oral folk practice to proclaim a message of Black Pride through the articulation of heroes. With this mission in mind, I consider three widely circulated Black Arts poems that use the toast to argue for Black Pride: Etheridge Knight's "Hard Rock Returns to Prison from the Hospital for the Criminal Insane" (1968), Haki Madhubuti's "But He Was Cool, or: he even stopped for green lights" (1969), and Nikki Giovanni's "Ego Tripping" (1970).[1]

Knight's "Hard Rock": The High Stakes of Communicative Imprisonment

Etheridge Knight was a master of the toast. A Mississippi-born and Indiana-raised Korean War veteran, he began writing poetry in the 1960s while serving an eight-year sentence in Indiana State Prison for snatching a purse from an elderly woman. Knight had developed an affinity and talent for toast telling from spending time with those practicing the oral tradition in his Indiana community, and his continuance of the practice in prison helped inspire him to develop his poetic talent through written work. He corresponded with and received encouragement from Dudley Randall, who published his first volume of poetry, *Poems from Prison*, with Broadside Press in 1968, just prior to Knight's release. The back cover of *Poems from Prison* includes Knight's autobiographical testimony: "I died in Korea from a shrapnel wound and narcotics resurrected me. I died in 1960 from a prison sentence and poetry brought me back to life." Knight considers poetry not only redemptive for the individual but redemptive for Black Americans collectively. He describes the work of the Black writer essentially as the work of the griot: "The Black Artist has a duty: to perceive and conceptualize the collective aspirations, the collective vision of black people, and through his art form give back to the people the truth that he has gotten from them. He must sing to them of their own deeds, and misdeeds" ("A Survey" 88). Further, the work that the Black writer "sings" serves an epideictic rhetorical function—the praising of new values of Black consciousness: "The Black Artist must create new forms and new values, sing new songs (or purify old ones); and along with other Black Authorities, he must create a new history, new symbols, myths and legends (and purify the old ones by fire)" (38). Part of this work for Knight involved celebrating folk poetic forms like the toast as the fire that would purify or birth conscious Black heroes.

In "Hard Rock Returns to Prison from the Hospital for the Criminal Insane," published in *Poems from Prison* and one of Knight's most anthologized works, Knight does the griot work of reinforcing values through story—specifically by underscoring the importance of preserving or creating defiant heroes as part of the struggle for Black consciousness. In "Hard Rock," Knight presents an anti-toast, charging the speaker with the task of narrating the ultimate defeat of a hero instead of cataloguing his triumphs. In order to do this, the speaker imbeds a celebratory toast of Hard Rock within the text. Drawing upon the idea of the toast as a collective ritual among the Black prisoners, the speaker establishes Hard Rock's story as representative of heroic myth. The opening lines of the poem introduce Hard Rock in the style of a traditional toast hero, quoting the common knowledge of Hard Rock as *bad*man:

> Hard Rock was "known not to take no shit
> From nobody," and he had the scars to prove it:
> Split purple lips, lumped ears, welts above
> His yellow eyes, and one long scar that cut
> Across his temple and plowed through a thick
> Canopy of kinky hair. (11)

But the poem turns quickly to flesh out the frame narrative of Hard Rock's fall from *bad*ness. "The WORD"—the communicative organ of the prisoners' oral community—is the vehicle through which the anti-toast, the story of Hard Rock's debilitation, passes. The speaker passes the WORD on to the reader: "The WORD was that Hard Rock wasn't a mean nigger / Anymore." Though this statement ominously indicates the truth of Hard Rock's undoing, it also points, with the word "anymore" emphasized by the line break, to Hard Rock's standing identity in the collective understanding as a "mean nigger."

The prisoners, denying that Hard Rock could have changed, briefly revive the old WORD, echoing toast-like accounts of his feats:

> . . . we wrapped ourselves in the cloak
> Of his exploits: "Man, the last time, it took eight
> Screws to put him in the Hole." "Yeah, remember when he
> Smacked the captain with his dinner tray?" "He set
> The record for time in the Hole—67 straight days!"
> "Ol Hard Rock! man, that's one crazy nigger."

The speaker identifies Hard Rock's story specifically as a myth: "And then the jewel of a myth that Hard Rock had once bit / A screw on the thumb and poisoned him with syphilitic spit" (12). (In the style of traditional toast heroes, Hard Rock here shows both fighting prowess and enough virility to give someone syphilis with one bite.) However, where the original WORD had supported Hard Rock as a toast-worthy *bad*man, this new distorted WORD undoes his myth, spreading a new narrative through the prisoners' oral community that negates the possibility of future heroics.

Hard Rock's fall results from the (presumably White) prison power holders' manipulation of his consciousness. Where many Black Arts writers refer abstractly to the warping of Black consciousness by White power and White values, Knight depicts this in excruciatingly physical terms: "the doctors had bored a hole in his head, / Cut out part of his brain, and shot electricity / Through the rest." The doctors literally destroy Hard Rock's mind, reducing his *bad*man defiance to a tame, lobotomized stupor. When they bring Hard Rock back, "Handcuffed and chained, he was turned loose, / Like a freshly gelded stallion, to try his new status" (11):

> The testing came, to see if Hard Rock was really tame.
> A hillbilly called him a black son of a bitch
> And didn't lose his teeth, a screw who knew Hard Rock
> From before shook him down and barked in his face.
> And Hard Rock did *nothing*. Just grinned and looked silly,
> His eyes empty like knot holes in a fence. (12)

Hard Rock, who had been a model of Black Power revolutionary heroics, had embodied for his community the possibilities of not only aggressive but violent defiance to White authority. The picture of the changed Hard Rock, however—grinning, silly, and compliant—strongly evokes an association to the caricatures of blackface minstrelsy, a type of performance popular in the nineteenth century that portrayed Black stereotypes enacted primarily by Whites for White amusement. The new Hard Rock resembles the "Sambo" minstrel character, an individual of childlike intellect contented by music, dance, and attention to bodily appetites (Rickford and Rickford 30). The doctors create the docile and grinning Hard Rock as the actualization of the Sambo ideal—a symbol Knight uses to show what happens when White people (literally) get inside your head. The two Hard Rocks seem to represent the distinction, widely circulated in Black Arts texts, between "Black" and "Negro" mentalities—an actualized selfhood versus the lack of self that results from adhering to White ideals. In fact, Knight raises the stakes: not only must individuals cast off the beliefs and aesthetics of Negro-hood to come to Black consciousness, but they must remain wary that White authority may reassert itself to the detriment of the actualized selfhood. The extremes to which the doctors go to make Hard Rock innocuous, however, stand as a last testament to Hard Rock's heroic toughness. That the speaker and others believe that the doctors would resort to lobotomy and electrocution to exert control shows their conception of the prison authorities as capable of dehumanizing moral compromise. That the prisoners believe that nothing less than this would take Hard Rock down allows them to extend his toast with one final assertion of his almost invincible *bad*ness—to lay a final claim to the WORD before resigning themselves to their hero's defeat.

The dynamic tension of the poem lies not in Hard Rock's story—a narrative we intersect only after the tragic fall—but in the story of the speaker and his fellow prisoners. The speaker links the possibility of his self-actualization and that of the other Black prisoners directly to Hard Rock's symbolic defiance. Only when they are able to posit a hero and, significantly, collectively *express* the possibility of aggressive and defiant action—"wrap themselves in the cloak of his exploits"—do they hold hope of it themselves. Conversely, deprived of a hero, they lose hope in the quest for selfhood, resigning themselves to the inevitability of defeat:

> And even after we discovered that it took Hard Rock
> Exactly 3 minutes to tell you his first name,
> We told ourselves that he had just wised up,
> Was being cool; but we could not fool ourselves for long,
> And we turned away, our eyes on the ground. Crushed.
> He had been our Destroyer, the doer of things
> We dreamed of doing but could not bring ourselves to do.

Knight's depiction of the prisoners' demoralization as collective (shown through the use of "we") underscores the importance of articulating heroes through myth. The speaker and the prisoners attach their collective identity to Hard Rock and express their admiration of him through collective ritual. If the celebration of a hyperbolic toast hero can, as Rickford and Rickford suggest above, help to heal collective castration, Knight suggests that defeat of the toast hero can produce equally detrimental effects. Although the prison authorities physically debilitate only Hard Rock, they achieve the psychological surrender of the other Black prisoners by removing the object of myth and symbol of powerful identity—sinking Shine with the *Titanic*. Knight goes on to express this defeat poignantly and expansively through the image of whipping scars: "The fears of years, like a biting whip, / Had cut grooves too deeply across our backs" (12). This image, which evokes the idea of enslaved people abused enough to shun the possibility of revolt or escape, connects Knight's depiction of the prisoners to the history of Black social marginalization and resonates strongly with the revolutionary ideology of the time. Knight's poem emphasizes the power of traditional oral art forms to affect collective consciousness but also portrays the danger of investing oneself in the collective without a stalwart selfhood. Although the prisoners value Hard Rock's defiance and invest themselves in his myth, they have no selfhood on which to rely for hope when their hero disappears. The tragic defeat of the prisoners in the poem serves as an argument for Black Arts writers' directive that they must first construct Black selves in order to sustain the fight for nationhood. When the call for Black nationhood faded, largely unachieved, from the political landscape, the idea of affirming the Black self, particularly through the articulation of Black heroes, remained as the movement's legacy.

Madhubuti's "But He Was Cool": From Soul Brother to Revolutionary

Haki Madhubuti, the poet formerly known as Don L. Lee who took his Swahili name in 1974, is one of America's best-selling authors. Born in Little Rock, Arkansas, and raised in Detroit, Madhubuti moved to Chicago after serving in the army from 1960 to 1963. In Chicago, he studied at Woodrow Wilson Junior College (now Kennedy-King College), Roosevelt University, and the University of Illinois and worked as an apprentice curator at the DuSable Museum of African American History, where he formed a relationship with Margaret Burroughs, an elder in Chicago's Black literary and arts scene. A former member of the Student Nonviolent Coordinating Committee (SNCC), the Congress of Racial Equality (CORE), and the Southern Christian Leadership Conference (SCLC), Madhubuti became central to the Black Arts Movement in Chicago in the 1960s, founding in 1967 the vital Third World Press publishing house, which, according to its origin story, he began in a South Side Chicago basement with fellow poets Carolyn Rodgers and Johari Amini, and developing the Writers' Workshop of the Organization of Black American Culture (OBAC), an organization at the center of Chicago Black Arts activity. Committed to the educative mission of BAM, Madhubuti also founded two independent schools in Chicago during the height of Black Arts: the Institute of Positive Education (IPE) in 1969 and the New Concept School in 1972.[2] For Madhubuti, the paideic mission of the Black artist, both inside and outside of formal institutions of education, involves the performance for the people of the richness of Black culture and history. In "Toward a Definition: Black Poetry of the Sixties (After LeRoi Jones)," an essay collected in Addison Gayle's *The Black Aesthetic*, Madhubuti reports, "Black poets have discovered their uniqueness, their beauty, their tales, their history, and have diligently moved to enlighten their people and the world's people in an art form that's called poetry, but to them is another extension of black music" (233). Madhubuti further attests that guiding individuals toward Black Pride involves not only the sharing of stories but also acknowledging the range of practices that constitute a distinct, living Black culture that is at once African and American: "We now know that there are nuances and ideas that are purely African. In the same vein, we can see things and ideas that are purely black, or African-American. We've talked about the music and we've seen it in the poetry, but that which we consider uniquely black can also be viewed in the way we prepare and eat food, the way we dance, our mode of dress, our loose walk, and in the way we talk and relate to each other" (232).

The hero of Madhubuti's toast poem "But He Was Cool, or: he even stopped for green lights," included in his 1969 volume *Don't Cry, Scream*, embodies this fully lived Black cultural pride. Celebrating the toast hero in the third-person form of the traditional narratives, the speaker of "But He Was Cool" toasts an individual who proves noteworthy not for fighting ability or sexual virility but as an extreme personification of the image of Black consciousness. The speaker introduces "Cool-cool," the otherwise unnamed Black consciousness *bad*man, by praising the physical darkness of his skin:

> super-cool
> ultrablack
> a tan/purple
> had a beautiful shade

Physically "ultrablack," Cool-cool proudly represents the idea that "Black Is Beautiful," embracing African phenotypical features as the new standard of beauty for those who accept and preach Black consciousness. He further shows pride in his Black physicality through his hair, perhaps the era's most visible sign of coming to Black consciousness, by wearing "a double-natural / that wd put the sisters to shame." Beyond the physical, Cool-cool's dress, his accessories, and even his linguistic acumen demonstrate that he has Pan-African access to the accoutrements of style, representing his African heritage to a *bad* extreme:

> his dashikis were tailor made
> & his beads were imported sea shells
>   (from some blk/country I never heard of)
> he was triple-hip.

> his tikis were hand carved
> out of ivory
> & came express from the motherland.
> he would greet u in swahili
> & say good-by in yoruba.

Cool-cool's direct and proud connection to artifacts and languages of the motherland constitute the crux of his praiseworthy heroics—of what makes him so cool. He not only unapologetically demonstrates Black Pride, but he has reestablished a connection with the aspects of African culture that Whites in power denied enslaved Africans and their descendants. Cool-cool has access to African dress, African art, and, perhaps most valuable, African speech. He embodies the pride of an individual who affirms his African heritage and declares that heritage as a history to be celebrated.

The toast teller heightens his praise of Cool-cool in the latter portion of the poem by engaging in extensive celebratory signifyin around the term "cool" itself. In the context of the toast as an oral performance, this section would be the climax, demonstrating the height of the speaker's energy and improvisational proficiency:

> woooooooooooo-jim he bes so cool & ill tel li gent
>   cool-cool is so cool he was un-cooled by
>   other niggers' cool
>   cool-cool ultracool was bop-cool/ice box
>   cool so cool cold cool
>   his wine didn't have to be cooled, him was
>   air conditioned cool
>   cool-cool/real cool made me cool—now
>   ain't that cool
>   cool-cool so cool him nick-named refrigerator.

As part of his praise for Cool-cool, the speaker shows off his own talent for signifyin and wordplay. The speaker begins to amplify the tone by talk-singing through phonetic exclamations and rhythmic pauses: "wooooooooooooo-jim he bes so cool & ill tel li gent," inventing the word "ill-telligent" to better describe Cool-cool as a sage of *bad*ness. Riffing on the word "cool" and its range of semantic meanings, the speaker alternates between metaphors that refer to cold temperatures and descriptions of the hero as deserving of respect in order to create semantic surprises: "cool-cool ultracool was bop-cool/ice box / cool so cool cold cool / his wine didn't have to be cooled, him was / air conditioned cool." The speaker further uses wordplay to emphasize the hero's coolness as something that sets him apart from regular folks and gives him the power to influence them: "cool-cool is so cool he was un-cooled by / other niggers' cool," "cool-cool/real cool made me cool—now / ain't that cool." This use of signifyin and wordplay, much of it composed in Black English grammar (using forms such as the habitual "be" and the zero copula), pays homage to the verbal prowess demonstrated by toast tellers in traditional oral performances. This invites the audience into the poem, marking the telling of Cool-cool's story as an act of participation in a common collective ritual.

Cool-cool's success story has one major issue, however, and the speaker varies from the traditional toast by pointing to the Achilles heel of the hero's hipness with some pointed signifyin at the end of the poem. Although Cool-cool so far has been *bad* in his representation of Black Pride, the speaker uses him as an example to teach a lesson—that the ultimate result of coming to Black consciousness for cultural nationalists is commitment to the political struggle:

> cool-cool so cool
> he didn't know,
> after detroit, newark, chicago &c.,
> we had to hip
>   cool-cool/ super-cool/ real cool
>   that
> to be black
> is
> to be
> very-hot.

Based on a simple play on linguistic opposites—"cool" and "hot"—this last line of the poem encapsulates the connection Madhubuti and other cultural nationalists believe exists between selfhood and nationhood. The speaker enforces the message rhetorically here through an indirect, ironic signifyin punch line. Although Cool-cool demonstrates all the stylistic signs of Black consciousness, his consciousness is not fully realized without his attending to the political dimension of the Black struggle. His undeniable soulfulness—a style and attitude that out-souls soul—establishes him in the mindset of the period as an individual who has achieved Black consciousness, but his lack of attention to the revolutionary imperative of Blackness leaves him an incomplete hero. The term "hot," like "cool," suggests the stylistically en vogue, but it also suggests both anger and activity. According to Smitherman's gloss, "hot" refers within Black semantics to "fast movement and action, or excessive energy generated in activity" (*Talkin and Testifyin* 53). The speaker extends these meanings to the idea of the revolutionary disposition by connecting "hotness" to "detroit, newark, chicago"—three vital hubs of Black Arts Movement activity: Detroit was the home of Dudley Randall and his publication machine, the Broadside Press; Newark was the home of Baraka and a symbol of advances in Black government; and Chicago was home to Madhubuti, Third World Press, and vital Black Arts organizations like OBAC. Because Black Arts writers directly connected their calls for selfhood and racial solidarity to the Black Power political impetus, "hot" here represents revolutionary activism—recalling the anger nationalists felt regarding White oppression as well as the fervency of activity needed to bring forth Black self-determination. The signified message, then, indicates that Cool-cool's Blackness, as cool as it is, is incomplete without attention to the collective struggle. Black selfhood, represented outwardly through soul style, must connect to the revolutionary project. Madhubuti's use of the toast here reinforces this argument: the *bad*dest, most defiant Black hero is one who fights for the cause.

Giovanni's "Ego Tripping": Pan-Africanism and the Creative Impulse

Nikki Giovanni, one of the Black Arts Movement's most provocatively outspoken young writers, was also one of its best selling. Born in Knoxville, Tennessee, and raised in Cincinnati, Ohio, Giovanni spent her summers down South in Knoxville with family. She points to her grandfather's love for classical myth and her grandmother's ardent Civil Rights activism as strong influences on her and admits, in reference to her family, that she comes from "a long line of storytellers" ("Nikki Giovanni"). Following her 1967 graduation from Fisk University, where she had studied in the Fisk Writers Workshop under Black activist writer John Oliver Killens and revived the university's chapter of SNCC, Giovanni quickly produced two volumes of poetry that appeared in 1968: *Black Feeling, Black Talk*, which the author self-distributed through

Afro-Arts Inc., and *Black Judgement*, whose publication was initially funded by the Harlem Council of Arts but was later published by Broadside Press. That year she gave a serendipitous first public reading to a packed house at New York City's famous jazz venue Birdland, propelling her into prominence on the Black Arts scene in New York. *Black Feeling, Black Talk* sold ten thousand copies in its first year, and *Black Judgement* sold six thousand copies in three months. A *New York Times* advertisement for an A&S and Brooklyn Arts and Culture Association poetry event in January 1978 lionized her as the "princess of black poetry" (A17), an appellation that spoke to both her youth and her public recognition as a Black Arts poet.

Giovanni first published "Ego Tripping," a first-person toast proclaiming the mythic power and vitality of the African diasporic self, in *Re: Creation* (1970), her third book of poems. Giovanni later chose the piece as the title poem of a volume for children, *Ego-Tripping and Other Poems for Young People* (1973). Her assumption that the poem could speak meaningfully to a broad audience that included both adults and children attests to its rhetorical function as the paideic educative material of the griot: the piece adapts the toast form to build Black Pride inclusively, inviting individuals across ages and across the African diaspora to celebrate with the speaker. Like the writing and oratory of many Black Arts and Black Power activists of the era, Giovanni's work here aesthetically and politically reflects the influence of Pan-Africanism encouraged by cultural nationalists like Maulana Karenga and Amiri Baraka. The Pan-Africanist work of Giovanni's "Ego Tripping" is to take a specifically African American poetic form and use it to build a mythical history in which Black individuals articulate their proud ancestral connection to Africa. For a people whose conventional "factual" history was denied and repressed, this assertion of pride in African roots depends necessarily on the creative power of myth.

The title of the poem, "Ego Tripping," announces a narrative of self-proclamation, placing the reader in the audience of a toast. While the poem maintains the epic tone and hyperbolic, signified metaphors of street toasts, it diverges thematically, focusing not on sexual virility or fighting ability but on the subject's creative prowess. A notable part of establishing this prowess, however, comes through the assertion, common to both literary and oral toasts, that "I am bad." In accordance with the episodic nature and fluid themes of toast narratives, the type of creative ability the speaker represents varies in size and scope. The speaker depicts, as the toast-hero, a giant-like corporeality that defies natural ability to survive and to create. She creates human wonders almost as a pastime:

> I was born in the congo
> I walked to the fertile crescent and built
>   the sphinx
> I designed a pyramid so tough that a star
>   that only grows every one hundred years falls
>   into the center giving divine perfect light
> I am bad

Both the creative prowess and the corporeality of the speaker are organically tied to the African landscape. She creates not only human masterpieces like the Sphinx and the pyramids but natural wonders—not through effort but as a byproduct of her own bodily functions:

> the tears from my birth pains
>   created the nile
>
> . . .
>
> My bowels deliver uranium
>   the filings from my fingernails are
>   semi-precious jewels
>   On a trip north
> I caught a cold and blew
> My nose giving oil to the arab world
>
> . . .
>
> The hair from my head thinned and gold was laid
>   across three continents

The speaker boasts a creative ability that is both inherent and fantastic—almost effortlessly natural but still indicative of divine worth. Significantly, though, the speaker is simultaneously divine and human; while she associates with gods and possesses the creative ability of divinity, she maintains a bodily existence, needing food and clothing for survival:

> I sat on the throne
>   drinking nectar with allah
> I got hot and sent an ice age to europe
>   to cool my thirst
>
> . . .
>
> I gazed on the forest and burned
>   out the sahara desert
>   with a packet of goat's meat
>   and a change of clothes
> I crossed it in two hours

The speaker expresses her simultaneous divinity and humanity in terms of Christian mythology as well, asserting, "I turned myself into myself and was / jesus / men intone my loving name / All praises All praises" (*Re: Creation* 37). This dual existence, the ability to be both human and divine, serves both as the basis for the speaker's boasting and as the poem's fundamental assertion of Black Pride.

The poem further thematically reinforces the idea of Pan-African Black Pride by celebrating the African and signifyin on the European. The speaker shows the African landscape as the bed of creation, of dynamism, but portrays Europe as frozen and unproductive, and made so at her will: "I got hot and sent an ice age to europe / to cool my thirst." Also, in a historical revision, the speaker shows Hannibal, as a toddler, having conquered Rome: "For a birthday present when he was three / I gave my son hannibal an elephant / He gave me rome for mother's day" (37). Rome, a symbolic root of Western aesthetic ideals, falls to the smallest of the speaker's children. Significantly, Noah and Hannibal, the speaker's offspring, become extensions of their mother's power, and they use this power to lift up the African at the expense of the European. The speaker, the collectivity of all Black selves, creates by nature and revolutionizes, metaphorically, by blood.

Relating this poem to the Black Arts Movement's concept of selfhood requires identifying the speaker—understanding the hero subjectivity that can boast this creative prowess. Formally emphasizing the poem's focus on the "I" through anaphora, Giovanni presents the "I" in such a way as to give a generality to the subject that can represent any and all Black selves. She accomplishes this representation of the collective in the subject with two devices: first, by depicting the subject's existence on a grand scale that defies time and space; and second, through the epic tone of the narrative, characteristic of toasts, which shows the speaker as an epic hero—the root and embodiment of a people. This epic hero, grounded in her references to the African landscape, establishes herself as Pan-Africanism personified—a representation of ethereal Blackness that is shared by all members of the diaspora. Although the speaker begins in a timeless African space by saying, "I was born in the congo" (a beginning one may read as a subtle revision of slave narratives, which generally begin with vague statements about the writer's date and place of birth), her reach extends to contemporary America: "My son noah built new/ark / I stood proudly at the helm" (37). While this pun extends the range of the subject's identity from African to African American, it also connects the reader specifically with Black nationalist movements. Newark, the home of movement leader Amiri Baraka and center of much of his activity within the movement, stands out politically. As Baraka notes in "The Practice of the New Nationalism," a 1970 article for the *Journal of Black Poetry*, the people of "New Ark" (as he refers to the city) elected a Black mayor and a majority (seven out of nine) of Black or Puerto Rican city council members in 1969 (*Raise* 163). At the time of Giovanni's writing, then, Newark metonymically represented the potential of the nationalist political project. The idea of "building Newark" in Giovanni's poem subtly alludes to the speaker and audience's collective ability to build political nationhood, and the image of the ark, as the place of those set apart and selected to survive, reinforces the promise of the politics of Black self-determination.

The toast form of the poem, then, underscores the message that the speaker demonstrates a natural creative prowess available intrinsically to those who share African heritage. The poem celebrates the creative abilities of the Black self through a form of verbal artistry familiar to and practiced by many speakers of Black vernacular at large. The toast serves characteristically as a way to show pride in one's selfhood to other members of the immediate community, and Giovanni represents creativity as a principle by which to value the self within a poetic form used by Black speakers to express self-pride. The poem implicitly serves both as call and as example, inviting the reader to identify with the heroism of the speaker and to take on the creative role of the speaker. This power, the speaker boasts, is accessible only through the vehicle of affirmed Black selfhood: "I cannot be comprehended / except by my permission" (*Re: Creation* 37).

Giovanni includes a performance of "Ego Tripping" on her 1971 record *Truth Is On Its Way*, a collection of ten of Giovanni's poems read along to gospel music accompaniment. In appealing to the gospel music crowd, Giovanni aimed "Ego Tripping" at a new audience for the toast—taking a "replete with funk" secular folk form and, by making it the proud testimony of a conscious Black diasporic speaker, dressing it up for church. The appeal of "Ego Tripping" extended not only across the secular-sacred divide in Black culture but also across generations. In 1999, Sacramento hip-hop group Blackalicious included a performance of the poem on their album *Nia* under the title "Ego Trip"—just one example, as I will discuss below, of Giovanni's later intersection with hip-hop culture. Giovanni is not alone among Black Arts poets in her significant impact on the attitudes and rhetorical strategies used by politically and socially conscious members of the hip-hop generation. In the remainder of the chapter, I examine the ways hip-hop music stands as a significant Black

Arts legacy, particularly through the poetic and rhetorical modes rappers inherited and adapted as ways to articulate proud Black heroes.

Hip-Hop and the Toast

The resistance inherent in toast stories is clear: the *bad*man represents the ultimate dominance of a marginalized figure over his conditions. He is a myth hero who subverts restrictions on language and action, flipping the script on Western morality and other suffocating confines of the social order. It is no surprise, then, that the toast serves as a central trope for the most widely consumed medium of contemporary Black resistance rhetoric: hip-hop music. As Smitherman characterizes it, "Hip Hop/Rap culture is a resistance culture. Thus, Rap music is not only a Black expressive cultural phenomenon; it is, at the same time, a resisting discourse, a set of communicative practices that constitute a text of resistance against White America's racism and its Euro-centric cultural dominance" (*Talkin That Talk* 271). Contemporary hip-hop is replete with examples of this phenomenon—of what Rickford and Rickford call the "wicked self-aggrandizement" that characterizes the heroics in hip-hop boasts (84). As I will discuss below, the work of Black Arts poets helped to facilitate not only the development of hip-hop but the modes of resistance rhetoric that voice the power and defiance of Black cultural heroes.

To contextualize, it is important to think historically about how the toast transformed into standard hip-hop rhetoric. There is no definitive point in time when hip-hop was "born," but it is generally accepted among hip-hop artists and scholars to have emerged from the South Bronx in the 1970s as a merger of traditional street language performance and the advent and development of improvisational DJing. Hip-hop historian Jeff Chang recounts what he calls the "creation myth" of hip-hop, which points to an outdoor party in the South Bronx in late August 1973. The innovative DJ Kool Herc (Clive Campbell) hooked up his father's sound system in the super-amplified style of Jamaican dancehall parties and used turntables to mix together the instrumental breaks from soul and funk songs, extending the dance time for partygoers by eliminating the silences between songs or during record flipping (67–70). The proliferation of parties like these throughout the Bronx and Brooklyn began to attract a community of individuals whose genres of artistic performance make up the five elements of hip-hop: DJing, in the break-mixing style developed by DJ Kool Herc and his contemporaries; MCing or rapping, delivering virtuosic rhymed verbal performances over the mixed breaks as accompaniment; breaking or breakdancing, a style developed by dancers in response to the high energy of these street parties and the extended dance time allowed by break mixing; graffiti, adopted as the visual art form of hip-hop culture because of the tagged walls in the areas of the Bronx where the early parties were held; and beatboxing, a type of performance that accompanies MCing in which performers use their mouths as rhythmic instruments, developed initially to substitute for beats from a sound system. For the sake of tracing the influence of Black Arts poetry on the development of hip-hop, I focus specifically on the emergence and popularity of rap music—hip-hop's verbally poetic practice that grew out of spontaneous MCing.

From the linguistic end, rap started out as entirely performative—an immediate art that depended on signifyin in the moment, on indirectly and ironically besting the braggadocio of one's linguistic opponents. The presence of profanity, the preponderance of themes of sexuality and violence, and the defiant, super-*bad* hero were already "on the street," as it were, from the traditional practice of toast telling and other forms of signifyin. It is a natural result that the themes of these existing linguistic practices formed the basis of developing rappers' repertoire. Literary and Hip-Hop Studies scholar Adam Bradley warns in his 2009 *Book of Rhymes: The Poetics of Hip Hop*, however, that "it is facile simply to draw a straight line between verbal expressions like the dozens and the toasts and rap. Rap is also music; it relies upon a rhythmic, and often a harmonic and melodic, relation to song. What rap shares with these earlier expressive practices is an attitude, a spirit of competition and a drive toward eloquence" (183). While rap's verbal performances certainly should not be considered just a reproduction of toast telling or other folk signifyin practices, the toast clearly served as a template, both formally and thematically, for one of rap's predominant rhetorical modes. The prevalent themes of violence and sex in rap narratives, evidence of consistency with the traditional toast themes of macho and mojo, allow rappers to use their rhymes as resistance rhetoric in the style of toasts by asserting dominance over the physical and social landscapes they inhabit. Often, this hero, whether celebrated in first or third person, is a complicated and iconoclastic figure: the hustler, the thug, the pimp. In one sense, the violent rhetoric of rap and the complicated presentation of these larger-than-life characters, drawn from the life experiences of the artists, implicate the oppressive conditions of urban America by airing them candidly to the broad audience of the music, which includes a significant young White contingent. The reliance on tropes and oral folk practices insular to Black communities, however, indicates that rap artists accomplish their primary mode of resistance as a legacy of the Black Arts poetic project: by articulating a vision of selfhood to those within the Black community. According to Rickford and Rickford, "Nothing thumbs its nose at conformity like the unrestrained African American vernacular. Although white suburban youngsters eat up hip-hop's edgy tales of money, sexual adventure, ghetto life, and racial injustice (and keep ghetto rhymes atop the pop charts), black urban youngsters are the genre's target audience. And black urban youngsters follow artists who roam the world implied by the neighborhood language of black urban youngsters" (87). Bradley traces the predominance of braggadocio and *bad*man hero creation in rap music from the following roots:

> In rap modesty is anything but a virtue. But how did extolling one's own greatness take on such a vital role in rap from its earliest days? Why is braggadocio so vital to the art form? The answers are as obvious as they are insufficient: partly as a consequence of rap's birth in the battle; partly as a consequence of rap's origins in a black oral tradition that celebrates individual genius; partly as a result of the interests and attitudes of its primary creators and consumers—young men; partly as a result of it being the creation of young *black* men seeking some form of power to replace those denied them. (188)

I suggest to add to this list of influences the work of Black Arts poets, who not only broadened the narrative range of toasts through Black Pride–themed poems and disseminated them to national audiences through print, performances, and recordings, but also asserted toast and signifyin practices as *poetic* language worthy of consumption as art. Partly as a legacy of the work of Black Arts poets, hip-hop musicians create hustlers as defiant cultural heroes in the *bad*man tradition, showing, however problematically, the possibility of asserting selfhood by defining one's own terms of survival in one's own adept poetic tongue.

Much in the same way that Black Arts writers describe the ideal Black poet (as in Larry Neal's passage that opens this chapter), Smitherman characterizes the rapper as "a postmodern African griot, the verbally gifted storyteller and cultural historian in traditional African society. As African America's 'griot,' the rapper must be lyrically/linguistically fluent; he or she is expected to testify, to speak the truth, to come wit it in no uncertain terms" (*Talkin That Talk* 269). Bradley also emphasizes that rappers must demonstrate poetic virtuosity—and must excel at it enough to boast about it: "From the beginning what made rap different from other forms of braggadocio is that it extolled excellence not simply in the stereotypically masculine pursuits—wealth, physical strength, sexual prowess—but in something new: in poetry, eloquence and artistry" (189). In one sense, rappers as inheritors of the Black Arts legacy accomplish one of Black Arts poets' seemingly unreachable goals: not only imitating musicians but themselves *becoming* musicians, attaining what Black aesthetic theorists felt was the most powerful rhetorical ethos within the Black community. Further, rap artists carry on, in their own way, the epideictic rhetorical project of blaming oppressive, racist cultural practices supported by White-controlled institutions and of praising Black culture as inherently valuable. As Smitherman puts it, "The Hip Hop Nation employs African American communicative traditions and discursive practices to convey the Black struggle for survival in the face of America's abandonment of the descendants of enslaved Africans" (*Talkin That Talk* 283). Where rap artists have *not* carried on the Black Arts legacy is in the lack of a connection to any active political program or movement. Smitherman points to, to use Larry Neal's term, the "spiritual sisterhood" between the Black Arts and Black Power Movements as precisely what hip-hop lacks. She observes, "In the absence of a national movement to provide a cohesive political framework, such as that which emerged during the 1960s–1970s, the Hip Hop Nation grapples with contradictions it lacks the political experience to resolve" (283). While the politics of the Black Arts Movement were certainly not tied to any singular platform or ideology, the movement's writers understood their aesthetic work to exist symbiotically with active Black nationalist movements, and most were themselves involved in or working to create and sustain activist institutions with specific political aims. Although in the wake of BAM hip-hop has evolved into a powerful aesthetic vehicle for political messages, those politics have not consistently been accompanied by activist engagement on the part of the artists nor tied to a specific set of political aims. Rhetorical scholar Gwendolyn Pough makes this point as well: "[R]ap music lacks an actual political program in the same way that the Black Arts Movement was connected to the political Black Power Movement. . . . In the case of rap music/Hip-Hop culture then, we have the rhetorical messages without the political work" (286). I argue that where rap artists have followed in the tradition of Black Arts poets even without overt political rhetoric is in their continued use of the toast and signifyin as resistance rhetoric and in their distribution of these communicative practices as popular art forms. Rap music as toast allows artists to continue to assert themes of Black Pride through the creation of contemporary *bad*man heroes—the next generation of first-person toasts that celebrate the defiant power of poetic skill.

Black Arts poets demonstrated to the soon-to-be hip-hop generation that recordings of poetic oral performances, specifically those accompanied by music, had a significant popular market. In an effort to disseminate the Black consciousness message to the people by any means necessary, many Black Arts poets distributed recordings of their poems, including Nikki Giovanni, as noted above, LeRoi Jones / Amiri Baraka (releasing records under both names), Don L. Lee / Haki Madhubuti, Jayne Cortez, and Sarah Webster Fabio, among others. Other Black nationalist poets, such as Gil Scott-Heron, the Last Poets, and the Watts Prophets, used recordings as their primary medium. Gil Scott-Heron, perhaps one of the most well-known voices of the era for his poem "The Revolution Will Not Be Televised," released four albums and seven singles or EPs between 1970 and 1978. The Last Poets, a varying group of artists whose original members collaborated in the East Wind Writers Workshop in Harlem and who purportedly established themselves as a group on Malcolm X's birthday in 1968, released seven albums between 1970 and 1977. Bradley accurately points to Scott-Heron and the Last Poets, along with "other masters of signifying like Muhammad Ali and H. Rap Brown," as "the fathers of rap" who helped spread the popularity of the toast and other Black vernacular practices "[i]n the decade before hip hop was born" (181). The work of these artists helped to coalesce and prime an audience that would be receptive to hip-hop records when they emerged in the 1970s.

Comparatively, though, the work of artists like the Last Poets stands out as decidedly and overtly more political than that of their hip-hop generation descendants. Although both the Last Poets and later rap artists employ Black oral traditions and insular communicative practices as rhetorical devices, the Last Poets signify to move their audiences clearly toward support of Black nationalist politics. In their piece "Niggers Are Scared of Revolution," included on their self-titled 1970 album, the artists employ some heavy signifyin to cleverly and ironically provoke their audience into leaving behind behaviors that thwart progress toward Black nationalist goals.[3] They declare,

> Niggers are scared of revolution but niggers shouldn't be scared of revolution because revolution is nothing but change, and all niggers do is change. Niggers come in from work and change into pimping clothes to hit the streets to make some quick change. Niggers change their hair from black to red to blond and hope like hell their looks will change. Niggers kill other niggers just because one didn't receive the correct change. Niggers change from men to women from women to men.
>
> Niggers change ... change ... change ... (Oyewole and Hassan 61)[4]

Engaging in complex wordplay with the word "change," the Last Poets argue that Black folks should be ready to embrace the revolution because they already practice every other kind of change—especially in those "Negro" (and here, more harshly, "nigger") behaviors that continue to repress and denigrate them: having to hustle to make enough money, privileging and longing for White phenotypical traits as measures of beauty, perpetuating crime within Black communities. The speaker continues his critique of "nigger" mentality as the impediment to Black revolution through further clever wordplay throughout the poem, asserting variously that "Niggers are actors" (61), "Niggers fuck" (62), "Niggers are players," "Niggers do a lot of shooting" (63), and "Niggers are lovers" (64), playing each descriptive keyword through its range of semantic possibilities to signify on behaviors that repress and hold the community back from political empowerment. For example, the speaker riffs on "fuck" as a versatile verb, adjective, expletive, and even noun that describes everything people do except TCB (take care of business) to support the revolution:

> Niggers fuck. Niggers fuck, fuck, fuck. Niggers love the word fuck. They think they're fucking cute. They fuck you around. The first thing they say when they're mad is "fuck it." You play a little too much with them they say "fuck you." Try to be nice to them, they fuck you over. When it's time to TCB niggers are somewhere fucking. Niggers don't realize while they're doing all this fucking they're getting fucked around. But when they do realize it's too late, so niggers do is just get fucked . . . up!
>
> . . . .
>
> Niggers would fuck fuck if it could be fucked. But when it comes to fucking for revolutionary causes Niggers say FUCK! . . . revolution. Niggers are scared of revolution (62, 63)

"Revolution" in this context—the type of change that the poets are advocating for their audience to accept instead—directs the audience clearly to the politics of Black nationalism. Within the social milieu in which this album was released, where Black Power rhetoric circulated widely and was the known political counterpart to Black Arts works, the call to revolution points to a specific political framework that suggests a specific set of actions. This pointedly political poetry, which represents much of the work the Last Poets produced through the late 1970s, makes sense in their rhetorical situation. Supported by a political movement, these artists could argue for their audiences to empower themselves without too much recourse to myth to assert Black heroes. As part of a movement that complemented an articulated political program, these proto-hip-hop artists boldly asked their listeners directly to put their lives on the line for the cause.

An interesting outgrowth of and contrast to this is the music of Public Enemy, a hip-hop group from Long Island, New York, who gained widespread popularity in the late 1980s and early 1990s. By the time of the group's formation in the early 1980s, various forces had converged or conspired to impede the political momentum of Black Power movements. Chang describes the federal government's targeting and persecution of Black Power activists as one of the crucial factors in the movements' waning strength: "A generation after COINTELPRO, Black radicalism had gone underground. Chuck's [Carlton "Chuck D" Ridenhour, Public Enemy's front man] striking logo for Public Enemy—a silhouette of a young black man in a gunsight—suggested exactly why." Purporting to bring "the return of the black radical" in this post–Black Power political and social climate (248), Public Enemy sought to wield the increasingly powerful popular medium of rap music to continue and revive the fight for Black consciousness. According to Chang, "For the hip-hop generation, popular culture became the new frontline of the struggle. While the political radicals fought a rear-guard defense against right-wing attacks on the victories of the Civil Rights and Black Power movements, the cultural radicals stormed the machines of mythmaking. Their intention was not only to take their message into the media, but take *over* the media with their message" (249–50). The artists who formed and launched Public Enemy inherited this work directly from the Black Arts and Black Power movements. As children in the early 1970s, Chuck D, Hank Shocklee (James Henry Boxley III), and Professor Griff (Richard Griffin) had attended a summer program on "The Afro-American Experience" at Hofstra and Adelphi universities that was organized and taught by Black Panthers, Black Muslims, and college students engaged in the push for Black Studies (235). Later as a college student at Adelphi University, Chuck D (along with Bill Stephney, Harry Allen, and Andre "Dr. Dré" Brown) took classes with Andrei Strobert, an African American Studies professor and jazz drummer who, according to Chang, had been "creatively and literally fed by the Black Arts movement" (240). Black Arts poet Sonia Sanchez even praised them by name as "the poets coming behind us in 1989" ("The Poetry of the BAM" 244). By the 1980s, however, Public Enemy and groups like it were left to produce conscious art without an explicit political program to which to direct their audiences. Instead, they worked centrally to advocate through art for Black Pride—sometimes through overt politicizing, but also powerfully through elevating MCs as *bad*man heroes.

Public Enemy's infamous "Fight the Power," released as a single in 1989 and included on their 1990 album *Fear of a Black Planet*, exemplifies hip-hop artists' cultivation of the political spirit of Black Power without the practical framework of a political program.[5] Chuck D, who delivers most of the lyrics in "Fight the Power" with occasional interjections from hype man Flavor Flav (William Drayton Jr.), calls early in the song for attention from a conscious Black audience, claiming, "Music hitting your heart cause I know you got soul / (Brothers and sisters, hey)."[6] He quickly shifts to the song's main theme—calling the audience to action against the "powers that be":

> Got to give us what we want
> Gotta give us what we need
> Our freedom of speech is freedom or death
> We got to fight the powers that be
> Lemme hear you say
> Fight the power
>
> Fight the power
> We've got to fight the powers that be

This invitation to political collectivity is as catchy and engaging as it is vague. Beyond asserting the vital need for freedom of speech—the most powerful tool of a poet-rhetor—Chuck D demands only "what we want" and "what we need" from unspecified "powers that be." The welcoming of all the soul brothers and sisters into political coalition to fight for their wants and needs is more sentimental than practical, but the call itself assumes that Black folks have common interests as a community and would benefit from collective activism.

Throughout the remainder of the song, Chuck D argues that a move toward political collectivity first involves strengthening one's own mind—the self-affirmation that the previous generation would have called Black consciousness. Chuck D points to his song and the power of art broadly as the vehicle that can help fortify this mental strength:

> As the rhythm designed to bounce
> What counts is that the rhyme's
> Designed to fill your mind
> Now that you've realized the pride's arrived
> We got to pump the stuff to make us tough
> From the heart
> It's a start, a work of art

The allusion to "pride" here serves as both a metaphor for the prowess of the Public Enemy ensemble and a reference to Black Pride—the result of immersing oneself in politically conscious Black art. And much like Black cultural nationalists, Chuck D asserts that fully empowered selfhood, selfhood primed to engage in liberatory politics, begins with the consumption of Black art, referring to his rhymes, "the stuff to make us tough," as "a start, a work of art." Later in the song, he more specifically points to "awareness" as one thing the collective needs. Calling upon the beloved community, he asks them to "get down to business" in strengthening their minds for the struggle by developing "mental self defensive fitness":

> What we need is awareness, we can't get careless
> You say what is this?
> My beloved let's get down to business
> Mental self defensive fitness

Public Enemy's urge that the people "fight the power" here becomes a call to strengthen their individual and collective consciousness as Black people, a notable inheritance from Black cultural nationalism that survived the dismantling of Black Power political structures.

The final verse of "Fight the Power" points to the need within the Black consciousness struggle to articulate Black heroes. Chuck D indicts Elvis, saying,

> Elvis was a hero to most
> But he never meant shit to me you see
> Straight up racist that sucker was
> Simple and plain
> Mother fuck him and John Wayne

Instead, he argues that heroes for the conscious Black community should come from an assertion of Black Pride, and the recovery of those heroes, many of them popularly unsung, should be part of the work of the artist:

> Cause I'm Black and I'm proud
> I'm ready and hyped plus I'm amped
> Most of my heroes don't appear on no stamps

Part of Public Enemy's broader project, alongside the expression of post–Black Power political consciousness, involved celebrating a new type of cultural hero, the *bad* MC, through the boast tradition of the toast.

"Public Enemy No. 1" gained popularity as a single off of the group's 1987 breakout album, *Yo! Bum Rush the Show*. Although Chuck D had composed the song several years earlier in response to animosity he confronted in his Long Island hip-hop community—making him feel like "Public Enemy No. 1"—the song became a defining piece of the group's identity. As part of their mission to articulate Black Pride and Black consciousness, the group presented the figure of "Public Enemy No. 1" as a metaphor for Black Americans, choosing as their logo the image of a Black male silhouette in rifle crosshairs, as Chang mentions above. Recalling his response to the group's taking the name Public Enemy, producer Bill Stephney affirmed, "The Black man is definitely the public enemy" (qtd. in Chang 247). In the song, Chuck D responds to the feeling of being the target of public enmity by establishing himself as a *bad*man MC. He boasts about his prowess in the style of first-person toasts, but he points to his verbal skills as the source of his fearsome power:

> Well I'm all in, put it up on the board
> Another rapper shot down from the mouth that roared
> 1-2-3 down for the count
> The result of my lyrics, oh yes, no doubt

Chuck D takes out his opponents with the same cold *bad*ness of a traditional toast hero like Stagger Lee, but the fight here takes place with words instead of literal weapons or fists. He signifies on the prospective opponent, the song's addressee, by using fists and guns as metaphors for his rhymes, warning the opponent not to disgrace himself by trying to battle—that the result would be Chuck D having to commit the crime of soundly beating him in competition:

> My rap's red hot, 110 degrees
> So don't start bassing, I'll start placing
> Bets on that you'll be disgracing
> You and your mind from my beating from my rhymes
> A time for a crime that I can't find
> I'll show you my gun, my Uzi weighs a ton
> Because I'm Public Enemy number one

Formally, Chuck D uses the rhymed couplet style characteristic of traditional toast poems, but he demonstrates his lyrical prowess by including internal consonant or assonant rhyme in many of the couplets, rhyming not only two words to create emphasis and semantic surprise, but three or more in each two-line unit: "bassing," "placing," and "disgracing"; "mind," "rhymes," "time," "crime," "find." Not only do skills like these make Chuck D verbally deadly to other rappers but, in the tradition of toast heroes, his powers make him successful as a lover. He boasts,

> Cause I can go solo, like a Tyson bolo
> Make the fly girls wanna have my photo
> Run in their room, hang it on the wall
> In remembrance that I rocked them all

The dual significance of "rocked" here—both a testament to the girls' enjoyment of his music but also a suggestion that they had been sexual conquests—helps to depict Chuck D as a *bad* lover in toast style. And perhaps most in line with toast traditions, Chuck D portrays himself as an iconoclast, a defiant lawbreaker who has no concern for boundaries set by the powerful—but specifically because of the way he wields his poetic verse:

> Cause I never pause, I say it because
> I don't break in stores but I break all laws
> . . . .
> I'm not a law obeyer, so you can tell your mayor
> I'm a non-stop, rhythm-rock, poetry sayer
> I'm the rhyme player, the ozone layer
> A battle what? Here's a bible so start your prayer

Chuck D closes his last verse with a summarizing self-description, one that connects his skill as a poet with his aims as a politically conscious Black artist: "Known as the poetic, political, lyrical son / I'm Public Enemy number one." Flavor Flav ends the song with "And that's the way the story goes / That's just the way the story goes," a closing that resonates with a traditional epilogue to hero stories in the Black oral tradition.[7]

Public Enemy's repertoire significantly includes both post–Black Power politically conscious verse and songs that continue the toast tradition by allowing the *bad*man hero to evolve into the untouchable MC. The group serves as a notable example of the way the cultural nationalist work of Black Arts poets influenced the development and the artistic resources of this powerful social phenomenon. Although even after the heyday of Black Power Black Americans still had reason to see themselves as Public Enemy No. 1, the next generation had inherited from Black Arts rhetors an appreciation of the power of poetry. This poetry still served as a powerful tool to spread the message of Black Pride and to strengthen the defiant heroes of the vernacular tradition.

Conclusion

In assessing the state of what she calls the "Hip Hop Nation," Geneva Smitherman suggests that one reason hip-hop has yet to develop into a movement is because "there is little help from their elders" (*Talkin That Talk* 283). To broaden the scope of my discussion of rap music as a legacy of the work of Black Arts poets, I conclude this chapter by pointing to instances in the development of hip-hop where there have been interventions and support from Black Arts elders. Although much of rap music has developed away from articulating overt political messages, there are some artists, as Gwendolyn Pough and others have pointed out, that voice messages similar to those articulated in Black nationalist politics of the sixties and seventies. Contemporary artists whose work is cosigned by Black Arts poets often fall into the category of "conscious" or "message" rappers. Black Arts poets' collaborations with these artists suggest ways that these poet-activists may conceive of their own legacies.

Nikki Giovanni stands as a vocal supporter of rapper Tupac Shakur, the legendary hip-hop artist who was also the son of two Black Panthers. Deeply affected by his murder in 1996, Giovanni wrote her 1997 book *Love Poems* in honor of him and includes in the book an elegy to him titled "All Eyez on U," a reference to Shakur's 1996 album *All Eyez on Me*. Her further tributes to Shakur include aiding in the publication of *The Rose That Grew from Concrete* (1999), a posthumous collection of Shakur's poems, her editorial decision to include his work in *The 100 Best African American Poems* (2010), and, perhaps most personal, her decision to tattoo Shakur's famous "Thug Life" tattoo on her arm. Although Giovanni's elder support of Shakur's work comes after his death, her work to sustain his legacy as an important poetic voice is heartfelt and extensive. In "All Eyez on U," she aligns his death with the suffering of activists and innocents she witnessed during the Civil Rights and Black Power eras:

> ... I saw
> them murder Emmett Till I saw them murder Malcolm X   I saw
> them murder Martin Luther King I witnessed them shooting
> Rap Brown I saw them beat LeRoi Jones I saw them fill their jails
> I see them burning churches

She further places the importance of his death next to those of Emmett Till and Malcolm X: "this generation mourns 2Pac as my generation mourned Till as we / all mourn Malcolm   this wonderful young warrior." Rising to the praise register of the elegy, she honors an individual whom she considered a fellow poet-activist: "what a beautiful boy graceful carriage melodic voice sharp wit intellectual / breadth what a beautiful boy to lose" (62).

The Last Poets make an appearance on "The Corner," a single from Chicago hip-hop artist Common's (Lonnie Rashid Lynn Jr.) 2005 Album *Be*. In a song where Common discusses the urban street corner as the violent, competitive space of inner-city drug trade and gang activity, the Last Poets' verses serve as a hopeful counterpoint—reminding the listener that the corner has in African American history been a vibrant center of culture. In lyrics steeped in deep description, Common characterizes the corner as the place "where struggle and greed fight," lamenting that "Corners leave souls opened and closed, hoping for mo' / With nowhere to go." Kanye West, who produced the track, describes the bleakness of the corner starkly in his lyrics for the hook: "On the corners niggas robbing, killing, / dying just to make a living." By contrast, the Last Poets' interludes, which appear after the hook between each of Common's verses, depict the vibrancy of urban street corners during the Black Power era. The corner, as the Last Poets recall it, was the center of Black Pride and political activism:

> The corner was our magic, our music, our politics
> Fires raised as tribal dances and war cries
> Broke out on different corners
> Power to the people
> Black power
> Black is beautiful

Despite the lament in much of the song about the brutal realities of the corner, the piece ends hopefully with the words of the Last Poets, suggesting the possibility that this space could be reclaimed in Black communities for positive action:

> The corner was our Rock of Gibraltar, our Stonehenge
> Our Taj Mahal, our monument
> Our testimonial to freedom, to peace, and to love
> Down on the corner

Common calls upon the elders here, drawing upon both the power of their words and their ethos as Black Power poet-rhetors to connect the stark present to more positive aspects of the past, cultivating hope for change.

"Everything Man," the first track on Brooklyn hip-hop artist Talib Kweli's (Talib Kweli Greene) 2007 album *Eardrum*, opens with a poem by Sonia Sanchez. The poem works much in the same way that an introduction by an established writer adds ethos to a young writer's volume of poems—Sanchez testifies that Kweli is, true to his name, a truth teller and griot:[8]

> But it seems like I've known him forever
> He who has moved through mornings and midnights
> Through deaths and dawns
> To document our bones our blood our lives

She urges the audience to listen to Kweli's verse, his "revolution of syllables," because of the empowerment he inspires through his words:

> Listen, listen to his exact wings
> Strumming mists from clouds
> Listen, listen, a man always punctual with his mouth
> Listen to his revolution of syllables
> Scooping lightning from his pores
> Keeping time, with his hurricane beat
> Asking us to pick ourselves up and become THUNDER

What follows in Kweli's song is his meditation on the seemingly impossible challenge of being an "everything man"—someone who is everything to everyone. In true hip-hop toast fashion, however, Kweli promises to rise to the occasion, citing his poetic virtuosity as the strength that enables him to be this hero:

> I believe, no, scratch that, I know this ain't my full potential
> Only usin 10 percent of my mental on instrumentals
> But incidentally my energy heavenly
> Can he be so ill there ain't no pill or no remedy
> . . . .
> I'm a hustler, I'm a gangster and a rebel with the rank of a general
> In the battle between God or the Devil
> I lay claim to your spirit, your religion, your belief system
> I'll do your hittin, your catchin, and your relief pitchin
> This kid proficient in every position
> The man of your dreams and your nightmares, commandin your vision

Amid these confident promises, though, Kweli admits his humanness: "I try to fit it in the same rhyme / But realize, I can't be everything to everyone at the same time." This is the hero that Sanchez endorses and to whom she passes the torch of the Black Arts project: the griot, the poet-rhetor who rides confidently on the pride generated by his culture and its traditions, but who also can touch down to deal plainly with his humanness.

In her poetic call for meaningful revolutionary messages in her 1970 poem "blk/ rhetoric," Sanchez astutely challenges her audience,

> who's gonna take
> the words
>   blk / is / beautiful
> and make more of it
> than blk / capitalism.
>   u dig? (*We a BaddDDD People* 15)

Sanchez's concern still needs answering, especially by those of us who point to hip-hop as a legacy of the Black Arts project. Hip-hop is an imperfect child of the Black Power era. Some of its challenges come from intolerances such as misogyny and homophobia, passed-down characteristics that reflect both the irreverence of the toast and the most strident rhetoric of Black nationalist movements—a topic that I will discuss in the next chapter. And certainly a thriving contingent in rap music seems to be concerned most about capitalism, whether the message that sells is about beauty or human uglinesses. There is hope, however, in conscious hip-hop artists' continued practice of the articulation of powerful cultural heroes—figures who through the rhetorical power of Black language traditions continue to embody the ideals of Black Pride.

CHAPTER 5

"Woman Power / Is / Black Power / Is / Human Power"

Resistance Rhetoric of Black Arts Women Poets

In September 1969, *Negro Digest* released its annual poetry issue dedicated to Gwendolyn Brooks, the movement's most recognized senior female poet. The issue presents the work of sixty-eight poets, twenty-three of whom are women. The cover of the issue features, alongside her photograph, Mari Evans's poem "I Am a Black Woman," whose final stanza reads,

> I
> am a black
> woman
> tall as a cypress
> strong
> beyond all definition still
> defying place
> and time
> and circumstance
>   assailed
>   impervious
>   indestructible
> Look
>   on me and be
> renewed.

With a total distribution of almost thirty-nine thousand copies ("Statement"), *Negro Digest*'s 1969 poetry issue reached a substantial audience.[1] An artifact that demonstrates both the reach of Black Arts poets and the diversity of those connected with the movement, the 1969 poetry issue also importantly stands as counterevidence that the notorious misogyny of some Black Arts Movement leaders (some of it purposely insidious and some of it unconscious sexism) drowned out the effective and dynamic presence of radical women writers. The lack of attention to women authors in some of the period's best-known poetry anthologies helps to suggest that women were largely absent from or minimally influential in the Black Arts Movement. In contrast to the inclusion in the September 1969 issue of *Negro Digest* of twenty-three women poets (just over a third of all those featured), New Black Poetry anthologies released contemporaneously with the poetry issue seem to privilege male writers significantly: in Amiri Baraka (who was then LeRoi Jones) and Larry Neal's 1968 anthology *Black Fire*, only three of the volume's fifty poets are women, and in Clarence Major's 1969 *The New Black Poetry*, twelve women are represented in the seventy-five poets included in the collection. Instead, the national audience that read the September 1969 issue of *Negro Digest* would perceive women poets as important, integral voices of the New Black Poetry—voices to be celebrated.

The second of the 1969 poetry issue's two feature articles (after LeRoi Jones's "The Black Aesthetic") is Chicago poet Carolyn Rodgers's "Black Poetry—Where It's At," a notable attempt early in the movement to descriptively taxonomize the kind of writing emerging as the New Black Poetry. Rodgers, an active and vocal member of Chicago's Black Arts scene, aimed in the piece to assert autonomy for Black writers as critics of their own work, wresting any claim to aesthetic authority over Black writing away from White critics, especially those who promote traditional Western aesthetic values. Referring hyperbolically throughout the article to the presumably White enemy of the movement as "the subhuman," Rodgers declares, "We do not (it cannot be said too often) want subhumans defining what we be doing" (16). Asserting dual-voicedly that "all Black poets don't write the same KIND of poetry, or all Black poems ain't the same kind" (7), Rodgers offers ten categories that describe poems by their theme and/or rhetorical purpose: *Signifying* poems are "used for constructive destruction," employing the Black vernacular practice of signifyin as "a way of saying the truth that hurts with a laugh, a way of capping on (shutting up) someone," with the goal of persuading the audience to change a problematic perspective or behavior (14).[2] A *teachin/rappin* poem "seeks to define and give direction to Black people," aiming the audience away from integrationist "Negro" identity and ideologies toward "Black" selfhood that supports self-determination (8). *Coversoff* poems "hip you to something, pull the covers off of something, or run it down to you, or ask you to just dig it—your coat is being pulled" (9). *Spaced* (spiritual) poems express "inner calm, . . . a mystical and positive way of looking at the Black man's relationship to the universe," sharing broad ontological insights "to expand our minds, to break the chains that strangle them, so that we can begin to imagine alternatives for Black people" (9, 10). *Bein* (self/reflective) poems show poets "[j]ust writing about the way they be, they friends be, they lovers be, the world be . . ." (12). *Love* poems include poems "from/about Black men and women" as well as "love poems for all Black people" (12). A *shoutin* (angry/cathartic) poem "usually tells the subhuman off. Or offs him with word bullets" (12–13), the kind of violent psogos poetry discussed in chapter 2. Rodgers lists two categories of music-inspired poems, *jazz* and *du-wah*, which may imitate these musical genres in style or may focus topically on musical heroes of the movement (notably John Coltrane). Her final category is *pyramid* poems, writing for "getting us together/ building/nationhood" (8).

Rodgers is significantly concerned with the rhetorical function of the poems in the categories she presents. Although all the types of poems she lists have both suasory and lyric functions, the categories highlight that certain poems work primarily to change minds—to "hip you to something" or "give direction to Black people." Further, her categories establish a spectrum for Black Arts poetry that ranges from the primarily hortatory to the primarily lyric. *Signifying*, *teachin/rappin*, *coversoff*, *shoutin*, and *pyramid* poems all have clear rhetorical goals that the poems convey thematically. In *spaced*, *bein*, *love*, *jazz*, and *du-wah* poems, the rhetorical aim exists in the poem's subtext, dependent upon the power of the poems' lyric expression. Rodgers suggests that many poets progress from more hortatory to more lyric writing as they move from blaming the enemy to praising exemplars of the new Black selfhood. For example, Rodgers suggests that "many Black poets, after writing a lot of *signifying*, *coversoff*, or *shoutin* poems," find an "inner calm" and begin to write *spaced* poems that convey "a mystical and positive way of looking at the Black man's relationship to the universe" (9). She further observes that "[f]or awhile," *shoutin* poems that relied on the violent rhetoric of "word bullets" "seemed to be the only kind of poem being written," but "we are now getting more, more & more love poems" (12).

Rodgers intends "Black Poetry—Where It's At" as a summary of the kind of work being done at the time by New Black Poets at large, as evinced by the range of examples she uses in the article to demonstrate her categories. But I would like to consider her formulations specifically in relation to the work of women poets of the Black Arts Movement. I argue that women poets used the forms and rhetorical strategies at both extremes of the hortatory-lyric spectrum—specifically those particular to Black English rhetorical practices—as a way to combat from within the movement restrictive conceptions of womanhood and female sexuality. Rodgers identifies *signifying* poems as the most specifically and powerfully persuasive to Black Arts poets' primary Black audiences. She gives the following explanation for calling *signifying* poetry "the most dynamic type of poetry I have mentioned": "No Black person can listen to some *signifying* without responding in some way. It pulls us in and we identify with the bad 'signifyer.' Obviously, this style of poetry has the power to involve Black people and to MOVE them" (16). Women poets took advantage of the linguistically and culturally rooted rhetorical power of *signifyin*, both in poems Rodgers would categorize specifically as *signifying* poems as well as in *teachin/rappin* and *coversoff* poems, to critique heterosexual-masculine-biased actions and policies among Black Arts and Black Power activists. On the other end of the spectrum, women poets used the Black English practice of *testifyin*, of telling the truth through story (Smitherman, *Talkin and Testifyin* 150), in *bein*, *love*, and *spaced* poems to present their own lived experiences of womanhood and female sexuality and to attest to the value of these experiences in informing the collective struggle for Black self-determination.

So despite the vocal masculinist discourse present in some Black Arts poetry, women writers of the movement considered themselves—and wrote asserting themselves to be—first-class citizens. In this chapter, I discuss how five Black Arts women poets, Sonia Sanchez, Carolyn Rodgers, Kay Lindsey, Mari Evans, and Audre Lorde, use rhetorical practices specific to Black English to problematize and resist from within the movement strict conceptions of womanhood and sexuality forwarded by some Black Arts proponents. Specifically, the work of these poets demonstrates (1) how the practice of signifyin serves as a primarily hortatory vehicle to argue against restrictive conceptions of femininity and homophobic prejudices and (2) how the practice of testifyin serves as a primarily expressive tool to celebrate womanhood through a communal lyric voice.

Rhetorical Resources: Signifyin and Testifyin

As I have argued throughout this book, understanding the rhetorical potential of these linguistic conventions depends on conceiving of Black English as having its own modes of discourse with specific and powerful rhetorical functions within Black speech communities. Women writer- and scholar-activists of the Black Arts era, such as Oakland poet and scholar Sarah Webster Fabio, sociolinguist Geneva Smitherman (whose work on Black English and education policy and practice I discuss in chapter 3), and pioneering sociolinguist

Claudia Mitchell-Kernan, were instrumental in working to codify and valorize the linguistic particularities of Black English.

Fabio contributed an article titled "What Is Black?" to a 1968 special issue of *College Composition and Communication* on "Intergroup Relations in the Teaching of English," in which she offers the following definition of "Black language": "Black language is direct, creative, intelligent communication between black people based on a shared reality, awareness, understanding which generates interaction; it is a rhetoric which places concretizations of abstractions, poetic usages of language, idiosyncrasies—those individualized stylistic nuances (such as violation of structured syntax) which nevertheless hit 'home' and evoke truth; it is an idiom of integrated insight, a knowledge emanating from a juxtaposition of feeling and fact which form a perspective of 'now' causing perpetual changes of meaning" (286). She further enumerates the following two characteristics as being true of Black language:

1. *The language particular to all biologically black persons; it is, to them, their own means of communication defying explanation.*
2. *A dialect of English; a means by which a black person can comfortably communicate with another black person without the fear of using improper rhetoric because he is correct every time his improvisational words ring true.* (286)

For Fabio, Black language combines what may traditionally be construed as opposite impulses: it is both rhetorical and poetic, both feeling and fact, and (though a tenuous and problematic claim) both biological and experiential. What Black language is fundamentally, though, is *the* most effective form of communication between Black speakers and audiences. Black speakers and listeners cocreate Black language by giving and receiving messages that, in the kairos of the moment, *"ring true,"* and by the sake of ringing true, the communication is *"correct."* In this sense, rhetorical effectiveness *defines* Black language.

Two of Smitherman's modes of discourse, signifyin and testifyin, specifically help to elucidate the power of women poets' resistance rhetoric. Similar to the way Rodgers characterizes signifyin as "constructive deconstruction," Smitherman defines signifyin, as noted in chapters 1 and 4, as the verbal art of insult in which a speaker humorously puts down the listener, "a culturally approved method of talking about somebody—usually through verbal indirection" (*Talkin and Testifyin* 118, 119). While, as discussed in detail in the previous chapter, there are rich performative uses of signifyin, the register of signifyin that elucidates the poetic resistance work of Black Arts women poets is a variety Smitherman calls "heavy" signifyin, which is used by a singular speaker to express emotion or integrated into dialogue or a statement for the sake of making a point. In this way, signifyin can be "a way of teaching or driving home a cognitive message but—and this is important—without preaching or lecturing" (120). This is the "constructive destruction" function to which Rodgers refers; signifyin is not antagonistic insult or criticism directed at an enemy, but a scolding directed at an insider in hopes of effecting a positive change. For example, Smitherman cites Malcolm X's heavy signification on Civil Rights nonviolent protests—"In a revolution, you swinging, not singing"—and Jesse Jackson's alliterative signifyin in a Breadbasket sermon—"Pimp, punk, prostitute, preacher, Ph.D.—all the P's—you still in slavery!" (qtd. in *Talkin and Testifyin* 120). The point of heavy signifyin like this, Smitherman argues, "is to put somebody in check, that is, make them think about and, one hopes, correct their behavior" (120–21).

In terms of audience, the speaker addresses signifyin only to those within the speech community, emphasizing interaction over insult, and the indirect nature of signifyin allows individuals to address an issue or problem while avoiding direct confrontation. Claudia Mitchell-Kernan, whose work in Black English sociolinguistics preceded and influenced Smitherman's, discusses in *Language Behavior in a Black Urban Community* (1971) the insider nature of signifyin audiences. She observes,

> The Black concept of *signifying* incorporates essentially a folk notion that dictionary entries for words are not always sufficient for interpreting meanings or messages, or that meaning goes beyond such interpretations. Complimentary remarks may be delivered in a left-handed fashion. A particular utterance may be an insult in one context and not another. What pretends to be informative may intend to be persuasive.... The context embeddedness of meaning is attested to by both our reliance on the given context and, most importantly, by our inclination to construct additional context from our background knowledge of the world. (69)

In many cases, the background knowledge needed to fully comprehend the indirect message of a signifyin text comes specifically from Black cultural experience—the "shared knowledge, attitudes, and values or signals" (90) that allow for the full metaphorical resonance of the message. In this way, when directed toward community insiders, signifyin actually works as a tool to strengthen community solidarity.

Alongside signifyin, testifyin, one of the traditions of narrative sequencing (or storytelling) within Black English speech culture introduced in chapter 1, serves as an important rhetorical mode for Black Arts women poets' resistance rhetoric. Testifyin is a communicative ritual that takes place in both sacred and secular spaces within Black culture in which an individual bears witness to a feeling or experience that resonates with the common experiences of the audience. Smitherman offers examples of secular testifyin that read interestingly similar to Rodgers's descriptions of *love, bein, shoutin, spaced, jazz*, and *du-wah* poems: "In the secular context, the subject matter includes such matters as blues changes caused by yo man or yo woman, and conversely, the Dr. FEELGOOD power of yo man or yo woman; experiences attesting to the racist power of the white oppressor; testimonials to the power of a gifted musician or singer." As a public narration and reenactment of experience, testifyin allows speakers to benefit from both the individual catharsis of having owned their truth and the affirmation of their collective identity from the responses of the audience. As Smitherman explains, "The retelling of these occurrences in lifelike fashion recreates the spiritual reality for others who at the moment vicariously experience what the testifier has gone through. . . . Thus one's humanity is reaffirmed by the group and his or her sense of isolation diminished" (*Talkin and Testifyin* 150). Testifyin, then, strengthens both the individual and the collective by healing and uplifting the individual members of the community and by solidifying their commitment to the community as a whole.

These modes of discourse, as rhetorical tools for Black Arts women poets, serve significant functions in their intra-community resistance against masculinist, misogynistic, and homophobic biases. By signifyin on restrictive conceptions within the community of womanhood or sexuality, Black Arts poets work to constructively deconstruct other activists' ideologies that would exclude or limit women's full participation in Black Arts and Black Power activism. By testifyin to their complex experiences as Black women, these Black Arts poets reaffirm their humanity and assert the validity of their identities within the activist communities they claim and serve.

Social Context: The New Black Womanhood

Black Arts women poets signify in their resistance writing on the idea of the "New Black Womanhood," a term referenced in the poetry that could refer to any of several strict conceptions among Black nationalist groups about how women should be to best support the revolution, the self-determination of the Black community. As many Black Arts poets were influenced by cultural nationalism, the New Black Womanhood likely refers in part to the strict prescriptions for gender roles advocated by cultural nationalist organizations. For example, *Black Woman's Role in the Revolution*, a 1969 publication authored by a women's group called the Mumininas of the Committee for Unified Newark (CFUN) and published by Amiri Baraka's Jihad Productions press, provides a telling, if extreme, snapshot of the strictures placed on women's roles by some within the cultural nationalist camp. A group that took its name from the Kiswahili word meaning "true believer," the Mumininas of CFUN were adherents to Maulana Karenga's cultural nationalist Kawaida philosophy, which asserted that the "natural" differences between men and women necessitated distinct and discrete roles for them in the revolution and in the family (Farmer 111). The pamphlet presents the argument that Black men and women should unify under the strategically essential banner of Black identity—"we are all Black and being oppressed by the same oppressor" (2)—but within the Black community men and women should have entirely discrete roles. Women, the authors assert, "have absolutely no business in man's discussions" or in public roles that would forward revolutionary goals. "Our duty," they affirm, "is to be a wife/mother. To raise our daughters to be proud, beautiful women; our sons to be men, kings, and kings of warriors." Specifically, this involves devotion to work in the domestic space: "Our homes should be clean, our smiles bright. Our husbands made to *feel like men*, after being downed for so long. His dinner should be prepared, his tensions relieved, and our understanding at its peak." Even when political discussion moves into the home, women should retreat further from the male rhetorical sphere: "Your only entrance should be to serve refreshments. Then what do we do until this is over? There's always something to keep us busy. Sewing, ironing, creating our own pieces of objects; planning menus—for healthy diets make a healthy mind; teaching our children" (4). The text charges that overlapping gender roles, especially those that involve women working outside the home, are just another form of White oppression, a way of extending the historical emasculation of Black men. Only White women, the pamphlet argues, "aspire to be men" (5)—not only in their desires to work outside the home but even in their insistence on literally wearing pants, clothes "designed by white faggots for devil women" (16). The authors insist overall that while Blackness is a unifying and equalizing valence of identity, gender identities must be understood and enacted as distinct and unequal. The frontline work of the revolution must be left to men: "Black women must understand that what the *brothers* are doing is serious business" (2, emphasis added).[3]

Beyond the specificity of the prescriptions in *Black Woman's Role in the Revolution*, concerns with gender roles common to cultural nationalist discourse can be described more broadly. Feminist scholar Patricia Hill Collins offers the following four ideas as representative of the gender ideology that permeated Black cultural nationalism: "(1) the importance attached to controlling Black women's reproduction and sexuality; (2) the significance of Black mothers in passing on Black culture; (3) the notion of complementary gender roles as points of departure in constructing Black masculinity and Black femininity; and (4) the symbolic association of Black women with the nation" (108). Incorporating into the foundations of Black cultural nationalism a normative understanding of the ideal family as heterosexual, nuclear, and patriarchal, many cultural nationalists forwarded a dichotomous, exclusive, and complementary conception of male and female gender roles. While men would serve as "warriors" for the Black nation, women would rule as "queens" of the home—by supporting and inspiring their men and, perhaps most importantly, by bearing and rearing Black children. The order and hierarchy of the patriarchal nuclear family was meant to serve as a blueprint for the power structure of the Black nation, and the idea of race as family (exemplified by the popularity of referring to any Black person as "brother" or "sister") for some included the understanding that deference to male authority would be part of racial filial duty. As Collins succinctly notes, "Race became family; racial family meant community; and Black community symbolized the 'imagined community' of nation" (100). In this formulation, Black women's adoption of strict gender roles that most valued willingness to procreate, serving as educators of and culture bearers to children, and confining their influence primarily to the domestic sphere demonstrated revolutionary commitment.

Prescriptions that limited women's role in the revolution were not unique to cultural nationalists but had proponents across the range of Black nationalist groups, including the Black Panther Party (BPP) and the Nation of Islam (NOI). Specifically, a number of nationalist organizations saw women's reproductive choices as affecting the progress of Black nationalist politics—most often condemning women's use of the birth control pill or choice to have abortions as complicity with White plans for Black genocide. In *The Black Woman in America* (1973), sociologist Robert Staples notes that "even revolutionary nationalist parties such as the Black Panther Party have held questionable views on the woman question," at one time holding as its official position that attempts to legalize abortion were a "genocidal plot" (175). In an essay collected in her 1970 anthology *The Black Woman* (a text I examine in detail later in this chapter) titled "The Pill: Genocide or Liberation," Toni Cade Bambara (then known as Toni Cade) recalls and critiques restrictions on women's sexuality put forward by Black nationalist groups at large. Describing one particular meeting she attended, Bambara states, "I don't recall who called the meeting or what organizations were present" (Cade, "The Pill" 162), but she goes on to describe the unrecalled or unnamed organization's distinct placement of women in domestic and background roles. The chairman's specific request during the meeting that the women be on kitchen duty for refreshments "would not have been so bad except that during the formation of work committees, the Sisters were arbitrarily assigned to man the phones and the typewriters and the coffeepots. And when a few tough-minded, no-messin'-around politico Sisters began pushing for the right to participate in policy-making, the right to help compose position papers for the emerging organization, the group leader would drop his voice into that mellow register specially reserved for the retarded, the incontinent, the lunatic, and say something about the need to be feminine and supportive and blah, blah, blah" (162–63). The main issue of concern to Bambara in this instance, however, was not the relegation of women to the domestic and, at best, the secretarial, but the voicing by male activists of an abandon-the-pill-for-the-revolution policy. One of the speakers, a "tall, lean dude," "went into deep knee bends as he castigated the Sisters to throw away the pill and hop to the mattresses and breed revolutionaries and mess up the man's genocidal program." The speaker's presentation made Bambara aware of this attitude as a broader part of Black nationalist policy: "the national call to the Sisters to abandon birth controls, to not cooperate with an enemy all too determined to solve his problem with the bomb, the gun, the pill; to instruct the welfare mammas to resist the sterilization plan that has become ruthless policy for a great many state agencies; to picket family-planning centers and abortion-referral groups, and to raise revolutionaries" (163). In the essay, Bambara's reasonable and measured objection to this call is to remind fellow nationalists that such a policy, beyond limiting the humanity of women, is just plain irresponsible: "It is a noble thing, the rearing of warriors for the revolution. I can find no fault with the idea. I do, however, find fault with the notion that dumping the pill is the way to do it. You don't prepare yourself for the raising of super-people by making yourself vulnerable—chance fertilization, chance support, chance tomorrow" (164). She argues further that the best way to support Black self-determination is to cultivate agency in the Black community's female citizens; as the future mothers of "super-people," women should have full resources, choices, and support from their partners when wielding their power to give birth to and raise revolutionaries.

In line with the encouragement in some nationalist camps of traditional, distinct gender roles, hyper-heterosexuality, and unencumbered procreation as actions and attitudes that bolster nationalist political goals, sexual identities and sexual behaviors that differed from these strict heterosexist recommendations were construed as "White" impediments to Black self-determination. As Henry Louis Gates Jr. notes, "[N]ational identity became sexualized in the sixties in such a way as to engender a curious subterranean connection between homophobia and nationalism" (qtd. in P. H. Collins 111). Patricia Hill Collins further observes about nationalist attitudes of the era, "Overall, those Black women who fail to have children or who reject the gender politics of the heterosexist nuclear family, face being labeled traitors to the race, too 'White,' or lesbians" (111). And although lesbian women certainly were heavily subject to these critiques, the brunt of heterosexist and homophobic criticism in Black Arts writing was aimed at gay men. Both male and female writers voiced antigay sentiments in their work, such as this graphic passage from Jayne Cortez's poem "Race," which appeared in her volume *Pisstained Stairs and the Monkey Man's Wares* (1969):

> Black men fucking Black men Now
> lapping chocolate shit sticks Now
> Parading in white gay bars Still
> soon to be like rabied dogs
> foaming—aging in jacked off old faggots homes
> Bowels caked with blood pleading to be fucked
> in the dry raisin hole that will not cry
> . . .
> Oh black man quick please the laxative
> so our sons can shit the White Shit of Fear out and Live

Cortez portrays gay sexuality here (and thematically throughout "Race") as a disease, a pathological impediment not only to Black revolutionary consciousness but to the life of "our sons." The source of this pathology in the poem is "the White Shit of Fear"—a social cause that can be evacuated by the "laxative" of Black men's reclaimed heterosexual masculinity. The antigay sentiment that pervaded the Black Arts Movement, like the anti-Semitic discourse discussed in chapter 2, certainly did not originate in Black communities during the Black Arts era, but the vehement voicing of homophobia and staunch heterosexism understandably made it difficult for LGBTQ writers to participate in or even voice support for cultural nationalist politics.[4]

Many scholars locate the beginning of BAM in 1965—the year of Malcolm X's assassination and of Amiri Baraka and Larry Neal's founding of the Black Arts Repertory Theater/School in Harlem. That year also saw the release of what became known as the Moynihan Report, a study conducted by sociologist and assistant secretary of labor Daniel Patrick Moynihan and published as *The Negro Family: The Case for National Action*. Begun as an investigation into a diverging relationship between the rate of Black male unemployment and the rate of Black welfare enrollment, the Moynihan Report purports to uncover a pathological crisis in Black families. According to the report, "[T]he Negro American community has . . . paid a fearful price for the incredible mistreatment to which it has been subjected over the past three centuries": the breakdown of the patriarchal nuclear family, which Moynihan believes significantly compounds the social and economic inequalities faced by Black Americans. Moynihan concludes, "In essence, the Negro community has been forced into a matriarchal structure which, because it is too out of line with the rest of the American society, seriously retards the progress of the group as a whole, and imposes a crushing burden on the Negro male and, in consequence, on a great many Negro women as well." Although Moynihan acknowledges that "there is, presumably, no special reason why a society in which males are dominant in family relationships is to be preferred to a matriarchal arrangement," he observes that American society at large expects and rewards institutions that promote male leadership and expresses that the presence of matriarchal structures in Black culture places Black people at "a distinct disadvantage." In some readings of the report, the Black woman as matriarch becomes, if not the cause of the problem, the fraught symbol of Black male emasculation and the downfall of the Black community.

Given that Black nationalist movements gained momentum in the mid-1960s alongside this public critique of the Black family, it is not surprising that prescriptions by nationalist groups for self-determined and self-sustaining Black communities seem to compensate for what Moynihan nationally proclaimed as the communities' weaknesses. Some cultural nationalists' strict delineation of gender roles, assigning men public "warrior" roles and women private nurturer roles, seems in particular to serve as a corrective to the pattern of families headed by Black matriarchs. Women in nationalist movements responded to these pressures in a variety of ways. Bambara writes in 1970 of her experience with women in nationalist movements eager to be considered anything but emasculating matriarchs: "Unfortunately quite a few of the ladies have been so browbeaten in the past with the Black Matriarch stick that they tend to run, leap, fly to the pots and pans, the back rows, the shadows, eager to justify themselves in terms of ass, breasts, collard greens just to prove that they are not the evil, ugly, domineering monsters of tradition" (Cade, "The Pill" 163). On the other end of the spectrum, a number of women activists, undeterred by the Black matriarch stigma, pushed for and achieved leadership positions in nationalist groups.

Women held prominent roles in the Black Panther Party in particular. Through a combination of tenacity, circumstance, and rhetorical savvy—emphasizing gender equality as necessary for socialist political moves—women like Kathleen Cleaver, Erica Huggins, and Elaine Brown served as lead party activists, seeming on the surface to make good on party cofounder Bobby Seale's public claim that the BPP was "moving on that principle of absolute equality between male and female: because male chauvinism is related to the very class nature of this society as it exists today" (Seale 394). Elaine Brown gives an anecdote about one of her small victories for women in the party as follows:

> I had introduced a number of women in the Party's administration. There were too many women in command of the affairs of the Black Panther Party, numerous men were grumbling.
>
> "I hear we can't call them bitches no more," one brother actually stated to me in the middle of an extraordinarily hectic day.
>
> "No, motherfucker," I responded unendearingly, "You may not call them bitches, 'no more.'" (362–63)

For many women participating in Black nationalist movements, however, the path for navigating through strict prescriptions about gender and participating fulfillingly in the movements' work fell somewhere between submissive antimatriarch and party figurehead. Black Arts women writers, many of whom were influenced by cultural nationalism, criticized and looked to change the strict prescriptions of the New Black Womanhood and often celebrated both women's vocal, public activism and their roles as mothers and nurturers. In fact, they argued for a complex understanding of Black womanhood that eschews prescription. Toni Cade Bambara models an appropriate answer to the question "Who is The Black Woman?" in the front matter of her anthology: "Who is The Black Woman? She is a college graduate. *A drop-out.* A student. *A wife.* A divorcee. *A mother.* A lover. *A child of the ghetto.* A product of the bourgeoisie. *A professional writer.* A person who never dreamed of publication. *A solitary individual.* A member of the Movement. *A gentle humanist.* A violent revolutionary. *She is angry and tender, loving and hating. She is all these things—and more"* (Cade, *Black Woman*). As demonstrated by the poems below, Black Arts women poets use signifyin and testifyin in their works to advocate for this kind of nuanced understanding of Black women and their role in the revolution, affirming women's ability to traverse both the public and private worlds, to be both "warriors" and "queens," both activists and mothers and many things in between—multifaceted women who would serve as the foundations of self-determined Black communities.

Signifyin Poems: The Heavy Humor of Constructive Deconstruction

Carolyn Rodgers's taxonomy of the New Black Poetry in *Negro Digest*'s 1969 poetry issue rings true with the kind of work she produced as one of the most prominent young artists of the Black Arts Movement in her native Chicago. A member of the Organization of Black American Culture (OBAC), Rodgers worked actively with their literary collective and studied poetry in workshops led by Gwendolyn Brooks. She received her bachelor's degree from Roosevelt University in 1965 and two years later joined fellow Chicago poets Haki Madhubuti and Johari Amini in founding Third World Press, a Black Arts publisher second in importance only to Dudley Randall's Broadside Press in Detroit. An outspoken woman who worked alongside men in several Black Arts organizations, Rodgers understandably found ironies in Black nationalist policies that looked to limit women's roles to domestic, secretarial, and reproductive contributions.

Carolyn Rodgers's poem "The Last M.F.," published in her 1969 volume *Songs of a Black Bird*, signifies on male cultural nationalists' advocacy of the dichotomous nature of gender roles. Rodgers sets up the poem as a rebuttal, using the first section to establish what "they say" about who and how a Black woman should be, and countering in the second half with an "I say" reply full of signifyin about how these recommendations misdirect energy that could be better focused on revolutionary goals. "They say" that the ideal woman socially presents "a more reserved speaking self," and that this woman who uses words gently and reservedly—one who acknowledges that the public forum is not her place—is more likely to win respect:

> they say,
> that i should not use the word
> muthafucka anymo
> in my poetry or in any speech i give.

> they say,
> that i must and can only say it to myself
> as the new Black Womanhood suggests
> a softer self
> a more reserved speaking self. they say,
> that respect is hard won by a woman
> who throws a word like muthafucka around
> and so they say because we love you
> throw that word away, Black Woman ... (37)

Ultimately, "they" ask the speaker as Black Woman to "throw that word away" "because we love you," indicating that this reining in of a woman's lexical and rhetorical range is for her own benefit.

In the "I say" section of the poem, the strength of the speaker's rebuttal lies in her ability to signify on semantics, playing with meanings and connotations of words to offer alternative perspectives on the ideas of "soft" womanhood and effective female speech:

> i say,
> that i am soft, and you can subpoena my man, put him
> on trial, and he will testify that i am
> soft in the right places at the right times
> and often we are so reserved, i have nothing to say (37)

The speaker flips the script on the idea of softness not by referring to it as reserved or polite demeanor but by celebrating the natural tactile softness of a woman's body. That kind of softness, she argues, seems to please men just fine, and her man will willingly attest to this. Softness for the speaker has nothing to do with speech but with sexual prowess, which she deploys to her and her man's satisfaction, with kairic savvy: "at the right times." This kind of feminine softness, the speaker wryly suggests, may lead to both her and her partner being quiet because of the extent of their sexual satisfaction: "often we are so reserved, i have nothing to say." The speaker signifies on the idea of ideal femininity as soft to resist the quieting of her voice, stating instead that, without the silencing of her public voice, she is already soft in a feminine way that pleases men just fine.

The crux of the semantic play in the poem lies in the speaker's litany of references to the floating and deeply contextual meaning of the word "muthafucka" in Black vernacular. The speaker asserts that she has the rhetorical savvy to use the word "muthafucka" without earning disrespect:

> i say,
>   that i only call muthafuckas, muthafuckas
> so no one should be insulted. only
> pigs and hunks and negroes who try to divide and
> destroy our moves toward liberation.

Reminding the reader that the term can be used, depending on context and audience, as either a compliment or a derogatory epithet, she asserts that the only people who should be insulted by her use of the word are enemies of Black nationalism, "only / pigs and hunks and negroes who try to divide and / destroy our moves toward liberation." Seeming to acquiesce to "their" advice, the speaker pledges, "this is the last poem i will write" using the word "muthafucka"—but this promise comes with a colorful demonstration of her semantic range:

> but they say that this new day
> creates a new dawn woman,
> one who will listen to Black Men
> and so i say
> this is the last poem i will write calling
> all manner of wites, card-carrying muthafuckas
> and all manner of Blacks (negroes too) sweet
> muthafuckas, crazy muthafuckas, lowdown muthafuckas
> cool muthafuckas, mad and revolutionary muthafuckas. (37)

Within this list, there are both compliments and insults, some of which depend on context that would be clear to insiders in the speaker's speech community: being called a "cool muthafucka" is a sign of respect or appreciation; no one wants to be around a "lowdown muthafucka"; and whether being a "crazy muthafucka" is good or bad depends on what they did. The speaker introduces this list in a tongue-in-cheek tone, suggesting that she plans to comply with the recommendation of the New Black Womanhood that she no longer use the term, but then demonstrating her dynamic ability to wield it in all of its complexity.

The poem's hardest hitting signifyin twist, however, comes in the last sentence of the poem when the speaker reminds the audience,

> But anyhow you all know just like i do (whether i say
> it or not), there's plenty of MEAN muthafuckas out
> here trying to do the struggle in and we all know
> that none of us can relax until the last m.f.'s
> been done in.

The indirect point of Rodgers's signifyin here is that the emphasis placed by some nationalists on the need for soft, reserved Black women who would not use the word "muthafucka" not only represses women's selfhood and rhetorical savvy, but is a waste of energy for nationalists as a whole. The poem suggests instead that activists should focus their energies on fighting enemies—the "MEAN muthafuckas"—who support and perpetuate anti-Black racism: "we all know / that none of us can relax until the last m.f.'s / been done in" (37). If instead of spending energy trying to eliminate un-soft words from women's public utterances nationalist groups would focus on fighting the oppressor, they would likely move closer to their collective goals for the Black nation.

Understanding the reach of "The Last M.F." as a signifyin poem, one that uses insular Black English tropes to talk about and attempt to correct problematic thinking or behavior within the community, requires recalling the rhetorical situation for Black Arts poems as received not only as writing, but significantly as performed to live audiences. Where the speaker's statement that "this is the last poem i will write" using the word "muthafucka" may seem to have more sincerity if the poem is consumed primarily as a finalized written text, one has to imagine Rodgers delivering the poem at multiple readings across the Black Arts scene in Chicago and nationwide. Writing one last poem full of "muthafuckas" that she will then not only publish and distribute in chapbooks but read in public places defies the mandate that women should stay out of the public sphere, allowing her through the wry, indirect voice of the poem to continue to assert herself through speech that is anything but soft and reserved. The message here is defiant: aimed at an insider audience of Black nationalists, the poem signifies with a litany of "muthafuckas" in order to emphasize the wrongheadedness in prescriptions for the New Black Womanhood. Rodgers asks her audience to focus instead on the broader collective goals of Black self-determination.

Kay Lindsey (later known professionally as Kay S. Lindsey), a Washington, D.C.–born poet, painter, Pacifica Radio producer, and Howard University graduate, echoes Rodgers's argument that Black nationalists focus on the revolution and not gender role distinctions. In her essay "The Black Woman as a Woman" (1970), Lindsey asserts that Black women have been "considered as a special subgroup within the Black community, which Black men should try to deal with as their own private extensions." The distraction of confining women to separate and limited roles within Black nationalist movements "is an illusion perpetuated on the Black man in order to deflect him from that task at hand, which is not to create a domestic niche for his woman, but to re-create society at large, a task which involves direct conflict with the white agency, which at the very least would overturn all its institutions, including the family" (86). Best known for her contributions to Bambara's *The Black Woman* anthology—in addition to "The Black Woman as a Woman" essay, she is one of only three poets (along with Nikki Giovanni and Audre Lorde) to be included in the collection—Lindsey argues not only that Black nationalists move away from prescribing roles for women, but specifically against the assertion that reproducing be women's main revolutionary contribution.

Lindsey's poetic piece in *The Black Woman* (simply titled "Poem") signifies on male nationalists' advocacy of limiting women's reproductive agency. Lindsey's poem presents an appropriately complex account of the relationship of the nationalist female speaker to the act of motherhood. Opening the poem with an ideological objection that women's political contributions be limited to birthing warriors, the speaker suggests that a woman is capable of more outward and public activism:

> I'm not one of those who believes
> That an act of valor, for a woman
> Need take place inside her.

She affirms in the second stanza that motherhood will not be part of her personal contribution to nationalist politics: "My womb is packed in mothballs / And I hear that winter will be mild." She complicates the issue, however, by sharing that she is already a mother and considers the act of giving birth one that should have been considered heroic before it was deemed useful to the cause:

> Anyway I gave birth twice
> And my body deserves a medal for that
> But I never got one.
>
> Mainly because they thought
> I was just answering the call of nature. (17)

Giving birth here is not revolutionary; it's natural. But the fact that it's a natural part of human existence does not detract from its extremity or its praiseworthiness. In fact, viewing giving birth as "just answering the call of nature"—especially for Black women who were then suffering and continue to suffer from disproportionately high adverse birth outcomes—is to be oblivious to the risk and sacrifice it takes to bear children. The understated tone in which the speaker conveys this sentiment allows her to signify on the stark disconnect between what is expected of Black women and what is valued.

Lindsey's speaker signifies more pointedly in the final two stanzas, using irony and indirection to critique issues of gender inequality within Black nationalist groups. Although in the opening of the fifth stanza the speaker sets the reader up to be hopeful that the new politics will lead to a new valorization of motherhood, she drops the signifyin punchline after the line break:

> But now that the revolution needs numbers
> Motherhood got a new position
> Five steps behind manhood.

The irony here is that even though the previously unheralded act of motherhood has received a bump in status in the revolutionary mindset to an "act of valor," this contribution—what some male nationalists considered women's main act of political importance—holds a status far from equal with men's efforts. The climactic signifyin moment of the piece arrives in the poem's closing couplet. Relying on the Black nationalist understanding of Civil Rights Movement integrationist politics as an outmoded political approach—the old, backward way of thinking—the speaker indicts the relegation of women to breeding roles for being just as backward and outdated:

> And I thought sittin' in the back of the bus
> Went out with Martin Luther King. (17)

She equates motherhood's position "five steps behind manhood" with "sittin' in the back of the bus," juxtaposing the racist inequality of de jure segregation with the ideal and practice of gender inequity within nationalist groups. The speaker wryly acts surprised that this kind of inequality and injustice persists within the movement, chastising in her final line that she thought it "Went out with Martin Luther King." Lindsey's use of signifyin here is an important rhetorical resource for her as a nationalist insider who is arguing for gender equity to an audience of other nationalists, both men and women. Concerned with the valorization of motherhood as the *only* worthy political contribution of female activists—and yet one that still does not earn equal status with male activism—Lindsey argues through indirection that those attitudes should not be part of radical Black politics. Such attitudes about gender inequity not only take the movement backward, but take it as far back as reinscribing the kinds of beliefs that perpetuated Jim Crow segregation.

Sonia Sanchez, active in the Black Arts and Black Studies Movements on both the East Coast and the West Coast and a staunch advocate of the rhetorical and aesthetic power of Black language (see chapter 3), also uses signifyin as a way to discourage other women activists from being caught up in the call to "hop to the mattresses and breed revolutionaries." "Memorial 3. rev pimps" appears in her first published poetry volume, *Home Coming* (1969). Including this piece in the "Memorial" series that appears in the volume, Sanchez uses the poem to declare that conceiving of sex as a revolutionary act is a way of thinking that should be dead and gone. She addresses the poem to a specific group of "Sisters" who are susceptible to the arguments that their sexuality be used in prescribed ways for nationalist political goals. Working to counsel her peers against this self-effacing impulse, Sanchez's speaker calls out the absurdity of asking women to support the revolution by having sex without birth control:

> hey.
>   Sisters
> git yr/blk/asses
> out of that re/
>   volution/
>   ary's
> bed.
>   that ain't no revolutionary
> thing com/munal
>   fuck/ing
> ain't nothing political
> bout fucking.
>   that's a white/
> thing u doing Sisters.

Sanchez wastes no time calling out the problematic equation of sex and Black revolution, conveying her speaker's emphatic tone through line breaks and punctuation with the slashes and separation of syllables reading like handclaps or vocal emphasis in a "real talk" conversation. Far from forward "Black" thinking, this kind of sexual behavior is a "white thing"—essentially an enemy action that keeps nationalist politics from progressing forward. The speaker accuses the men in the poem of using Black nationalist rhetoric as a way to run game, thinking only of their individual sexual conquests and not of any community-minded activism:

>   and that so/
> called/brother there
> screwing u in tune to

>   fanon
>   and fanon
>   and fanon
>   ain't no re
>   vo/lution/
>   ary

Sanchez signifies here on the use of revolutionary rhetoric as game with the imagery of "fanon / and fanon / and fanon" as the sounds these men would make during sex, suggesting that the women the poem addresses are naïve enough to believe that anyone who alludes to Martinican psychoanalyst, philosopher, and freedom fighter Frantz Fanon, whose writings were foundational texts in the ideological development of the Black Power and Black Arts Movements, must have revolutionary intentions at heart. The speaker closes the poem with a cutting metaphor, challenging the female audience,

> the game he's running
> ain't called no
>   post/office
> cuz. u show me
> a revolutionary/fuck &
> i'll send my ass   C.O.D.
> to any Revolutionary.
>   u dig? (31)

The speaker, who asserts herself as a revolutionary, is so sure that the "hop to the mattresses" policy is game and not politics that she is willing to mail herself to the mattress if anyone can make a legitimate case that sex is part of the path to Black self-determination. Sanchez's rhetorical strategy here falls into the category of heavy signifyin—using pointed wry humor to shed light on and correct problematic gender relations between male and female nationalists. The "u dig?" in the last line of the poem, which bookends the "hey. / Sisters" that opens the piece, underscores that this conversation is addressed to peers for their benefit. Sanchez's speaker is using signifyin to have a tough-love talk with other women to help keep them from being exploited by those who purport to be working to uplift the Black community.

The poems of Audre Lorde importantly use signifyin to extend the critique of gender roles and relationships within Black nationalist groups to include questioning attitudes toward LGBTQ sexualities. In particular, Lorde's work addresses the problematic trope of homosexuality as White pathology that pervades much of Black Arts and cultural nationalist writing. Lorde, a publicly out lesbian in the Greenwich Village writing scene since the mid-1950s, is an exceptional case of an LGBTQ author openly affiliating with the Black Arts Movement. Including nationalist messages in her work and publishing four books of poetry with Broadside Press between 1968 and 1974, Lorde stands as an important and defiant Black Arts voice. Expressing her sense of being an outsider in *The Cancer Journals* in 1980, Lorde sheds light on earlier phases of her life as well, including her intersection with Black nationalist politics: "I am defined as other in every group I'm part of. The outsider, both strength and weakness. Yet without community there is certainly no liberation, no future, only the most vulnerable and temporary armistice between me and my oppression" (12–13). In her Black Arts–era poetry, Lorde emphasizes this tension between the need to define community and the danger of defining too strictly who gets included in or excluded from that community. In the brief signifyin poem "Revolution Is One Form of Social Change" from her 1974 volume *New York Head Shop and Museum,* Lorde analogizes the gender hierarchizing that took place within nationalist movements and "the man['s]" process of "making niggers":

> When the man is busy
> making niggers
> it doesn't matter
> much
> what shade
> you are.
>
> If he runs out of one
> particular color
> he can always switch
> to size
> and when he's finished
> off the big ones
> he'll just change
> to sex
> which is
> after all
> where it all began (38)

Lorde uses enjambment here to underscore how forces in power persistently aim to emphasize and exploit difference: the reader hears an end to the clause at the line break after "it doesn't matter," but the speaker continues, "much /

what shade / you are"; she employs the same technique with "and when he's finished / off the big ones." "The man" comes full circle back to emphasizing and exploiting differences of "sex / which is / after all / where it all began." The process of "making niggers," of arbitrarily subordinating one group to another for the sake of gaining or maintaining power, began with hierarchizing the sexes. The point here is not to eliminate difference or become blind to difference, whether in shade, size, or sex—in fact, all of these examples of difference are substantially biological and cannot be erased from the body. Instead, the speaker uses irony and indirection to ask her audience to consider carefully which differences become rationales for oppression.

In her poem "Hard Love Rock #II," which also appears in *New York Head Shop and Museum*, Lorde critiques the irony of nationalists participating in the process of emphasizing and hierarchizing difference. Lorde opens the poem with an inclusive, affectionate direct address to men in the movement, which she quickly complicates:

> Listen brother love you
> love you love you love you dig me
> a different colored grave

With the enjambment between the second and third lines, she introduces the technique she will use throughout the poem to establish the tension and division between the speaker and the "brother." Where the line break suggests that the speaker is asking her addressee if he "digs" (understands, feels) her affection, reading the line through the break causes the clause to read, "you dig me / a different colored grave," accusing the male addressee of rejecting her affection and camaraderie, of segregating her away with finality in a "different colored grave." She continues the strategy of conveying irony through enjambment in the subsequent lines, with the line break suggesting a reading of "we are both lying" as an admission that both the speaker and the brother have been untruthful:

> we are both lying
> side by side in the same place
> where you put me
> down
> deeper still
> we are
> aloneness unresolved by weeping
> sacked cities not rebuilt

> by slogans
> by rhetorical pricks
> picking the lock
> that has always been
> open. (24)

Reading through the enjambment produces "we are both lying / side by side in the same place," indicating that, despite the brother's desire to separate himself from the speaker, they are both relegated to the same oppression from the White ruling class, put down in the same grave of anti-Black racism. The indictment of the brother goes further; the speaker accuses him of "put[ting her] / down / deeper still," of further oppressing her even though they are both already in the ground because of assaults from a common enemy. Referring to "rhetorical pricks" that are "picking the lock / that has always been / open," the speaker allusively indicts some nationalists' calling for women to devote their sexuality to the revolution. Like the speaker in Sanchez's poem above, Lorde's speaker suggests that sex should not be used as a means to a political end but should be valued as an essential human intimacy—that that "lock" "has always been / open" without "pricks" needing to come at it "rhetorically." Moving beyond the implication of Sanchez's poem above, however, Lorde's speaker here laments not only the claiming of women's sexuality for political goals but the insistence that their sexuality be heterosexual. The metaphor of the segregated graves for the speaker and the brother suggests something irresolvable, something un-integrable, about the two individuals' identities—something as charged as the assertions by some nationalists that homosexuality is a White perversion that cannot be part of the new Black community. The speaker asserts that their individual and communal oppression, "aloneness unresolved by weeping / sacked cities not rebuilt," will not be ameliorated by rhetorical maneuvering that insists on divisions between them based on prescribed definitions of Black identity. As Lorde expresses in "Now," which appears in the same volume, "Woman power / is / Black power / is / Human power" (20): as much as the Black Power struggle is a fight for human rights, Black women's fight for empowerment is part of the fight for the Black community as a whole. Creating divisions within nationalist movements that limit women's participation or that condemn and ostracize LGBTQ people does not help to ameliorate the "aloneness" of facing prejudice or to rebuild the "sacked cities" of Black communities.

Lorde builds to the climax of her signifyin critique in the poem's last two short stanzas. Again using enjambment for semantic surprise, Lorde writes,

"Black is," coaxing the reader to fill in "beautiful" at the end of the line to echo one of Black Power and Black Arts' most memorable slogans. Instead, the speaker of the poem refuses to endorse the slogan, asserting that

> Black is
> not beautiful baby
> beautiful baby beautiful
> lets do it again (24)

Lorde certainly does not take issue with the project of affirming the beauty of Black physicality or culture or of flipping the aesthetic connotation of "Black" from negative to positive. The poem's speaker objects instead to Black being beautiful when the definition of Black identity excludes her and others like her based on homophobia. "Black is beautiful" as a definition of a people may be effective in conveying nationalist movements' strategic essentialism with rhetorical pith. It does not, however, describe for Lorde the united coalition that will most effectively move forward nationalist political goals. The argument of the poem is not against strategic essentialism but *for* it—that her lesbianism not be a factor that excludes her from the Black collective, that Black identity be broad and inclusive enough to embrace all those who are willing to make it a primary category of identity for the sake of political change.

The speaker, then, calls upon the addressee of the poem (both the brother and the larger audience) to "do it again"—to come up with a working definition of Black identity that includes all self-identifying Black people as full members of the political coalition, regardless of sexual identity or gender. The last stanza begins this process of redefinition with the poem's most pointed moment of signifyin. What "Black is," for the speaker, starts with a new understanding about what Black "is not":

> It is
>
> not
> being screwed twice
> at the same time
> from on top
> as well as
> from my side. (24)

The ironic and poignantly indirect argument here is that those within the Black nationalist coalition cannot subject each other to the same kinds of segregation and oppression that Black Americans have consistently been subjected to by Whites. Being "screwed . . . from the top" should be enough to bind individuals together in political coalition without the same kinds of "screwing" tactics being carried out on subgroups within the coalition. The sexual nature of the metaphor drives home Lorde's indignation that this kind of division, of segregated grave digging, happens on the basis of gender and sexuality.

The poems above demonstrate Black Arts women poets' strategic use of signifyin as a way to argue against limiting conceptions of gender and sexuality within nationalist movements. Rhetorically, signifyin here serves a primarily hortatory function, speaking out against what *is* to argue for what *ought to be*. It is important to view these arguments by Black Arts women rhetors as carefully employing insular community rhetorical practices to work for the constructive deconstruction of problematic gender attitudes and practices. Far from putting their nationalist comrades on blast to their political foes, these women writers used indirection, irony, and wry humor to argue for change in a voice that would be clear and compelling to community insiders without sacrificing political unity.

Testifyin Poems: From Black Matriarch to Black Queen

In the poems I examine below, Black Arts women poets use the Black English rhetorical mode of testifyin as a means to assert that women do and should fill a range of roles in public and private spheres. Testifyin both affirms the significance of one's individual life experience and, through the resonance of these experiences among others in the community, confirms that individual's membership in and importance to that community. The primacy of sharing experience here makes these poems centrally lyric. Different from the Black Arts Movement's programmatic poems or the specifically addressed and primarily hortatory signifyin poems above, testifyin poems couch argument within the expressive voices of speakers presenting versions of their lives.

Mari Evans's poem "I Am a Black Woman," the piece that appears on the cover of the September 1969 poetry issue of *Negro Digest*, testifies to women's role throughout African American history as both fighters and nurturers. Born in Toledo, Ohio, educated at the University of Toledo where she studied fashion design, and active in Indianapolis as an educator and television producer for a program called *The Black Experience*, poet, playwright, and children's book author Mari Evans understood the community-building power of conveying individual experience through rhetorical modes that are part of collective ritual within Black culture. In "I Am a Black Woman," Evans's speaker testifies through a lyric voice that is at once individual and collective. Amplifying the rhetorical circumstances for testifyin, the poem's speaker individually represents Black women's experiences from the Middle Passage through the present—an experience she conveys metaphorically as "some sweet arpeggio of tears":

> I am a black woman
> the music of my song
> some sweet arpeggio of tears
> is written in a minor key
> and I
> can be heard humming in the night
> Can be heard
>   Humming
> in the night

As testimony, the poem formally emphasizes the significance of the lyric "I." Evans begins all of the poem's stanzas with "I," leaving the "I" on its own as the first line of the last stanza, and she breaks the line on "I" on two other occasions. The suggestions in the poem that the text is supposed to be performed further emphasize its nature as community testimony. The repetition in the first stanza of "[I] Can be heard / Humming / in the night," with "Humming" capitalized and on its own line, suggests that the speaker might vocalize these words or hum in a minor key. The speaker also confesses in the following lines of the poem to an action she has done "/with these hands/," the slash marks emphasizing the parenthetical interruption as an implicit stage direction: the speaker shows her hands to the audience as part of her testimony. These formal aspects of the poem indicate to the reader that the poem relates a deeply personal (or personalized, in the sense of the "I" representing all Black women) experience that is meant to be heard and understood by others. The testimony itself promises to heal and affirm both speaker and community.

The speaker presents the content of her testimony in the second stanza, tracing her experience living in a state of war—of having seen herself and those around her literally struggle for life—since her forced transport across the Atlantic:

> I saw my mate leap screaming to the sea
> and I/with these hands/cupped the lifebreath
> from my issue in the canebrake
> I lost Nat's swinging body in a rain of tears

and heard my son scream all the way from Anzio
for Peace he never knew. . . . I
learned Da Nang and Pork Chop Hill
in anguish

She witnessed her "mate leap screaming to the sea," choosing suicide over imminent enslavement upon arrival in the Americas. She confesses that "I/with these hands/cupped the lifebreath / from my issue in the canebrake," having chosen after suffering in slavery to kill her child rather than have them live enslaved as well. The speaker goes on to reveal her presence in and loss during historically recorded instances of war and rebellion. She "lost Nat's swinging body in a rain of tears," indicating her grief at the execution of Nat Turner after his leadership of a slave rebellion. She refers to the poignant irony of her son having fought and died in World War II for freedoms abroad when those same freedoms were denied him at home: "heard my son scream all the way from Anzio / for Peace he never knew." She expresses her "anguish" at the equally ironic losses of her own at "Da Nang and Pork Chop Hill," battles in the Vietnam and Korean wars, respectively.

The speaker then importantly places herself in the present on the field of battle:

Now my nostrils know the gas
and these trigger tire/d fingers
seek the softness in my warrior's beard

It is significant that the speaker, the symbolic representative of all Black women, locates her role in the contemporary struggle as a soldier—as someone not only who has pulled the trigger but whose hands have grown weary from shooting, someone whose nostrils have experienced the gas enough times to "know" it. The speaker is at once this fighter and the loving partner who "seeks the softness in my warrior's beard," who has been a mother and mourns the loss of her children. Although the speaker is the keeper, the collective memory, of a tragic history, she does not consider herself a tragic figure. Describing herself in terms of military fortifications in the last stanza, the speaker asks her audience to be inspired by her strength:

I
am a black woman
tall as a cypress
strong
beyond all definition still

>   defying place
>   and time
>   and circumstance
>   assailed
>   impervious
>   indestructible
>   Look
>   on me and be
>   renewed

Purposely enjambing the last line to allow for the surprise of the speaker's self-characterization as empowered and empowering, Evans writes, "Look / on me and be / renewed." The speaker, voicing the collective experience of Black women throughout African American history, is both nurturer and warrior—and the force that will compel others to remain brave and strong in the current fight.

In two sequential poems in *Songs of a Black Bird* (1969), Carolyn Rodgers also reflects on the complex role of Black women as mothers, but this time from the perspective of the daughter. Written as testimonial reenactments of and reflections on two interactions in which the speaker's mother was trying to take care of her, the poems use the rich linguistic resources of Black English grammar, phonetics, and tonal semantics to craft mother and daughter voices both personal to the speaker and familiar to a broader Black audience to address the community problem of the often-fraught interaction between nationalist youth of the 1960s and 1970s and their elders. The first poem, "Jesus was Crucified, or, It Must be Deep (an epic pome)," details a phone conversation in which the speaker's mother has called to check in on her because she has been ill. The discussion quickly turns to the mother's concern that the illness stems from the speaker's having "too much hate" in her, fearing "it's somethin wrong wid yo mind girl." The source of the problem, according to the mother, is her association with and political support of what the reader understands to be Black nationalists, but whom her mother confuses with "communists":[5]

>   talking bout hatin white folks & revolution
>   & such and running round wid NegroEs
>   WHO CURSE IN PUBLIC!!!! (she sd)
>   THEY COMMUNIST GIRL!!! don't yuh know that???

Her mother finds this behavior especially upsetting because she feels it doesn't represent the sacrifices she made to raise her daughter to be "decent":

> ... the way i worked my fingers to the bone in
> this white mans factori to make u a de-cent some-
> bodi and here u are actin not like decent folks (9)

The poem portrays the mother as caring but entirely out of touch with the oppressive racial circumstances in which they live and confused by and afraid of Black nationalists' strategies to address the circumstances. The speaker recounts her mother's concerns ironically and responds tersely and sarcastically to her mother's pleas that she turn (back) to Christian religion for guidance. The poem's title moment comes from the speaker's wry response to her mother's insistence on the truth of the Bible:

> ... she sd it is it is and deep deep down
> in yo heart u know it's true
>   (and i sd)
>   it must be d
>   eeeep (11)

The poem represents the stark divide that Black Power and Black Arts activists felt between themselves and advocates of integrationist politics. As Molefi Kete Asante (formerly Arthur L. Smith) observes in *Rhetoric of Black Revolution* (1969), those who supported Civil Rights integrationism tended to be older and to have faith in Christian religion and in the organizing power of Black churches; Black Power supporters tended to be a younger, increasingly college-educated contingent and often voiced a strong secularism in their call for Black political, social, and economic self-determination (Smith 67). Within the poem, the speaker wants to distance herself not only from her mother's Christian faith and belief in the authority of the church, but also from her mother's conception of "decency" that vests some value in acceptance by White-dominated society. In this sense, the mother's proud declaration of her sacrifice for her daughter, of "work[ing] my fingers to the bone in / this white mans factori to make u a de-cent some- / bodi," serves for the speaker as evidence of her mother's dependence on White institutions. For Black nationalists advocating self-determination for their communities, being financially dependent on a job in a White-owned factory demonstrates problematic entrapment in White power structures. And perhaps more troubling for Black consciousness advocates like the cultural nationalists in Rodgers's Chicago cohort, the speaker's mother doesn't realize that she has bought in to the system of values that oppresses her.

Further, in addition to the critique the mother receives from her young Black nationalist daughter, women of the mother's generation were also under fire from White authorities. It was figures like the speaker's mother, female heads of household working to support their families financially, that Moynihan feared were family-killing, emasculating forces. The mother is a strong, working, independent mother (the only male figures mentioned in the poem are the White factory owner and the mother's White pastor)—a seemingly positive characterization, but this is exactly the type of matriarchal figure that the Moynihan report maligns. In this sense, the mother figure symbolizes an impediment to Black social and political progress to critics both inside and outside the Black community.

In "It Is Deep," the poem that immediately follows "Jesus was Crucified" in *Songs of a Black Bird*, Rodgers's speaker complicates and softens the disdain she presents in the first poem. Where "Jesus Was Crucified" functions primarily as a signifyin poem that critiques the mother's lack of Black consciousness, "It Is Deep" mollifies this critique by testifyin to the importance of the mother's nurturing to both the individual and collective strength of nationalists. The subtitle indicates the nature of the poem as testimony. Admonishing herself and the reader, "don't never forget the bridge / that you crossed over on," the speaker prefaces the poem with the lesson to be learned from her story, the communal takeaway to be demonstrated by the sharing of her individual experience. The speaker tells her audience about a surprise visit her mother made to her home out of concern about the speaker's disconnected phone. Depicting her mother, like in the first poem, as deeply Christian and proudly down-home, the speaker changes her tone. Instead of being wryly critical of her mother's lack of political awareness, the speaker describes her mother's deep love and indefatigable nurturing with sentimental respect:

> My mother, religiously girdled in
> her god, slipped on some love, and
> laid on my bell like a truck,
> blew through my door warm wind from the south
> concern making her gruff and tight-lipped
>   and scared
> that her "baby" was starving. (12)

Although the speaker doesn't consider herself a "baby," she understands her mother's concern and her instinct to nurture; being worried about a child you can't reach and whose bills are past due is a natural maternal response, not the domineering act of a "matriarch." After examining what the speaker has in the house to eat, her mother

>   ... pressed fifty
>   bills in my hand saying "pay the talk bill and buy
>   some food; you got folks who care about you ..." (13)

The speaker portrays here not an oppressive matriarch or White-fearing enemy of the revolution, but a woman whose personal sacrifices and place within the Black community allow for the speaker to have developed her own Black consciousness, written her own "book of / Black poems," and spent her time and energy working toward Black self-determination.

And although, also as in the first poem, the speaker acknowledges the generational differences between her mother and her, particularly in terms of their politics, she recognizes that the political reach of her generation necessitates standing on the shoulders of the one before. The speaker remains critical of her mother's lack of Black consciousness, observing that her mother

> thinks that I am under the influence of
> **communists**
> when I talk about Black as anything
> other than something ugly to kill befo it grows.

The speaker further admits that "in any impression [my mother] would not be / considered 'relevant' or 'Black'" and is "not able to understand, what she had / been forced to deny" (12). But the speaker uses her testimony here to complicate the issue of writing off the elders. In contrast to depicting her mother as complicit with White values and institutions as in the first poem, the speaker recalls moments when her mother has acknowledged and expressed anger about having been subjected to institutionalized racism:

>   ... I grew hearing her
> curse the factory where she "cut uh slave"
> and the cheap j-boss wouldn't allow a union,
>   ... I heard the tears when
> they told her a high school diploma was not enough[6]

Although this awareness is not the Black consciousness of the Black Power advocates, the speaker recognizes here that her mother has suffered through injustices and that her perseverance in the face of that struggle should be recognized. The speaker closes the poem with a brief encomium to her mother as the "bridge" that carried her to her own Black consciousness:

> My mother, religious-negro, proud of
> having waded through a storm, is very obviously,

>   a sturdy Black bridge that I
>   crossed over, on. (13)

Beyond working to heal the generational rift between Black nationalist youth and their elders, the poem is significant in recognizing and elevating women in both activist and nurturer roles. The speaker, who has written a "book of Black poems," has a public, active role in the revolution, but she is bolstered by the support of her community, the "folks who care about you," and specifically by her independent, hardworking mother. Rodgers emphasizes the specific need for mother-love in a short poem called "Untitled No. Hurt" that appears in the same volume. Addressing a potential love interest, the speaker accuses him of being unable to love her because of his resentment toward his mother:

>   you were all my men and in
>   you, i glimpsed the meaning of
>   so many words like strength and beauty—
>   but you could not love me,
>   because you hate your
>   Black
>   momma. (21)

There is a suggestion here of the damage that buying into the Moynihan Report could wreak on nationalist goals to rebuild Black communities. The self-determined community, according to Black nationalist ideologies, begins with the strong, devoted love of partners, with the family as the microcosm of broader community health. Rodgers here suggests that momma-hate, like accusations of emasculation that followed the Moynihan Report, can impede the establishment of loving partnerships. In this poem and those above, Rodgers testifies to lessons learned about building strong relationships and communities upon the foundation of strong women, whether they work in or outside of the home. Instead of wrongheadedly condemning Black matriarchs or relegating women solely to reproductive and domestic roles, nationalists should respect both the "sturdy Black bridges" and the women activists crossing over on them in the name of the revolution. Rodgers's speaker testifies here to her community to recount this lesson learned, and in doing so she, like the speaker in Evans's poem above, makes a statement about the broad range of roles that should be available to women if Black nationalism is to make effective political strides.

Conclusion

Toni Cade Bambara's anthology *The Black Woman* first appeared in 1970 at the height of the Black Arts Movement, and the first edition of the text serves as an interesting artifact for gauging the currents affecting Black women activists' political commitments. The back cover of the book reads, "Today America is witnessing two great human revolutions. One is that of burgeoning Black pride and militancy. The other is the rising demand by women for liberation from their chattel-like roles in a male-dominated society. This volume presents the eloquent writings of those vitally involved in both—Black women, speaking of themselves and for themselves." This text points to the inclination of women within Black nationalist movements to belong simultaneously to both struggles—believing or hoping that Black nationalism and women's liberation were not at odds but had, essentially, liberatory goals cut from the same cloth. This inclination is an early version of what feminist scholar Kimberlé Crenshaw would later call intersectionality, or what Black Left activists like Claudia Jones and Louise Thompson Patterson had named "triple oppression" a generation before BAM: the understanding that an individual experiences the world through multiple axes of identity and that one's relationship to individual or social empowerment relies not on one aspect of identity but on their intersection. Indeed, these issues of addressing the fundamental complexity of identity would become central both to politics and to scholarship in a range of fields. For example, literary scholar Bernard W. Bell identifies thirteen aspects of selfhood whose "complex relationship" are "both a product and a process" that compose an individual's identity: chromosomes, color, ethnicity, class, gender, geography, age, culture, sexuality, consciousness, commitment, conscience, and choice (*Contemporary* 8). These discussions have important roots in the work of Black women activists of the 1960s and 1970s to assert the importance of being all ways free—as Audre Lorde might put it, of asserting oneself against the powers that come at you from the top and as well as from those on the side.

At the same time, however, Black women activists perceived that their specific concerns seemed to be the priority of neither Black nationalist movements nor the White-led feminist movement. Kay Lindsey describes what she calls this "serious dilemma" in "The Black Woman as a Woman": "[T]he Black movement is primarily concerned with the liberation of Blacks as a class and does not promote women's liberation as a priority. Indeed, the movement is for the most part spearheaded by males. The feminist movement, on the other hand, is concerned with the oppression of women as a class, but almost totally composed of white females." The crucial irony, as Lindsey presents it, is that "[t]hus the Black woman finds herself on the outside of both political entities, in spite of the fact that she is the object of both forms of oppression" (85). As things stood in 1970, Black women participating in either movement were subject to the leadership of their liberating movement replicating the kind of discrimination practiced by the White patriarchal forces they were fighting.

The rhetorical strategies exemplified by the work of the Black Arts women poets above are an indicator of how some Black women activists approached this dilemma. Unlike other poems of the movement that were meant to be primarily heard by Black audiences but also overheard by White audiences, the poems that signify on and testify to women's roles in Black communities were meant to be heard and understood solely by community insiders. Signifyin and testifyin as rhetorical modes are specific to Black English speech communities; these writers, then, crafted their hortatory messages for an audience of other Black folks. The implication is that, by signifyin to promote "constructive deconstruction" and by testifyin to affirm identities within the communities, Black Arts women poets were looking to work *within* Black nationalist movements to strengthen them. For many women, this strategy preceded defecting to White feminist movements or arguments for Black feminism as a struggle that should displace advocacy for Black self-determination. Lindsey attests to this in her essay, arguing that the White institutions (such as the "white agency" that identified the Black matriarch as a pathological force in Black communities) that oppress Black women on both axes of identity should be considered the primary enemy, and the revolutions promoted by Black nationalist groups would be more likely than the feminist movement to take on these institutions as a whole. She writes, "What we truly are as women or as Black women or human beings or groups is an unknown quantity insofar as we have not determined our own destiny. We have an obligation as Black women to project ourselves into the revolution to destroy these institutions which not only oppress Blacks but women as well, for if those institutions continue to flourish, they will be used against us in the continuing battle of mind over body" (89).

Rhetorical analysis of women's writing from the heyday of BAM, then, contradicts arguments that women activists within the movement caused divisiveness by choosing the feminist fight over Black politics. The historical eventuality of these issues remaining unresolved during the height of Black Power resulted in many Black feminists' subsequent turn to womanism, a movement in which, according to novelist and poet Alice Walker, a woman activist "will recognize that, along with her consciousness of sexual issues, she must incorporate racial, cultural, national, economic, and political considerations into her philosophy" (21). But this turn in the early 1980s took place subsequent to the dismantling of Black Power institutions. More importantly, attention to the vocality and complexity of women's writing from the Black Arts Movement helps counter assertions that the masculinist policies of some nationalists succeeded in stifling women's voices or activism. As the 1969 poetry issue of *Negro Digest* demonstrates, women writers constituted a strong contingent of dynamic voices within the movement and used their writing to advocate for a multiplicity of roles in the struggle and in the ideal community the struggle was to bring about.

It is impossible to know if these attempts to argue for change from within would have been successful if the Black Arts and Black Power Movements had thrived longer than they did. Although organizations like the Black Panther Party did pronounce openness to ideas of gender equity and allowed women to hold prominent positions, this change came about in part because of group infighting and persecution by COINTELPRO, depleting the group's male leadership and resulting in the de facto promotion of women in the party. And although women served in prominent and public capacities in Black Arts organizations, such as Gwendolyn Brooks's leadership of a number of initiatives in the cultural nationalist Chicago Black Arts scene, pronouncements that would correct or revise the strict gender prescriptions in public statements like *Black Woman's Role in the Revolution* did not appear to a significant degree. What did thrive following the ebb of Black Arts influence were powerful political movements arguing specifically for significant changes in attitudes toward gender and sexuality, including the Black Feminist / Womanist Movement and the Gay Rights Movement, and the flowering of Black women's writing that evolved through the 1970s and 1980s. Nikki Giovanni models this shift in her 1970 poem "Revolutionary Dreams":

> i used to dream militant
> dreams of taking
> over america to show
> these white folks how it should be
> done
> . . . .
> then i awoke and dug
> that if i dreamed natural

> dreams of being a natural
> woman doing what a woman
> does when she's natural
> i would have a revolution (Re: Creation 20)

The revolution for Giovanni here is still possible, but the terms of engagement have shifted to necessarily include recognizing the ways gender and sexuality inflect the struggle. The kinds of arguments Black Arts women writers articulated in their poetry helped pave the way for activists and artists to embrace an intersectional rhetorical battle for rights that would take place with a broader audience and with notable, lasting effects.

CODA

"A Language That We Been Speaking"

Twenty-First-Century Echoes of the Black Arts Movement

Superstar Beyoncé Knowles-Carter's controversial performance at the 2016 Super Bowl Halftime Show reads interestingly as a legacy of the Black Arts Movement. Beyoncé designed the performance as an homage to Black Power, emerging on the field in the Bay Area's Levi's Stadium, forty miles from where the Black Panther Party was founded fifty years earlier, wearing black leather and two bandoliers, accompanied by a cadre of all-female dancers with natural hairstyles and Black Panther–style berets. During their performance of "Formation," the single Beyoncé had released online as a video the night before and that had accumulated more than seven million views prior to the start of the Super Bowl (Doubek), the dancers formed an X on the field in seeming tribute to Malcolm X and raised fists in an echo of the Black Power salute (Zaru). Following the show, photographs circulated on Twitter of several of the dancers standing on the sidelines with raised fists and holding a sign reading "Justice for Mario Woods," a Black man killed in December 2015 by San Francisco police (@jamilahking). Although the Super Bowl performance itself included no references to police shootings, the photograph, which resonated with the imagery in the "Formation" video that drew attention to the Black Lives Matter movement's call for an end to police violence against Black people in America,[1] marked both the song and Beyoncé's portion of the show as concerned with the politics of Black Lives Matter. Melina Abdullah, a California-based Black Lives Matter activist, praised Beyoncé and artists like her for their "willing[ness] to raise social consciousness and use their artistry to advance social justice" ("Beyoncé's Super Bowl Show"), and Ilyasah Shabazz, Malcolm X's daughter, said of the performance, "She entertained us with a purpose" (Colangelo).

Although a broad swath of fans responded positively to Beyoncé's performance, the show put Black Lives Matter opponents on the defensive, a response that is transparent and easily documentable in the era of social media.

Following the show, a number of police departments around the country, including those in Raleigh, Miami, and Nashville, called both the Super Bowl performance and the video for "Formation" "anti-cop" and urged officers not to do off-duty security work for Beyoncé's upcoming tour performances in those cities (France). Former New York City mayor and vocal conservative Rudy Giuliani publicly criticized Beyoncé's performance as "ridiculous" and "terrible," registering his outrage that she used the Super Bowl "as a platform to attack police officers who are the people who protect her and protect us, and keep us alive" (Zaru). Republican New York congressman Peter King critiqued what he called "her pro-Black Panther and anti-cop video 'Formation' and her Super Bowl appearance" as "just one more example of how acceptable it has become to be anti-police" ("Beyoncé's Super Bowl Show"). Among the public, the performance ignited a Twitterstorm of critique from White folks calling the performance racist and spouting righteous indignation that the sacred space of the Super Bowl Halftime Show had been defiled by divisive politics.

Significantly, the source of Beyoncé's message and the controversy it sparked is an aesthetic text—one that demonstrates the substantial inheritance the current moment of generative pro-Black activism has received from the rhetorical successes of the Black Arts Movement. Thematically, the politics within the song's lyrics, especially the truncated version that was performed at the Super Bowl, are subtle, with the most overt political statement being the reference to getting "in formation," which conjures the double meaning of aesthetic formation (dancers taking their positions) and military formation.[2] This insinuation of armed resistance by Black folks echoes the rhetorical work of Black Arts poets to put the enemy on the defensive, to allow them to overhear a text meant for a primary Black audience that praises Black cultural values and indicts White America in broad strokes. Beyond the threat of Black America's getting in formation, the song is saturated with affirmations of Black Pride and Black Is Beautiful: Beyoncé embraces her personal family heritage as a descendant of Black parents from Texas and Louisiana, celebrates the beauty of her daughter's natural hair and the phenotypical characteristics of what she calls her own "Negro nose," and toasts her own financial success as a Black entrepreneur. These utterances echo the key rhetorical topoi that Black Arts poets engaged as part of their project to cultivate Black consciousness in their listeners. Beyoncé's delivery of her lyrics straddles the line between sung text and a rhythmically rich poetic reading, a legacy of BAM's influence on the development of Spoken Word poetry and hip-hop. She personifies the ideal poet-performer that Larry Neal conceptualized in 1967: "loud, gaudy, and racy" (in the best possible ways); powerfully attuned to context; able to "sing, dance, and chant" her way "into the substance of... individual and collective experiences" (22). And "Formation" suggests a more accurate history of women's participation in and of the vital presence and resilience of queer culture within Black nationalist movements of the 1960s and 1970s: here a cadre of women, inspired by New Orleans "Queen of Bounce" Big Freedia's assertion in the song's prologue that she "came to slay," assert their place as central to the active and public work of the resistance—and Beyoncé carries the ammunition.

Given this rhetorical inheritance, the public response to "Formation"—both the adoration and resentment—should actually be understood as the expected outcome of effective Black nationalist rhetorical poetics. The obvious irony of the conservative White response, of course, is that neither the Black Lives Matter movement nor much of the art that underscores the imperatives of the movement is about White people at all. In the case of Beyoncé in particular, beyond the straightforward command to police to "stop shooting us" that appears in the "Formation" video, her work since 2016 has significantly focused on themes of Black Pride and Black self-love aimed at those within the Black community, messages that appear front and center in her 2018 Coachella performance and in *Homecoming*, the 2019 film documenting the creation and realization of the performance. Conceived as a Homecoming celebration at an imaginary HBCU, the show is an emphatic celebration of Black excellence, featuring a full HBCU-style marching band and dance line, probates pledging an imaginary fraternity who step and stroll, and a variety of talented solo dancers who take center stage along with Beyoncé. In a segment early in *Homecoming* that shows footage of Beyoncé's dancers and musicians during rehearsals, the film includes in voiceover a segment from an interview with singer and activist Nina Simone speaking about "To Be Young, Gifted, and Black" at the time of its release in 1970. Simone explains her motivation for making conscious Black art, and in particular art that celebrates the beauty, history, and culture of Black people:

> I think what you're trying to ask is why am I so insistent upon giving out to them that Blackness, that Black Power..., pushing them to identify with Black culture.... I have no choice over it. In the first place, to me we are the most beautiful creatures in the whole world, Black people. And I mean that in every sense, outside and inside. And to me we have a culture that is surpassed by no other civilization, but we don't know anything about it.... My job is to somehow

make them curious enough or persuade them, by hook or crook, to get more aware of themselves and where they came from and what they are into and what is already there, and just to bring it out. This is what compels me to compel them, and I will do it by whatever means necessary.

Beyoncé uses Simone's Black Arts–era statement as a declaration of her rhetorical mission as an artist in the era of Black Lives Matter. In a cultural context where it is virtually impossible to avoid being overheard, Beyoncé boldly composes her music and performances around messages of Black Pride and Black Is Beautiful and deploys them as ways of decolonizing mainstream performance venues. Her message itself is not to the White audience but to the Black one, and the message is meant to be the work of rhetorical education: to use Simone's words above, a "persuasive" and "compelling" aesthetic account of the beauty of Black selves and Black culture. Accomplishing this rhetorical work stands as one of the primary successes and most meaningful legacies of the Black Arts Movement, and the fact that movement's influence has inflected the work of one of the most popular and influential artists of the twenty-first century is a powerful demonstration of this legacy.

The Black Lives Matter movement itself, founded by three women activists, Patrisse Cullors, Alicia Garza, and Opal Tometi, two of whom identify as queer, demonstrates the profoundly important legacies of and lessons from the Black Arts Movement and from Black Power more broadly. The aims of Black Lives Matter are arguably as cultural as they are purely political, for the long history of police violence against Black people in America is inextricably tied to the institutionally embedded and continually reinscribed racist depictions of Black people in broader American culture. If we take the words "Black Lives Matter" as a true distillation of the movement's argument, the cultural rhetorical work is fundamental: activists must convince America that Black people are worthy of human rights to make meaningful inroads in the fight against legacies of slavery and mass incarceration. This begins with a reaffirmation of pride within the Black community itself, the movement's primary audience, although the movement's message is intended to be broadly overheard by White and mainstream America in hopes of establishing a coalition of people willing to follow Black leaders in the slow work of excavating deeply rooted cultural beliefs and traditions that fertilize overt and subtle practices of anti-Black racism from generation to generation. In line with the rhetoric of the movement's Black nationalist predecessors, Black Lives Matter has strategically and powerfully deployed radical epideixis, blaming the hero worship of police officers and the criminalization of Black and Brown bodies in mainstream American culture for allowing acts of racism or excessive violence to occur with impunity and to go unpunished. Each publicized case sparks a burst across social media of rhetorical vilification of the implicated officer and rhetorical objectification of the police at large, aiming to unify the Black audience and to communicate an alternative set of values to overhearers: police are fallible, and there are some who end up killing innocent people because, consciously or unconsciously, they see Black and Brown people as criminals before they see them as humans. The values being praised by Black Lives Matter's epideixis boldly depart from the terms of respectability politics, asserting that victims need not be infallible for their deaths to be unjust: It doesn't matter what Trayvon Martin was wearing. It doesn't matter that Eric Garner sold loose cigarettes. It doesn't matter that Sandra Bland argued with a police officer. It doesn't matter that Tamir Rice was playing with a toy gun. It doesn't matter that George Floyd tried to spend a suspicious twenty-dollar bill. What mattered was their lives.

Importantly, Black Lives Matter has grown not only from the successes but from the limitations of the Black Power movements of the 1960s and 1970s, redefining Black nationalism for a new era. As evinced by its published guiding principles, the movement affirms that unapologetic Blackness need not preclude intersectional concerns or a love of diversity within and outside of Black identity. As Cullors explains in a statement for a 2015 news article, "[Black Lives Matter] was created from not just a politic of 'blackness,' but it was created from the intersections of blackness, womanness, and queerness" (Brydum). The movement works proactively to "build a space that affirms Black women and is free from sexism, misogyny, and environments in which men are centered," to "dismantle the patriarchal practice that requires mothers to work 'double shifts' so that they can mother in private even as they participate in public justice work," to "disrupt the Western-prescribed nuclear family structure requirement by supporting each other as extended families and 'villages' that collectively care for one another," to "foster a queer-affirming network . . . [to free] ourselves from the tight grip of heteronormative thinking," and to "make space for transgender brothers and sisters to participate and lead" while "do[ing] the work required to dismantle cisgender privilege and uplift Black trans folk" ("What We Believe"). This broad inclusiveness, an explicit revision of the strictures placed by 1960s and 1970s Black nationalist movements on revolutionary identity, has not gone without controversy, with some activist groups reviving the argument that focusing on any identity but Blackness dilutes the purpose of the struggle.[3] But the work to build a broad coalition of activists and to acknowledge the intersectional dynamics of Blackness has not gone unacknowledged, even by the movement's critics from the Civil Rights Movement generation. For example, 1960s civil rights activist Barbara Reynolds, writing in a 2015 op-ed for the *Washington Post* that Black Lives Matter has been wrongheaded for lacking clear leadership, using disruptive protest tactics, refusing to use respectability to show Black humanity, and failing to clearly articulate strategies or goals, does concede that the attention that Black Lives Matter has given to Black women, Black LGBTQ people, and others, including their public prominence as movement leaders, has been one way that "BLM has improved on the previous generation" (Reynolds).

And many still active Black Arts writers will openly admit that this kind of improvement is in order. During a weeklong visit in March 2013 to Penn State University as a visiting scholar, Black Arts poet Sonia Sanchez announced more than once to audiences composed of students, faculty, and community members, "I am not a revisionist." Advocating contemporary activism grounded in ideals of inclusivity and respect that aims ultimately for peace, Sanchez does not try to erase or ignore the strident, violent, or exclusive utterances that appeared in her poetry of the 1960s and 1970s. Instead, she acknowledges them as part of her historical and literary presence and recognizes they are part of her journey as a person and an artist. In deepening our understanding of the work and legacies of BAM, it is important to follow Sanchez's lead: to recognize that damaging utterances exist next to constructive, life-giving ones—and to use the poetry of this juxtaposition to inspire activism.

A profound inheritance from the Black Arts Movement is that the new generation of Black activists does not seem to question that art can be a powerful weapon in this fight, and Black Lives Matter leaders have purposely made room for art to play a rhetorical role in the struggle. Movement founder Cullors, who has been working as an artist since 2005 and earned an MFA from the University of Southern California in 2019, is a dancer and theater artist trained in "Theatre of the Oppressed," the aesthetic method Brazilian playwright Augusto Boal developed in the 1970s that uses theater to educate communities for social and political activism. Cullors describes her own performance-based work as art that "ultimately asks the audience to identify themselves in relationship to various forms of violence, be it coded in silence behind jail walls or in the coming out stories of people of color," aiming to "render bare the narratives of state-induced trauma while lifting up a path towards healing." She writes that she uses the tool of "discomfort" to invite audiences to "shed complicity and engage broader questions of systemic violence and spiritual rejuvenation" (Cullors)—a kind of aesthetic and rhetorical purposefulness that echoes the aims Amiri Baraka articulated for Black art in "The Revolutionary Theatre" in 1964.

Beyond Cullors's individual identity and work as an artist, Black Lives Matter's website has included calls for and announcements about artwork since 2016. The organization currently fundraises by offering merchandise for sale designed by a rotating group of "featured artists." This significantly includes featuring former Black Panther minister of culture Emory Douglas, with whom they partnered to commemorate the fifth anniversary of Black Lives Matter by reprinting Douglas's collage "We Shall Survive, Without a Doubt." As the Black Lives Matter website describes it, the piece, which first appeared on the back cover of the *Black Panther* newspaper in 1971, "features Black Panther cubs in their full joy, experiencing the revolutionary social programs the Panthers created for the Black community," and they call the partnership with Douglas a way to "honor to our movement's radical roots while imagining our triumphant future" ("Emory Douglas"). Cullors has similarly acknowledged radical roots from the Black Arts Movement specifically, quoting Sonia Sanchez in the introduction to her 2018 memoir *When They Call You a Terrorist* in an epigraph that reads, "I write to keep in contact with our ancestors and to spread truth to people" (Khan-Cullors and Bandele). Although those producing art connected to and inspired by Black Lives Matter—from hip-hop artists to literary writers to fashion designers—have not coalesced into a broad, multigenre "sister" movement akin to Black Arts, Black Lives Matter is broadly benefitting from a cultural shift back to legitimizing "political" art, as evinced by a 2018 essay that U.S. Poet Laureate Tracy K. Smith wrote for the *New York Times Book Review*, whose title declares, "Political Poetry Is Hot Again."

One of the earliest manifestations of "political poetry" deployed in support of Black Lives Matter—and the manifestation of Black Lives Matter arts activism that most closely resembles the work of Black Arts poets—is Black Poets Speak Out (BPSO), a hashtag video campaign sparked by the 2014 grand jury decision not to indict police officer Darren Wilson for the killing of Mike Brown in Ferguson, Missouri—the event that also ignited nationally televised protests and fueled Black Lives Matter's momentum as a political movement. Conceived and organized by poets and Cave Canem fellows Amanda Johnston, Jericho Brown, Mahogany Browne, Jonterri Gadson, and Sherina Rodriguez-Sharpe, BPSO aims, according to Browne, "to centralize in one space hundreds of poems, songs, prayers and testimonies speaking on behalf of black mothers, black fathers, black brothers and sisters—thousands of voices insisting on justice" as a "collective outcry for our black lives." Poets are asked to record videos of themselves reading poetry, either their own or others', and to preface the reading with the statement, "I am a black poet who will not remain silent while this nation murders black people. I have a right to be angry." Organizers of the campaign have explicitly tied the effort to the politics of Black Lives Matter, hashtagging all of the videos posted to Tumblr with the dual declarations #blacklivesmatter and #blackpoetsspeakout. BPSO's programmatic statement asserts that "[i]n light of the continuous murders of black people across the nation," Black poets are standing "in solidarity with those who refuse to accept these atrocities as a normal condition of black life." They openly identify poetry as their medium for calling for "an absolute transformation" in the policies and practices of the criminal justice system toward Black people in America: "We are using the force of our art to transform policy. . . . We will not be done until we see justice for the murder of black people." As organizer Amanda Johnston iterates this understanding of her role as an artist, "As a poet, I believe it is my responsibility to not look away and use art as a tool to raise awareness and create change" ("About Us").

Housed on Tumblr, BPSO has produced hundreds of videos shared across social media platforms. And in the months following the protests in Ferguson, the campaign expanded its efforts from an online video campaign to other forms of activism, including a series of community readings in the United States and abroad that they dubbed "poetry protests," a digital letter-writing campaign aimed at elected officials in which writers were asked to attach a BPSO video of their choice to the correspondence, a set of lesson plans for incorporating BPSO videos into secondary school classrooms distributed through *Mosaic* literary magazine, and the publication of a special issue of *Pluck! The Journal of Affrilachian Arts and Culture* featuring original poetry by BPSO activists. The description organizers give about the poetry protests is telling about the ways that BPSO has inherited the rhetorical tactics of the Black Arts Movement. The readings feature no headlining writers or book sales and offer no introductory bios of any of the readers, aiming to be democratic events that equalize the participation of established poets and community members: "no one voice headlines over the fallen, no one person's sorrow owns the spotlight." As both poetry readings and protests, the events provide an opportunity for collective ritual, a space to testify about "the shared stories and experiences of the poets and the people" as a "call to action against police violence" (Browne). The community-based sharing of poetry, with an eye to raising consciousness through testimony about collective Black experience, serves as a call to build the movement for fully realized Black humanity. Among the poems voiced by BPSO activists are pieces by Black Arts poets Gwendolyn Brooks, Lucille Clifton, Nikki Giovanni, June Jordan, and Audre Lorde. The work of these poets literally speaks to the rhetorical circumstance of Black Lives Matter.

And it is not surprising that BPSO poets feel a connection to the poets of the Black Arts generation, for despite the critiques outlined in the introduction to this book, the writing and activism of Black Arts poets have both subtly and overtly inflected the work of poets who followed them. As Cave Canem fellows, the BPSO founders have benefitted from the "home for Black poetry" that poets Toi Derricotte and Cornelius Eady launched in 1996 "to remedy the under-representation and isolation of African American poets in the literary landscape" ("Mission and History"). According to Joanne Gabbin, literary scholar and founder of the vibrant Furious Flower Poetry Center at James Madison University, the first academic center in the United States dedicated to Black poetry, Derricotte was inspired to create Cave Canem after attending the first Furious Flower Conference in 1994, which Gabbin held to bring together the younger and older generations of Black poets to establish a continuity of the tradition. Dedicated to Gwendolyn Brooks, the conference celebrated Sonia Sanchez, Nikki Giovanni, Haki Madhubuti, and Amiri Baraka and connected them with then-newly celebrated poets like Rita Dove to bridge a chasm that had been created by the backlash against the Black Arts Movement in the intervening decades ("About the Center"). Since then, Gabbin has held two more historic Furious Flower conferences, in 2004 and 2014, continuing to gather successive generations of Black poets and scholars of Black poetry into a cohesive community.[4] And while the faces and names of the "young poets" have changed with each successive meeting, Black Arts poets have continued to come and celebrate and educate as elders and mentors, as poet-rhetors and griots and wielders of nommo. They have not gone anywhere. And many are, in fact, still doing the work.

As this book has demonstrated, the Black Arts Movement deserves its accolades as an African American literary renaissance, one whose writers, working as poet-rhetors, made significant contributions by expanding the generative cultural possibilities of rhetorical aesthetics. The rich example of the Black Arts Movement highlights the importance of considering the rhetorical aims and effects of poetic works and the movements that produce them. I suggest, then, that scholars add a rhetorical dimension to their conceptions of what a "successful" literary movement looks like. The evidence in the case of BAM is strong. Black Arts writers redefined literature on their own terms; established independent institutions and employed creative methodologies to bring that work to a broad community of Black readers and audiences; invigorated readership and artistic consumption in segments of the Black community that had been broadly ignored; asserted the aesthetic and rhetorical value of culturally unique Black language practices; used their works to persuade their people to love themselves, to see their own beauty, and to take pride in their history and cultural heroes; and advocated for the weakening or destruction of insidious systems of institutional racism. And much of this advocacy worked. The most significant result of the rhetorical work of the Black Arts Movement is that activists succeeded to a great degree in winning the struggle for Black consciousness. As the anecdotes I have presented above underscore, the movement's influence is far-reaching and palpable in the twenty-first century, particularly in the widespread cultural presence of positive assertions of Blackness, in the continuing fight to validate the beauty and richness of Black language practices, in the populist dissemination of Black vernacular culture through both writing and popular music, and in the ongoing conversations about the aesthetic and political intersections of race with gender and sexuality. Although intimately connected to practical political aims that would benefit the collective—aims they did not fully realize—the movement achieved its broadest influence through the cultural impact of changing individual attitudes and perceptions about Blackness. This is the work that Black Lives Matter now continues. As BPSO cofounder Mahogany Browne says of her work, crafting her description in the poignant grammar of Black English, her activism "is rooted in a language that we been speaking. It is a truth that we been feeding our children and whispering into their hair when they sleep" (Browne)—a testimony not only to the power of poetry to educate and awaken but also to the presence of the ancestors, from the Black Arts Movement and long before, in the new generation's activist voices.

Notes

INTRODUCTION

1. Seventeen-year-old Trayvon Martin was shot and killed on February 26, 2012, while walking back from a convenience store in the Florida neighborhood where he was visiting his father. George Zimmerman, then a neighborhood watch captain, had called 911 to report Martin as "suspicious" and ultimately confronted and shot the unarmed teenager after being warned by the 911 operator not to approach him ("Trayvon Martin Shooting Fast Facts"). Martin's death and the subsequent acquittal of Zimmerman for his murder sparked what would become the Black Lives Matter movement in 2013.

2. Rowell divides the poets into categories of "Precursors" and "Heirs," with the Precursors section including those identified as "Modernists" representing the 1940s to 1960s and poets from "The 1960s and Beyond" divided into camps of "The Black Arts Movement" and "Outside the Black Arts Movement." The "Heirs" section, which demonstrates the anthology's focus on contemporary writers, is divided into three "waves" of post-1960s poets.

3. See George Schuyler, "The Negro-Art Hokum"; Langston Hughes, "The Negro Artist and the Racial Mountain"; and W. E. B. Du Bois, "Criteria of Negro Art."

4. See "Writers Symposium," *Negro Digest*.

5. These periodizations, particularly the distinction between the New Negro Movement and the Harlem Renaissance, continue to be matters of scholarly debate. In *The Afro-American Novel and Its Tradition* (1987), literary and African American Studies scholar Bernard W. Bell offers this formulation of African American literary periods: liberation or slave narratives as the first flowering, the generation of Dunbar and Chesnutt as the second, the Harlem Renaissance and New Negro Movement as the third, the Black Arts Movement as the fourth, and the women novelists of the 1970s and 1980s as the fifth.

6. To be fair, Gates also levels a critique at artists of the Harlem Renaissance: "Not only were their dreams of political advancement to remain unfulfilled, but in terms of formal literary achievement, they mostly failed to raise their art to its adulthood" ("Black Creativity").

7. Gates's *Time* article was truly a public-intellectual crossover piece. He published a similar article in the journal *Critical Inquiry* in 1997, which includes the same passages quoted above. See "Harlem on Our Minds."

8. The first conference was held at the University of California, Merced on March 1–2, 2014. The conference for which Gates wrote the blurb took place at Dillard University in New Orleans on September 9–11, 2016.

9. Although scholars and writers who had participated in or been influenced by the Black Arts Movement had produced critical texts such as Stephen Henderson's introduction to his anthology *Understanding the New Black Poetry* (1973), Addison Gayle's *The Black Aesthetic* (1971), Don L. Lee's *Dynamite Voices* (1971), Amiri Baraka and Larry Neal's *Black Fire* (1968), and Eugene Redmond's *Drumvoices* (1976), very little other scholarship that assesses not only the flaws but the merits of the Black Arts Movement appeared prior to the twenty-first century. Kalamu ya Salaam's long-awaited *The Magic of Juju: An Appreciation of the Black Arts Movement*, which he writes from the perspective of "participant and critic," was finally published in 2016, although portions of the manuscript had been circulating informally since the late 1990s (Rambsy, "Magic of Juju").

CHAPTER 1. "Art for All Our Sake"

1. Black Arts writer and theorist Larry Neal calls the Black Arts Movement the "aesthetic and spiritual sister of the Black Power concept" in his 1968 essay "The Black Arts Movement." See Neal, *Visions of a Liberated Future* 62.

2. As literary and cultural historian James Smethurst thoughtfully observes in *The Black Arts Movement*, it is an oversimplification to think of these nationalist schools of thought as entirely distinct, firm categories, and there are other useful ways to distinguish the range of Black nationalist ideologies that circulated during the 1960s and 1970s. For example, Maulana Karenga divides nationalists into religious nationalists (such as the NOI), political nationalists (such as the BPP), economic nationalists (such as the Black cooperative movement), and cultural nationalists (such as US). See Smethurst, *Black Arts Movement* 16.

3. It is worth noting that while RAM and BPP were both revolutionary nationalist groups, their approaches to the role of culture in the revolution diverged. See Smethurst, *Black Arts Movement* 170–71.

4. For example, Larry Neal was involved in the revolutionary nationalist RAM and Uptown Writers Group and was also influenced by the NOI. Carolyn Rodgers, an active member of the cultural nationalist group Organization of Black American Culture (OBAC) in Chicago, wrote poems supporting the efforts of the Black Panthers. Sonia Sanchez, whose work expresses strong cultural nationalist perspectives, was also a member of NOI from 1972 to 1975.

5. For a thorough insider history of the founding, flowering, and broad impact of the Black Arts Movement, see ya Salaam, *Magic of Juju* (2016).

6. See ya Salaam, *Magic of Juju* (2016), and Smethurst, *Black Arts Movement* (2005), for detailed accounts of the activist histories and contributions of Neal and Touré.

7. While Black Arts initiatives began and operated locally, local cadres were invigorated by the understanding that they were part of a national movement, and this energy helped to enrich the local manifestations of the movement. Kalamu ya Salaam calls this the local-national-local (L/N/L) model for understanding the history of BAM (ya Salaam, *Magic of Juju* x–xi).

8. See, for example, Fabio, "Tripping with Black Writing" (1972).

9. While there have been a number of other terms that linguists since the 1970s have developed to describe African American language culture, including "Ebonics," "African American English" (AAE), and "African American Vernacular English" (AAVE), I have chosen to use "Black English" throughout this project in keeping with the term of the Black Arts era.

10. For an extended discussion of the significance of the blues to the African American ethos, see LeRoi Jones, *Blues People* (1963), Baraka's (then Jones) influential sociocultural study of the blues continuum as the origin of American music.

11. Literary scholar Howard Rambsy II discusses this broadly in *The Black Arts Enterprise and the Production of African American Poetry* (2011), and literary scholar James Sullivan focuses specifically on the Broadside Press Broadside Series in *On the Walls and in the Streets* (1997).

12. *Negro Digest* experienced a publishing hiatus from 1951 to 1961 because it had difficulty in the 1950s competing for readership with *Ebony* and *Jet*. Its success when relaunched in 1961 can be attributed to the editorial acumen of Hoyt Fuller.

13. Historian Jonathan Fenderson thoughtfully examines Fuller's impact and his work to negotiate the challenges of building *Negro Digest / Black World* as a Black institution in *Building the Black Arts Movement: Hoyt Fuller and the Cultural Politics of the 1960s* (2019).

14. The poem first appeared in print in the January 1966 issue of the *Liberator*.

15. I use the term "signifyin" and a number of others as Smitherman does, purposely writing them without a final "g."

16. For the remainder of this project, I use the word "griot" to refer to both male and female figures who serve this role, although I recognize that in traditional West African cultures griots and griottes may have distinct duties and responsibilities.

17. It should be noted that Black Arts activists differed markedly from the ancient Greeks in insisting on an expansive and class-inclusive audience. Ancient paideic educators used a curriculum founded on the heroic epics of Homer to establish an essential Greek identity in citizen-class males, and this education marked them as socially elite. Black Arts writers, on the other hand, hoped to invite *all* Black people into the national fold (see Amiri Baraka's poem "SOS").

CHAPTER 2. "Our Distaste for the Enemy, Our Love for Each Other"

1. I am concerned, however, with the openness of Rountree and other critics (such as Vinzenz Buccheit) to the assertion that "Aristotle's 'speech of Blame was . . . only theoretical as a complement (to the speech of praise)'" (294). My concern with preserving psogos rhetoric as an actual and not merely theoretical Aristotelian category stems from an interest in investigating what the dearth of examples of psogos oratory in Aristotle's text means in both ancient and modern contexts in terms of epideictic rhetoric's power to reinscribe or challenge cultural values—values that serve as the basis for judgment across rhetorical species and genres. Rountree is correct in noting that Aristotle defines the speech of blame "indirectly, in opposition to his conception of the speech of praise" (298); in introducing and defining the topics of epideictic rhetoric in book I, Aristotle merely states that "blame is derived from the opposites" of praise (1.9.41). But this tactic appears in discussions all over the treatise, likely for efficiency in Aristotle's lecture notes. Citing this as evidence that Aristotle conceived of epideictic blame only as a theoretical category is akin to saying that Aristotle believes shamelessness exists only in theory because he mentions it only as constituting the opposite of shame, which he discusses at length (2.6.14–27).

2. See Walker, *Rhetoric and Poetics in Antiquity* (2000).

3. The national development of Black Studies programs at previously resistant institutions is an example of instances when fear of Black Power uprisings resulted in political successes. I would argue that Black Power and Black Arts rhetoric, though significantly accompanied by a number of campus takeovers, won space in universities for Black Studies—a rhetorical victory.

4. Aristotle additionally advises, "And one should speak of whatever is honored among each people as actually existing [in the subject praised], for example, among the Scythians or Laconians or philosophers. And all in all, attribute what is honored to what is honorable, since they seem related" (*Rhetoric* 1.9.30).

5. "Black Art" is anthologized in, for example, *Black Fire*, *The Black Poets*, *Understanding the New Black Poetry*, *Call and Response*, the *Norton Anthology of African American Literature*, and *African American Literature* (Penguin Academics).

6. "True Import" is referenced in Eugene Redmond's *Drumvoices* and in criticism by Phillip Brian Harper and Cheryl Clarke, to give a few examples. Dudley Randall does include the poem in his anthology *The Black Poets* (1971).

7. I specifically address the anti-Semitic and misogynistic language of the poem—and of writing of the movement generally—later in this section.

8. It is difficult not to read Baraka's own biographical circumstances into the relatively lighter treatment he gives mulattos here: Baraka had mixed-race daughters whom one would imagine he would rather rehabilitate with Black consciousness than destroy.

9. This phenomenon was not entirely restricted to the work of male writers. See, for example, Nikki Giovanni's "Of Liberation," in *Black Feeling, Black Talk, Black Judgement*, 45, or Jayne Cortez's "Race," in *Pisstained Stairs and the Monkey Man's Wares*.

10. In fact, the homophobic language in "Black Art" specifically again strikes a reader familiar with Baraka's life as strange and ironic. African American Studies scholar Jerry Gafio Watts argues in *Amiri Baraka: The Politics and Art of a Black Intellectual* (2001) that the homophobic statements in his work of this era "were part of his broader strategy to bury his own homosexual past" (335).

11. A third biographical irony here: Baraka had been married to and had two children with a Jewish woman, Hettie Cohen.

12. Tom W. Smith provides data that confirm the generational split: "On the 1982 GSS the term 'Black' was favored by 61 percent of those born after 1942, by 55 percent of those born between 1933 and 1942, and by 40 percent born before 1933. Conversely, on the 1979–80 National Black Survey 'Negro' and 'colored' were found to be unacceptable to 32.5 percent of Blacks born before 1933, 48 percent born from 1933 to 1942, and 64 percent born after 1942. Nomenclature choice is strongly influenced by generation" (503).

13. Gilyard shared this point as part of a class on the rhetoric of the Civil Rights Movement, Penn State University, Spring 2008.

CHAPTER 3. "A Tradition of Beautiful Talk"

1. Smitherman notes that this characteristic conforms to grammatical patterns of West African languages. See Smitherman, *Talkin and Testifyin* 22.

2. Baraka's short poem "SOS" begins with and repeats the lines "Calling black people" and "Calling all black people" as a call for broad racial unity and community (Baraka, "SOS" 181).

3. It should be noted that Bernard W. Bell's *The Folk Roots of Contemporary Afro-American Poetry* (1974) appeared contemporaneously with Henderson's *Understanding the New Black Poetry*. However, I am referring here to Bell's first major and influential work in vernacular criticism on the African American novel, *The Afro-American Novel and Its Tradition*, which was published in 1987.

4. See Smitherman, *Talkin and Testifyin* 1.

5. The proceedings of the conference and participants' recommendations for further steps in educational advocacy are collected in Smitherman, *Black English and the Education of Black Children and Youth* (1981).

6. The poem Smitherman references, "Blackman/an unfinished history," appears in Don L. Lee, *We Walk the Way of the New World* (1970).

CHAPTER 4. "Most of My Heroes Don't Appear on No Stamps"

1. Notably, Geneva Smitherman points to these poems in her early scholarship as powerful examples of the New Black Poetry utilizing the rhetorical resources of Black English. In "The Power of the Rap: The Black Idiom and the New Black Poetry" (1973), she briefly discusses Knight's "Shine" and "Hard Rock" and Giovanni's "Ego Tripping" as representative of the toast and Madhubuti's "But He Was Cool" as an example of signification (signifyin).

2. Madhubuti established a third educational institution in Chicago, the Betty Shabazz International Charter Schools Network, in 1998.

3. I deal in depth with the concept of heavy signifyin—specifically its use by women poets of the Black Arts Movement to complicate gender expectations within Black nationalist movements—in the following chapter.

4. The text of the original recorded piece was printed, with some minor textual changes, under the title "Niggers R Scared of Revolution" in *The Last Poets on a Mission: Selected Poems and a History of the Last Poets* in 1996. The text I quote here comes from this later printed version.

5. Public Enemy titled the song "Fight the Power" and incorporated the refrain "Fight the powers that be" in homage to a 1975 Isley Brothers song of the same name.

6. The lyrics in parentheses indicate Flavor Flav's contributions to Chuck D's main text.

7. For example, Ralph Ellison frames his modern toast tale "Mister Toussan" with rhymes from what he calls "Negro slave stories." He ends the story, "Iron is iron / And tin is tin / And that's the way / The story ends." See Ralph Ellison, *Flying Home and Other Stories* 31–32.

8. *Kweli* is a Kiswahili word for "truth" or "true."

CHAPTER 5. "Woman Power / Is / Black Power / Is / Human Power"

1. For perspective, selling two thousand copies of a published volume of poetry in the United States would currently put a book on the list of best sellers ("Poetry Print Runs"). Additionally, readership of a text is almost always estimated to be significantly larger than the number of copies distributed to account for multiple readers using the same document.

2. While Rodgers and some others (including Gates and Mitchell-Kernan) refer to the term "signifying" with a final "g," I use Smitherman's spelling, "signifyin," to refer to the practice throughout this book.

3. Historian Ashley D. Farmer argues that the Mumininas, led in part by Amiri Baraka's wife Amina Baraka, later pushed back from within CFUN on the strictly defined gender roles, using subsequent publications like *Mwanamke Mwananchi (The*

Nationalist Woman) (1971) to redefine expectations for African (or Afrikan) womanhood within Kawaidism. See Farmer, *Remaking Black Power* (2017).

4. In fact, I have not been able to find a single openly gay male writer who identified as a Black Arts proponent. Hoyt Fuller, who served as a central figure in the Black Arts Movement as the publisher of *Negro Digest / Black World*, was gay but remained largely closeted (see Fenderson, *Building the Black Arts Movement*). The only openly gay male writer I have found with a relationship to Black Power initiatives is James Baldwin, who was an instrumental part of the Black Studies Movement at the University of Massachusetts Amherst. Additionally, Cheryl Clarke notes that Amiri Baraka eulogized Baldwin by stating that Baldwin's play *Blues for Mister Charlie* predicted the Black Arts Movement's ideology, but Baraka had not mentioned this connection until after Baldwin's death (50).

5. A subtle irony of the poem is that the Black Panther Party advocated a socialist political platform, something the speaker's mother would probably not have been aware of. The mother's fear here is of communists in the post–World War II American sense of dangerous subversives and enemies of democracy.

6. The term "j-boss" in this passage reads as an anti-Semitic reference to the boss of the factory. For a discussion of anti-Semitic language in Black Arts poetry, see chapter 2.

Coda

1. The video for "Formation" includes shots of Beyoncé sinking into flood waters on top of a New Orleans police car, a little boy in a hoodie dancing in front of a line of police and then holding his hands up, and graffiti saying "stop shooting us."

2. Even the leather and bandoliers can be read less politically as a tribute to Michael Jackson, an imitation of the gold and black outfit he wore during his Super Bowl Halftime performance in 1993.

3. For example, the Atlanta metro area is home to two groups claiming affiliation with Black Lives Matter. Black Lives Matter Atlanta, which is listed as an official chapter on the Black Lives Matter website, aligns itself with the national organization's principles of inclusivity and intersectional justice. A second group, Black Lives Matter of Greater Atlanta, formed not as a way to expand coverage into the metro area but because of dissension about the necessity of articulating a focus on LGBTQ issues as part of the fundamental mission. See Mo Barnes, "Why There Is a Beef with Black Lives Matter Activists in Atlanta, Part 1" (2018).

4. The first Furious Flower Conference in 1994 was themed "A Revolution in African American Poetry," the conference in 2004 was themed "Regenerating the Black Poetic Tradition," and the conference in 2014 was themed "Seeding the Future of African American Poetry."

Bibliography

Abdul-Ghani, Casarae Lavada. *Start a Riot! Civil Unrest in Black Arts Movement Drama, Fiction, and Poetry.* University Press of Mississippi, 2022.
"About the Center." *Furious Flower Poetry Center,* https://furiousflower.org/about/.
"About Third World Press Foundation." *Third World Press Foundation,* https://thirdworldpressfoundation.org/about/.
"About Us." *Black Poets Speak Out,* https://blackpoetsspeakout.tumblr.com/About.
Advertisement for A&S. *New York Times,* 25 Jan. 1978, A17, https://search.proquest.com/docview/123846423?accountid=11824.
"Angles of Ascent: A Norton Anthology of Contemporary African American Poetry." *Amazon,* www.amazon.com/Angles-Ascent-Anthology-Contemporary-American/dp/0393339408/ref=sr_1_1?keywords=angles+of+ascent&qid=1562883031&s=books&sr=1-1.
Aristotle. *On Rhetoric: A Theory of Civic Discourse.* Translated by George A. Kennedy. 2nd ed. Oxford University Press, 2007.
Asante, Molefi, editor. *Language, Communication, and Rhetoric in Black America.* Harper & Row, 1972.
———. *The Voice of Black Rhetoric: Selections.* Allyn & Bacon, 1971.
Baker, Houston A., Jr. *Afro-American Poetics: Revisions of Harlem and the Black Aesthetic.* University of Wisconsin Press, 1988.
———. *Blues, Ideology, and Afro-American Literature.* University of Chicago Press, 1984.
Baldwin, James. "Negroes Are Anti-Semitic Because They're Anti-White." *The Price of the Ticket: Collected Nonfiction 1948–1985,* St. Martin's, 1985, pp. 425–34.
Baraka, Amiri. *The Autobiography of LeRoi Jones.* Freundlich Books, 1984.
———. *The LeRoi Jones/Amiri Baraka Reader.* Edited by William J. Harris. Thunder's Mouth, 1991.
———. "A Post-Racial Anthology?" *Poetry,* vol. 102, no. 2, 2013, pp. 166–73.
Baraka, Amiri, and Larry Neal, editors. *Black Fire: An Anthology of Afro-American Writing.* 1968. Black Classic Press, 2007.

Baraka, Imamu Amiri (LeRoi Jones). *Raise, Race, Rays, Raze: Essays since 1965.* Random House, 1971.

———. "SOS." *The Black Poets*, edited by Dudley Randall, Bantam Books, 1971, p. 181.

Barnes, Mo. "Why There Is a Beef with Black Lives Matter Activists in Atlanta, Part 1." *Rollingout*, 23 Mar. 2018, https://rollingout.com/2018/03/23/why-there-is-a-beef-with-black-lives-matter-activists-in-atlanta-part-1/.

Bell, Bernard W. *The Afro-American Novel and Its Tradition.* University of Massachusetts Press, 1987.

———. *Bearing Witness to African American Literature: Validating and Valorizing Its Authority, Authenticity, and Agency.* Wayne State University Press, 2012.

———. *The Contemporary African American Novel: Its Folk Roots and Modern Literary Branches.* University of Massachusetts Press, 2004.

———. *The Folk Roots of Contemporary Afro-American Poetry.* Broadside, 1974.

Beyoncé. "Formation." *Lemonade*. Parkwood Entertainment, 2016, www.beyonce.com/album/lemonade-visual-album/.

———. "Formation." Super Bowl 50 halftime show, 7 Feb. 2016, Santa Clara, CA.

———. *Homecoming: A Film by Beyoncé*. Parkwood Entertainment, 2019, www.netflix.com/watch/81013626.

"Beyonce's Super Bowl Show Brings Praise and Criticism." *CBSNews*, 9 Feb. 2016. www.cbsnews.com/news/beyonces-super-bowl-show-brings-praise-and-criticism/.

"Black Arts Movement Conference—Southern Style." Dillard University, June 2016. Flyer.

Black Lives Matter, https://blacklivesmatter.com.

Bloom, Harold. *The Western Canon: The Books and School of Ages.* Riverhead Books, 1994.

Bolden, Tony. *Afro-Blue: Improvisations in African American Poetry and Culture.* University of Illinois Press, 2003.

Boyd, Melba Joyce. *Wrestling with the Muse: Dudley Randall and the Broadside Press.* Columbia University Press, 2003.

Bradley, Adam. *Book of Rhymes: The Poetics of Hip Hop.* BasicCivitas, 2009.

Brooks, Gwendolyn, editor. *A Broadside Treasury.* Broadside Press, 1971.

———. *Family Pictures.* Broadside Press, 1970.

———. *Report from Part One.* Broadside Press, 1972.

Brown, Elaine. *A Taste of Power: A Black Woman's Story.* Anchor Books, 1994.

Brown, H. Rap. *Die, Nigger, Die!* Dial Press, 1969.

Browne, Mahogany. "Black Poets Speak Out." Poetry Society of America, 2015, https://www.poetrysociety.org/psa/poetry/crossroads/black_poets_speak_out/.

Brydum, Sunnivie. "Patrisse Cullors Knows That We Are Not Separate." *Advocate*, 8 Dec. 2015, www.advocate.com/40-under-40/2015/12/08/patrisse-cullors-knows-we-are-not-separate.

Burroughs, Margaret. "What Shall I Tell My Children Who Are Black (Reflections of an African-American Mother)." *Poetry Foundation*, www.poetryfoundation.org/poems/146263/what-shall-i-tell-my-children-who-are-black-reflections-of-an-african-american-mother.

Cade, Toni, editor. *The Black Woman: An Anthology*. Washington Square Press, 1970.

———. "The Pill: Genocide or Liberation." *The Black Woman: An Anthology*, edited by Toni Cade, Washington Square Press, 1970, pp. 162–69.

Carmichael, Stokely. "Toward Black Liberation." *Black Fire*, edited by LeRoi Jones and Larry Neal, William & Morrow, 1968, p. 119.

Chang, Jeff. *Can't Stop Won't Stop: A History of the Hip-Hop Generation*. Picador, 2005.

Cicero. De Oratore. *The Rhetorical Tradition: Readings from Classical Times to the Present*, 2nd ed., edited by Patricia Bizzell and Bruce Herzberg, Bedford/St. Martin's, 2001, pp. 289–338.

Clarke, Cheryl. *"After Mecca": Women Poets and the Black Arts Movement*. Rutgers University Press, 2005.

Colangelo, Lisa L. "Daughter of Malcolm X Lauds Beyoncé's Controversial Super Bowl Halftime Performance." *Daily News*, 29 Feb. 2016, www.nydailynews.com/new-york/malcolm-x-daughter-praises-beyonce-super-bowl-act-article-1.2548175.

Collins, Lisa Gail, and Margo Natalie Crawford, editors. *New Thoughts on the Black Arts Movement*. Rutgers University Press, 2006.

Collins, Michael S. *Understanding Etheridge Knight*. University of South Carolina Press, 2013.

Collins, Patricia Hill. *From Black Power to Hip Hop: Racism, Nationalism, and Feminism*. Temple University Press, 2006.

Common, featuring Kanye West and The Last Poets. "The Corner." *Be*. Geffen Records, 2005.

Cortez, Jayne. *Pisstained Stairs and the Monkey Man's Wares*. 1969. Phrase Text, 1970.

Crawford, Margo Natalie. *Black Post-Blackness: The Black Arts Movement and Twenty-First-Century Aesthetics*. University of Illinois Press, 2017.

Cullors, Patrisse. "Art." *Patrisse Cullors*, https://patrissecullors.com/art/#.

Doubek, James. "With 'Formation,' Beyoncé Lights Up the Internet. Here's What People Are Saying." NPR, 7 Feb. 2016, www.npr.org/2016/02/07/465934070/with-formation-beyonc-lights-up-the-internet-heres-what-people-are-saying.

Dubey, Madhu. *Black Women Novelists and the Nationalist Aesthetic*. Indiana University Press, 1994.

Du Bois, W. E. B. "Criteria of Negro Art." *Crisis*, vol. 32, no. 6, Oct. 1926, pp. 290–97.

———. "The Souls of Black Folks." *Three Negro Classics*, Avon Books, 1965, pp. 207–390.

"Dudley Randall and Broadside Press." *Broadside Lotus Press*, www.broadsidelotuspress.org/dudley-randall-broadside-press.

Ellison, Ralph. *Flying Home and Other Stories*. Vintage, 1998.

"Emory Douglas." *Black Lives Matter*, https://blacklivesmatter.shop.capthat.com/dept/featured-artist?cp=101422_104350_103425.

Evans, Mari. "I Am a Black Woman." *Negro Digest*, Sept. 1969, front cover.

Fabio, Sarah Webster. *Black Back: Back Black*. S.W. Fabio, 1973.

———. *Boss Soul*. Smithsonian Folkways, 1973.

———. *A Mirror: A Soul. A Two-Part Volume of Poems*. Richardson, 1969.

———. "Tripping with Black Writing." *The Black Aesthetic*, edited by Addison Gayle Jr., Anchor Books, 1972, pp. 173–81.

———. "What Is Black?" *College Composition and Communication*, vol. 19, no. 5, 1968, pp. 286–87.

Farmer, Ashley D. *Remaking Black Power: How Black Women Transformed an Era*. University of North Carolina Press, 2017.

Fenderson, Jonathan. *Building the Black Arts Movement: Hoyt Fuller and the Cultural Politics of the 1960s*. University of Illinois Press, 2019.

Forsgren, La Donna. *In Search of Our Warrior Mothers: Women Dramatists of the Black Arts Movement*. Northwestern University Press, 2018.

———. *Sistuhs in the Struggle: An Oral History of Black Arts Movement Theater and Performance*. Northwestern University Press, 2020.

Fowler, Virginia C. *Nikki Giovanni: A Literary Biography*. Praeger, 2013.

France, Lisa Respers. "Why the Beyoncé Controversy Is Bigger Than You Think." *CNN*, 24 Feb. 2016, www.cnn.com/2016/02/23/entertainment/beyonce-controversy-feat/index.html.

Fuller, Hoyt W. "Towards a Black Aesthetic." *The Black Aesthetic*, edited by Addison Gayle Jr., Anchor Books, 1972, pp. 3–11.

Gates, Henry Louis Jr. "Black Creativity: On the Cutting Edge." *Time*, 10 Oct. 1994, https://content.time.com/time/magazine/article/0,9171,981564,00.html.

———. *Figures in Black: Words, Signs, and the "Racial" Self*. Oxford University Press, 1987.

———. "Harlem on Our Minds." *Critical Inquiry*, vol. 24, no. 1, 1997, pp. 1–12.

———. "Preface to Blackness: Text and Pretext." *Within the Circle: An Anthology of African American Literary Criticism from the Harlem Renaissance to the Present*, edited by Angelyn Mitchell, Duke University Press, 1994, pp. 235–55.

———. *The Signifying Monkey: A Theory of African-American Literary Criticism*. Oxford University Press, 1988.

Gayle, Addison, Jr., editor. *The Black Aesthetic*. Anchor Books, 1972.

———. "Cultural Strangulation: Black Literature and the White Aesthetic." *The Black Aesthetic*, edited by Addison Gayle Jr., Anchor Books, 1972, pp. 38–45.

Gilyard, Keith. "Introduction: Aspects of African American Rhetoric as a Field." *African American Rhetoric(s): Interdisciplinary Perspectives*, edited by Elaine B.

Richardson and Ronald L. Jackson II, Southern Illinois University Press, 2004, pp. 1–18.

———. *Let's Flip the Script*. Wayne State University Press, 1996.

———. *Liberation Memories: The Rhetoric and Poetics of John Oliver Killens*. Wayne State University Press, 2003.

———. *Voices of the Self*. Wayne State University Press, 1991.

Giovanni, Nikki. *Black Feeling, Black Talk, Black Judgement*. William Morrow, 1970.

———. *Love Poems*. William Morrow, 1997.

———. *Re: Creation*. Broadside Press, 1970.

———. *The Women and the Men*. William Morrow, 1975.

Gross, Elizabeth. "Criticism, Feminism and the Institution: An Interview with Gayatri Chakravorty Spivak." *Thesis 11*, no. 10/11, 1984–85, pp. 175–87.

Hale, Thomas A. "Griot." *The Oxford Encyclopedia of African Thought*, vol. 1, edited by F. Abiola Irele and Biodun Jeyifo, Oxford University Press, 2010, pp. 419–21.

Harper, Philip Brian. "Nationalism and Social Division in Black Arts Poetry of the 1960s." *Critical Inquiry*, vol. 19, no. 2, 1993, pp. 234–55.

Harrison, Paul Carter. *The Drama of Nommo*. Grove Press, 1972.

Hauser, Gerard. "Aristotle on Epideictic: The Formation of Public Morality." *Rhetoric Society Quarterly*, vol. 29, no. 1, 1999, pp. 5–23.

Henderson, Stephen. *Understanding the New Black Poetry: Black Speech and Black Music as Poetic References*. William Morrow, 1973.

Hughes, Langston. *The Collected Works of Langston Hughes*, vol. 1: *The Poems: 1921–1940*. Edited by Arnold Rampersad. University of Missouri Press, 2001.

———. "The Negro Artist and the Racial Mountain." *Nation*, vol. 122, 23 June 1926, pp. 692–94.

Jaeger, Werner. *Paideia: The Ideals of Greek Culture*. 2nd ed., 3 vols. Translated by Gilbert Highet. Oxford University Press, 1965.

@jamilahking. "Beyonce's Dancers Paid Tribute to #MarioWoods, Black Man Killed by San Francisco Police." *Twitter*, 7 Feb. 2016, https://twitter.com/jamilahking/status/696526158335229952.

Jones, LeRoi. *Blues People: The Negro Experience in White America and the Music That Developed from It*. William Morrow, 1963.

———. *Home: Social Essays*. William Morrow, 1966.

———. "A Poem for Black Hearts." *Negro Digest*, vol. 14, no. 11, 1965, p. 58.

Jones, Meta DuEwa. *The Muse Is Music: Jazz Poetry from the Harlem Renaissance to Spoken Word*. University of Illinois Press, 2011.

Joyce, Joyce Ann. *Ijala: Sonia Sanchez and the African Poetic Tradition*. Third World Press, 1996.

"June Jordan." *Poetry Foundation*, www.poetryfoundation.org/poets/june-jordan.

Karenga, Maulana. "Black Art: A Rhythmic Reality of Revolution." *Negro Digest*, vol. 27, no. 3, 1968, pp. 5–9.

———. "Black Cultural Nationalism." *The Black Aesthetic*, edited by Addison Gayle Jr., Anchor Books, 1972, pp. 31–37.

———. "Nommo, Kaiwaida, and Communicative Practice: Bringing Good into the World." *Understanding African American Rhetoric: Classical Origins to Contemporary Innovations*, edited by Ronald Jackson and Elaine Richardson, Routledge, 2003, pp. 3–22.

Kgositsile, William Keorapetse. "Paths to the Future." *The Black Aesthetic*, edited by Addison Gayle Jr., Anchor Books, 1972, pp. 234–45.

Khan-Cullors, Patrisse, and Asha Bandele. *When They Call You a Terrorist: A Black Lives Matter Memoir*. St. Martin's, 2018.

Knight, Etheridge. *Poems from Prison*. Broadside Press, 1968.

———. "A Survey: Black Writers' Views on Literary Lions and Values." *Negro Digest*, vol. 17, no. 3, 1968, pp. 37, 87–88.

Kweli, Talib, featuring Sonia Sanchez and Res. "Everything Man." *Eardrum*. Blacksmith Records, 2007.

The Last Poets. "Niggas Is Scared of Revolution." *The Last Poets*. Douglas Records, 1970.

Leak, Jeffrey B. *Visible Man: The Life of Henry Dumas*. University of Georgia Press, 2014.

Lee, Don L. *Black Pride*. Broadside Press, 1968.

———. "Directions for Black Writers." *Black Scholar*, Dec. 1969, p. 55.

———. *Don't Cry, Scream*. Broadside Press, 1969.

———. "Gwendolyn Brooks: Beyond the Word Maker—The Makings of an African Poet." *Report from Part One*, by Gwendolyn Brooks, Broadside Press, 1972, pp. 13–30.

———. "Introduction/or entrance into a blk/thing." *Black Back: Back Black*, by Sarah Webster Fabio, S. W. Fabio, 1973, pp. iv–v.

———. *Think Black!* Broadside Press, 1969.

———. "Toward a Definition: Black Poetry of the Sixties (After LeRoi Jones)." *The Black Aesthetic*, edited by Addison Gayle Jr., Anchor Books, 1972, pp. 222–33.

———. *We Walk the Way of the New World*. Broadside Press, 1970.

Lindsey, Kay. "The Black Woman as a Woman." *The Black Woman: An Anthology*, edited by Toni Cade, Mentor, 1970, pp. 85–89.

———. "Poem." *The Black Woman: An Anthology*, edited by Toni Cade, Mentor, 1970, p. 17.

Locke, Alain. "Negro Youth Speaks." *The New Negro: An Interpretation*, edited by Alain Locke, Albert and Charles Boni, 1925, pp. 47–53.

Lorde, Audre. *The Cancer Journals*. Spinsters Ink, 1980.

———. *New York Head Shop and Museum*. Broadside Press, 1974.

MacLeish, Archibald. "Ars Poetica." *Poetry Foundation*, https://www.poetryfoundation.org/poetrymagazine/poems/17168/ars-poetica.

Mailloux, Steven. *Reception Histories: Rhetoric, Pragmatism, and American Cultural Politics*. Cornell University Press, 1998.

Malcolm X. "Message to the Grassroots." *Blackpast*, 16 Aug. 2010, www.blackpast.org/african-american-history/speeches-african-american-history/1963-malcolm-x-message-grassroots/.

———. "Speech at the Founding Rally of the Organization for Afro-American Unity." *Blackpast*, 15 Oct. 2007, www.blackpast.org/african-american-history/speeches-african-american-history/1964-malcolm-x-s-speech-founding-rally-organization-afro-american-unity/.

Marcoux, Jean-Philippe. *Jazz Griots: Music as History in the 1960s African American Poem*. Lexington Books, 2012.

Marcuse, Harold. "Reception History: Definition and Quotations." University of California, Santa Barbara, Department of History, 6 Mar. 2009, https://marcuse.faculty.history.ucsb.edu/receptionhist.htm.

Mathes, Carter. *Imagine the Sound: Experimental African American Literature after Civil Rights*. University of Minnesota Press, 2015.

"Mission and History." *Cave Canem*, https://cavecanempoets.org/mission-history/.

Mitchell-Kernan, Claudia. *Language Behavior in a Black Urban Community*. Language Behavior Research Laboratory, 1971.

———. "Signifying and Marking: Two Afro-American Speech Acts." *Directions in Sociolinguistics: The Ethnography of Communication*, edited by John J. Gumperz and Dell Hymes, Holt, Rinehart and Winston, 1972, pp. 161–79.

Moynihan, Daniel Patrick. *The Negro Family: The Case for National Action*. U.S. Department of Labor, Mar. 1965, www.dol.gov/general/aboutdol/history/webid-moynihan.

Mullen, Harryette. "The Black Arts Movement: Poetry and Drama from the 1960s to the 1970s." *African-American Writers*, 2nd ed., vol. 1, edited by Valerie Smith, Scribner's, 2001, pp. 51–58.

National Council of Teachers of English. "Students' Right to Their Own Language." *NCTE*, 1974, www.ncte.org/library/NCTEFiles/Groups/CCCC/NewSRTOL.pdf.

Neal, Larry. *Visions of a Liberated Future: Black Arts Movement Writings*. Edited by Michael Schwartz. Thunder's Mouth, 1989.

Nielsen, Aldon Lynn. *Black Chant: Languages of African-American Postmodernism*. Cambridge University Press, 1997.

———. *Integral Music: Languages of African American Innovation*. University of Alabama Press, 2004.

"Nikki Giovanni." *Poetry Foundation*, www.poetryfoundation.org/poets/nikki-giovanni.

Okpewho, Isidore. *African Oral Literature: Backgrounds, Character, and Continuity.* Indiana University Press, 1992.

Ongiri, Amy Abugo. *Spectacular Blackness: The Cultural Politics of the Black Power Movement and the Search for a Black Aesthetic.* University of Virginia Press, 2009.

Oyewole, Abiodun, and Umar Bin Hassan, with Kim Green. *The Last Poets on a Mission: Selected Poems and a History of the Last Poets.* Henry Holt, 1996.

Perelman, Chaim, and Lucie Olbrechts-Tyteca. *The New Rhetoric: A Treatise on Argumentation.* Translated by John Wilkinson and Purcell Weaver. University of Notre Dame Press, 1969.

Phelps, Carmen L. *Visionary Women Writers of Chicago's Black Arts Movement.* University Press of Mississippi, 2012.

"Poetry Print Runs." *Verylikeawhale,* https://verylikeawhale.wordpress.com.

Pough, Gwendolyn D. "Seeds and Legacies: Tapping the Potential in Hip-Hop." *That's the Joint! The Hip-Hop Studies Reader,* edited by Murray Forman and Mark Anthony Neal, Routledge, 2004, pp. 283–89.

Poulakos, Takis. "Isocrates' Civic Education and the Question of *Doxa.*" *Isocrates and Civic Education,* edited by Takis Poulakos, University of Texas Press, 2004, pp. 44–68.

Public Enemy. "Fight the Power." Single, Motown, 1989.

———. "Public Enemy No. 1." *Yo! Bum Rush the Show.* Def Jam & Columbia Records, 1987.

Rambsy, Howard, II. *The Black Arts Enterprise and the Production of African American Poetry.* University of Michigan Press, 2011.

———. "The Magic of Juju and Black Arts Scholarly Discourse." *Cultural Front,* 26 Sept. 2016, www.culturalfront.org/2016/09/the-magic-of-juju-and-black-arts.html.

Randall, Dudley, editor. *The Black Poets.* Bantam Books, 1971.

Randall, Dudley, and Margaret G. Burroughs, editors. *For Malcolm: Poems on the Life and the Death of Malcolm X.* Broadside Press, 1967.

Reid, Margaret Ann. *Black Protest Poetry: Polemics from the Harlem Renaissance and the Sixties.* Peter Lang, 2001.

Reynolds, Barbara. "I Was a Civil Rights Activist in the 1960s. But It's Hard for Me to Get Behind Black Lives Matter." *Washington Post,* 24 Aug. 2015, https://www.washingtonpost.com/posteverything/wp/2015/08/24/i-was-a-civil-rights-activist-in-the-1960s-but-its-hard-for-me-to-get-behind-black-lives-matter/.

Richardson, Elaine. *African American Literacies.* Routledge, 2003.

Rickford, John Russell, and Russell John Rickford. *Spoken Soul: The Story of Black English.* John Wiley, 2000.

Rock, John S. "Whenever the Colored Man Is Elevated, It Will Be by His Own Exertions." *Let Nobody Turn Us Around: Voices of Resistance, Reform, and Renewal: An African American Anthology,* edited by Manning Marable and Leith Mullings, Rowman & Littlefield, 2009, pp. 107–11.

Rodgers, Carolyn. "Black Poetry—Where It's At." *Negro Digest*, Sept. 1969, pp. 7–16.

———. *Songs of a Black Bird*. Third World Press, 1969.

Rountree, Clarke. "The (Almost) Blameless Genre of Classical Epidectic." *Rhetorica*, vol. 19, no. 3, 2001, pp. 293–305.

Rowell, Charles Henry, editor. *Angles of Ascent: A Norton Anthology of Contemporary African American Poetry*. Norton, 2013.

Sanchez, Sonia. *Home Coming*. Broadside Press, 1969.

———. "The Poet as Creator of Social Values." *Black Scholar*, vol. 16, no. 1, 1985, pp. 20–28, https://www.jstor.org/stable/41067138.

———. "The Poetry of the BAM: Meditation, Critique, Praise." *SOS—Calling All Black People: A Black Arts Movement Reader*, edited by John H. Bracey Jr., Sonia Sanchez, and James Smethurst, University of Massachusetts Press, 2014, pp. 243–53.

———. "Sounds Bouncin Off Paper: Black Language Memories and Meditations." *Talkin Black Talk: Language, Education, and Social Change*, edited by H. Samy Alim and John Baugh, Teachers College Press, 2007.

———. *We a BadddDDD People*. Broadside Press, 1970.

Schultz, Kathy Lou. *The Afro-Modernist Epic and Literary History: Tolson, Hughes, Baraka*. Palgrave Macmillan, 2013.

Schuyler, George. "The Negro-Art Hokum." *Nation*, vol. 122, 16 June 1926, pp. 662–63.

Seale, Bobby. *Seize the Time: The Story of the Black Panther Party and Huey P. Newton*. Black Classic Press, 1991.

Shockley, Evie. *Renegade Poetics: Black Aesthetics and Formal Innovation in African American Poetry*. University of Iowa Press, 2011.

Simone, Nina. "Nina Simone: That Blackness." *YouTube*, 4 Feb. 2013, www.youtube.com/watch?v=c3ClwX7oyXk.

Sipiora, Phillip. "Introduction: The Ancient Concept of Kairos." *Rhetoric and Kairos: Essays in History, Theory, and Praxis*, edited by Phillip Sipiora and James S. Baumlin, State University of New York Press, 2002, pp. 1–22.

Smethurst, James Edward. *The Black Arts Movement: Literary Nationalism in the 1960s and 1970s*. University of North Carolina Press, 2005.

———. *Behold the Land: The Black Arts Movement in the South*. University of North Carolina Press, 2021.

Smith, Arthur. *Rhetoric of Black Revolution*. Allyn & Bacon, 1969.

Smith, David Lionel. "The Black Arts Movement and Its Critics." *American Literary History*, vol. 3, no. 1, 1991, pp. 93–110, www.jstor.org/stable/489734.

Smith, Tom W. "Changing Racial Labels: From 'Colored' to 'Negro' to 'Black' to 'African American.'" *Public Opinion Quarterly*, vol. 56, no. 4, 1992, pp. 496–514, www.jstor.org/stable/2749204.

Smith, Tracy K. "Political Poetry Is Hot Again. The Poet Laureate Explores Why, and How." *New York Times Book Review*, 10 Dec. 2018, https://www.nytimes.com/2018/12/10/books/review/political-poetry.html.

Smitherman, Geneva. "English Teacher, Why You Be Doing the Thangs You Don't Do?" *English Journal*, vol. 61, no. 1, 1972, pp. 59–65, www.jstor.org/stable/812897.

———. "Introduction." *Black English and the Education of Black Children and Youth: Proceedings of the National Invitational Symposium on the King Decision*, Wayne State University Press, 1981, pp. 11–31.

———. "The Power of the Rap: The Black Idiom and the New Black Poetry." *Twentieth Century Literature*, vol. 19, no. 4, 1973, pp. 259–74.

———. "'Students' Right to Their Own Language': A Retrospective." *English Journal*, vol. 84, no. 1, 1995, pp. 21–27.

———. *Talkin and Testifyin: The Language of Black America*. Wayne State University Press, 1977.

———. *Talkin That Talk: Language, Culture, and Education in African America*. Routledge, 1999.

Snellings, Rolland. "'Keep on Pushin': Rhythm & Blues as a Weapon." *SOS—Calling All Black People: A Black Arts Movement Reader*, edited by John H. Bracey Jr., Sonia Sanchez, and James Smethurst, University of Massachusetts Press, 2014, pp. 86–89.

Sollors, Werner. *Amiri Baraka / LeRoi Jones: The Quest for a "Populist Modernism."* Columbia University Press, 1978.

Staples, Robert. *The Black Woman in America: Sex, Marriage, and the Family*. Nelson-Hall, 1973.

"Statement of Ownership, Management, and Circulation." *Negro Digest*, vol. 19, no. 1, Nov. 1969, p. 78.

Sullivan, James D. *On the Walls and in the Streets: American Poetry Broadsides from the 1960s*. University of Chicago Press, 1997.

Thomas, Lorenzo. "Neon Griot: The Functional Role of Poetry Readings in the Black Arts Movement." *Close Listening: Poetry and the Performed Word*, edited by Charles Bernstein, Oxford University Press, 1998.

Thompson, Julius E. *Dudley Randall, Broadside Press, and the Black Arts Movement in Detroit, 1960–1995*. McFarland, 1999.

Touré, Askia M. *From the Pyramids to the Projects: Poems of Genocide and Resistance!* Africa World Press, 1990.

"Trayvon Martin Shooting Fast Facts." *CNN*, 14 Feb. 2022, https://www.cnn.com/2013/06/05/us/trayvon-martin-shooting-fast-facts/index.html.

Ture, Kwame, and Charles V. Hamilton. *Black Power: The Politics of Liberation in America*. 1967. Vintage, 1992.

Van Deburg, William L. *New Day in Babylon: The Black Power Movement and American Culture*. University of Chicago Press, 1992.

Walker, Alice. "Womanist." *The Womanist Reader*, edited by Layli Phillips, Routledge, 2006, pp. 19–20.

Walker, Jeffrey. "Aristotle's Lyric: Re-imagining the Rhetoric of Epideictic Song." *College English*, vol. 51, no. 1, 1989, pp. 5–28.

———. *Rhetoric and Poetics in Antiquity*. Oxford University Press, 2000.

Warren, Nagueyalti. "Pan-African Cultural Movements: From Baraka to Karenga." *Journal of Negro History*, vol. 75, no. 1/2, 1990, pp. 16–28.

Watts, Jerry Gafio. *Amiri Baraka: The Politics and Art of a Black Intellectual*. New York University Press, 2001.

"What We Believe." *Black Lives Matter*, https://blacklivesmatter.com/about/what-we-believe/.

Widener, Daniel. *Black Arts West: Culture and Struggle in Postwar Los Angeles*. Duke University Press, 2010.

"Writers Symposium." *Negro Digest*, vol. 17, no. 3, Jan. 1968, pp. 10–48.

ya Salaam, Kalamu. "The Black Arts Movement." *Neo-Griot*, 30 Sept. 2016, http://kalamu.com/neogriot/2016/09/30/essay-the-black-arts-movement-2/.

———. *The Magic of Juju: An Appreciation of the Black Arts Movement*. Third World Press, 2016.

Zaru, Deena. "Beyonce Gets Political at Super Bowl, Pays Tribute to Black Lives Matter." *CNN*, 8 Feb. 2016, www.cnn.com/2016/02/08/politics/beyonce-super-bowl-black-lives-matter/index.html.

Credits

A portion of chapter 5 was previously published in "a thunderin/lightenin poet-talkin / female / is a sign of things to come": Ntozake Shange and the Womanist Legacy of the Black Arts Movement," *The Langston Hughes Review*, vol. 28, no. 1, 2022, pp. 25–48, https://doi.org/10.5325/langhughrevi.28.1.0025. Used with permission from Penn State University Press.

Permission to print poems in this book is given below.

Haki Madhubuti (Don L. Lee), "The New Integrationist," "A Poem to Complement Other Poems," "Two Poems," and "But He Was Cool, or: he even stopped for green lights" from *Groundwork: New and Selected Poems*. Copyright © 1996 by Haki R. Madhubuti. Reprinted by permission of Third World Press Foundation. "In a Period of Growth" from *Think Black!* Copyright © 1967 by Haki R. Madhubuti. Reprinted by permission of Third World Press Foundation. "The Self-Hatred of Don L. Lee" from *Liberation on Narratives: New and Collected Poems 1966–2009*. Copyright © 2009 by Haki R. Madhubuti. Reprinted by permission of Third World Press Foundation.

Nikki Giovanni, excerpts from "The True Import of Present Dialogue: Black vs. Negro," "Ego Tripping," and "Revolutionary Dreams" from *The Collected Poetry of Nikki Giovanni*. Copyright © 2003 by Nikki Giovanni. Used by permission of HarperCollins Publishers.

Amiri Baraka (Leroi Jones), "Black Art" from *S. O. S.: Poems 1961–2013* Copyright © 2014 by The Estate of Amiri Baraka. Used by permission of Grove/Atlantic, Inc.

Margaret Burroughs, "What Shall I Tell My Children Who Are Black?" Courtesy of the Estate of Dr. Margaret Burroughs.

Joyce Whitsitt, "For Malcolm" from *For Malcolm: Poems on the Life and Death of Malcolm X*. Edited by Dudley Randall and Margaret Burroughs. Copyright © 1967 by Joyce Whitsitt. Reprinted by permission of Broadside Lotus Press.

Ted Joans, "My Ace of Spades" from *For Malcolm: Poems on the Life and Death of Malcolm X*. Edited by Dudley Randall and Margaret Burroughs. Copyright

© 1967 by Joyce Whitsitt. Reprinted by permission of Broadside Lotus Press

Sonia Sanchez, "Malcolm" from *Shake Loose My Skin: New and Selected Poems*. Copyright © 1999 by Sonia Sanchez. Reprinted by permission of Beacon Press. "we a baddDDD people" and "blk/rhetoric" from *We a BaddDDD People*. Copyright © 1970 by Sonia Sanchez. Reprinted by permission of Broadside Lotus Press. "Memorial. 3. rev pimps" from *Homecoming*. Copyright © 1967 by Sonia Sanchez. Reprinted by permission of Broadside Lotus Press.

Clarence Major, "Brother Malcolm: Waste Limit" from *For Malcolm: Poems on the Life and Death of Malcolm X*. Edited by Dudley Randall and Margaret Burroughs. Copyright © 1967 by Broadside Press. Reprinted by permission of Broadside Lotus Press.

Edward Spriggs, "For Brother Malcolm" from *For Malcolm: Poems on the Life and Death of Malcolm X*. Edited by Dudley Randall and Margaret Burroughs. Copyright © 1967 by Broadside Press. Reprinted by permission of Broadside Lotus Press.

Gwendolyn Brooks, "The Life of Lincoln West." Reprinted by consent of Brooks Permissions.

Sarah Webster Fabio, "Black Back" from *Black Back: Back Black*. Fisk University, John Hope and Aurelia E. Franklin Library Special Collections, Sarah Webster Fabio Collection, box 9, folder 7.

Audre Lorde, "Naturally" from *The Collected Poems of Audre Lorde*. Copyright © 1968 by Audre Lorde. Used by permission of W. W. Norton. "Hard Rock Love #II" from *The Collected Poems of Audre Lorde*. Used by permission of W. W. Norton. Copyright © 1974 by Audre Lorde. "Revolution is One Form of Social Change" from *The Collected Poems of Audre Lorde*. Copyright © 1974 by Audre Lorde. Used by permission of W. W. Norton.

Etheridge Knight, "I Sing of Shine" and "Hard Rock Returns to Prison from the Hospital for the Criminal Insane" from *The Essential Etheridge Knight*. Copyright © 1986 by Etheridge Knight. Reprinted by permission of the University of Pittsburgh Press.

The Last Poets, (Abiodun Oyewole and Umar Bin Hassan with Kim Green), "Niggers R Scared of Revolution." Excerpt from *On a Mission: Selected Poems and a History of the Last Poets*. Copyright © 1996 by Abiodun Oyewole and Umar Bin Hassan. Reprinted by permission of Henry Holt and Company. All Rights Reserved.

Public Enemy, "Fight the Power" from *Do the Right Thing*. Words and music by Carlton Ridenhour, Hank Shocklee, Eric Sadler, and Keith Shocklee. Copyright © 1990 by Songs Of Reach Music, Terrordome Music, Shocklee Music, Keith Shocklee Music, Your Mother's Music and Songs Of Universal. All Rights on behalf of Songs Of Reach Music, Terrordome Music, Shocklee Music, Keith Shocklee Music and Your Mother's Music Administered by BMG Rights

Management (U.S.). All rights reserved. Reprinted by permission of Hal Leonard.
"Public Enemy No. 1." Words and music by Carlton Ridenhour and James Boxely III. Copyright © 1987 by Songs of Universal, Reach Music Publishing, Terrordome Music Publishing and Shocklee Music all rights for Reach Music Publishing, Terrordome Music Publishing LLC and Shocklee Music controlled and administered by Reach Global. All Rights Reserved Used by Permission Reprinted by Permission of Hal Leonard.

Common, featuring Kanye West and The Last Poets. "The Corner." Words and music by Kanye West, Lonnie Lynn, Umar Hassan, and Leon Moore. Copyright © 2005. Emi Blackwood Music, Please Gimme My Publishing, Irving Music, Stripe Music, Songs of Universal, Senseless Music, and Be Bop or Be Dead Music. All rights for Please Gimme My Publishing controlled and administered by Emi Blackwood Music. All rights for Stripe Music controlled and administered by Irving Music. All rights for Senseless Music controlled and administered by Songs of Universal. All rights reserved. International copyright secured. Used by permission of Hal Leonard.

Carolyn Rodgers, "The Last M.F.," "Jesus was Crucified, or, It Must be Deep (An Epic Poem)," "It Is Deep," and "Untitled No. Hurt" from the book *Songs Of A Black Bird*. Copyright © 1973 by Carolyn Rodgers. Reprinted by permission of Third World Press Foundation.

Index

Abdullah, Melina, 189
aesthetics: BAM's lack of, according to Gates, 3; change in standards of, 79–80; politics relationship to, 1–2; superficiality of White, 119. *See also* Black aesthetics; Western art/Western aesthetics
African revolutions, 24
African rhetorical tradition: basic facts about, 36, 37; community-orientation of, 33–34, 36; and contemporary Black poetry, 100; grammatical patterns of West Africa, 83, 203n1; and hip-hop, 147; nommo, 37, 104; and rap, 139, 140; in toasts, 204n7; for uplift and survival, 36. *See also* griots and griottes
Afro-American Novel and Its Tradition, The (Bell), 106, 199n5, 203n3
After Mecca (Clarke), 12
"All Eyez on U" (Giovanni), 148–149
American Literary History, 4
Amini, Johari, 31, 128, 165
Amiri Baraka: The Politics and Art of a Black Intellectual (Watts), 203n10
amplification, 52–53, 202n4
"And Shine Swam On" (Neal), 27, 122–123
Angles of Ascent: A Norton Anthology of Contemporary African American Poetry (Rowell), 1–2, 6
Annie Allen (Brooks), 89
anti-Semitism: in "Black Art," 59, 60–62; Jews as representing broader White culture, 60–62, 183, 205n6; and language of violence, 22; source of Black, 59–60

antistrophos, 44
Aristotle, 45–47, 48, 52–53, 202n1, 202n4
art, meaningfulness of, 27
artistic freedom, 18
Asante, Molefi Kete: highly diverse nature of Black Americans, 50; rhetorical justification of revolution's claims and aspirations, 49; rhetorical vilification, 57; rhetoric of Black revolutionaries, 52–53, 62; supporters of integration of Civil Rights era and Black Power movement, 181
audience(s): as activist, 53–54; age of, 133; artist's relationship to, 18; of BAM, 48–49, 50–51; Black, as cocreators in "Black Art," 63; of Black Arts poets and poetry, 97, 186; Black communities' access to Black Arts works, 51; of BLM, 192; classical Greek, versus Black activist, 201n17; as cocreators in call-response, 34; and derogatory references to Jews, 61–62; and dissemination of Black literature, 29–32; of Harlem Renaissance, 25–26; of hip-hop, 138–39; of Malcolm X's nationalist rhetoric, 73–74; meaning of "bad" to different, 83–84, 203n1; performative aspect of arts and, 29; poetry as considered in relation to, 102; and production of mixed-media works, 32; of recorded toasts, 136; and saturation of Black poetry, 102; and signifyin, 34–35, 157, 167; size for poetry, 152, 204n1 (chapter 4); and testifyin, 35, 158; and toasts, 35, 119; and use of Black English, 26, 103; and

audience(s) *(continued)*
    Western/White aesthetics in literature, 25; White, for "True Import of Present Dialogue," 78

*bad*man (hero): and Black Arts poets, 139; and Black Pride, 129–132; and community empowerment, 120; described, 117, 120; in hip-hop, 143–45, 147; as mythic hero, 137; roots of, in rap, 139; toasted in "Hard Rock," 125
Baker, Houston, 105
Baldwin, James, 59–60, 205n4 (chapter 5)
"Ballad of Birmingham" (Randall), 31
Bambara, Toni Cade, 160–61, 163–65, 169, 185
Baraka, Amina, 204n3 (chapter 5)
Baraka, Amiri: on artistic freedom, 18; and BART/S, 16, 70; basic facts about, 14–15; Black Americans as cultural nation, 51; Black art to liberate Black Americans, 6; Black consciousness as leading to revolution and Black nationalism, 54; and BPSO, 197; call for racial unity and community, 203n2; eulogy for Baldwin, 205n4 (chapter 5); family of, 61, 203n11; gender and inclusion in *Black Fire*, 153; goals of BAM, 6; and Jihad Productions press, 159; and Karenga's theories, 18; and "literary Negroes," 25; and Malcolm X, 15–16, 70; music as communicative ideal, 27; New Ark as representative of aspirations of Black nationalists, 135–36; and Pan-African ideology, 24; review of *Angles of Ascent*, 1–2, 6; role of art in revolutions, 53–54; sexuality of, 203n10. *See also* "Black Art" (Baraka)
Be (Common), 149
beatboxing, 138
bein poetry, 154–55
Bell, Bernard W., 203n3; African American literary periods, 199n5; African Americentric rhetorical theories, 32–33; African Americentric scope of theoretical foundations of BAM, 8; critical works of, 200n3; roots of Black Arts poetry, 105–106

Beyoncé Knowles-Carter, 189–92, 205nn1–2
Big Freedia, 191
Black Aesthetic, The (Gayle), 18–21, 25, 129
Black aesthetics: "African Americentric" rhetorical theories to evaluate Black Arts, 32–33; and BAM, 17, 74; and Beyoncé's Super Bowl Halftime Show (2016), 190, 192; and Black consciousness, 115; and Black English, 81–83; Blackness in, 21, 90–91; collective nature of, 17–18; and music, 27; need for, 19–21; and privilege of White features, 99; value of intrinsic Blackness of work, 100; and vernacular theory of Black literature, 106. *See also* "Black Back" (Fabio)
Blackalicious, 136
Black Americans: as BAM's primary audience, 48–49; as BAM's secondary audience, 50–51; Black English as mother tongue of, 93; as BLM's primary audience, 48–49, 192; as cultural nation, 51; extolling African heritage of, 129–32; as highly diverse audience, 50; importance of articulating heroes, 127; importance of folk heroes and history of, 122–24; importance of myth to, 133; language of educated elite versus language of "Black masses," 28–29; matriarchal structure of families, 163; "Public Enemy No. 1" as metaphor for, 146; as readers, 29–30; roots of culture of, 33; suffering of, compared to Jewish Americans, 60; Whites' fear of Black masculinity, 72. *See also* Black English
Black Americans, as collective: and African rhetorical tradition, 36; Black consciousness includes love of, 22; and Black English, 82–83; and blame rhetoric, 58, 61; and BPSO, 196–197; call to, for political activity in hip-hop, 144–45; criteria for, 17–18; family as microcosm of, 184; individual as representing, 93, 135, 178–79; music as community ritual, 27; need to define and danger in defining, 173–74; need to include all sexualities, 176–77; race as family, 160; role of praise

rhetoric, 44, 52; and testifyin, 158; toasts as community ritual, 131; White segregation and oppression as unifier, 176–77; women's historic membership in and significance to, 177–78

"Black Art" (Baraka): in anthologies, 55, 200n5; anti-Semitism in, 59, 60–62; as *ars poetica* of BAM, 56; connection between poetry and life, 54–55; first appearance of, 32, 201n14; functionalism in, 61; as misogynistic and homophobic, 58–59, 203n10; Negro mentality as correctable, 56–57; poem itself as actor in violence depicted, 62–64; removal of White influence as necessary for development of Black consciousness, 56; verbal violence in, 56; violence against authority figures, 57–58; worthiness of poems, 54

"Black Art: A Rhythmic Reality of Revolution" (Karenga), 44

Black Arts Movement (BAM): as "aesthetic and spiritual sister" of Black Power movement, 12, 200n1; African Americentric scope of theoretical foundations of, 8; and *Angles of Ascent*, 1–2; as "artless" and "old school," 1–2; and Black aesthetics, 17; "Black Art" as *ars poetica* of, 56; Black Arts as rhetorical catalyst for revolution, 17, 22; Black audiences, 48–49, 50–51; and BLM, 194–95; and BPSO, 196–97; constructive epideictic mission of, 53–54; criteria for, 17–19; and cultural nationalists, 14; derivation and critiques of, 19; and development of Black consciousness, 5, 7, 49, 198; dissemination of written works, 29–32; early influences on, 15, 201n7; "egregious extremes" of, 4; as failure, 43; and functionalism, 17, 21; Gates on, 3–4; goals of, 2, 6, 14, 44, 49; as homophobic, 59, 162, 203n10, 205n4 (chapter 5); hubs of activity of, 132; ideology of accessibility, 29; as instrument of political education, 6, 12–13, 16–17, 18; international conferences on, 3–4, 200n8; as literary period, 199n5; literature to inspire nationalistic consciousness, 39–40, 201n17; and *Negro Digest/Black World*, 30; origins of, 14–15, 27; and Outside the Black Arts Movement, 199n2; reassessment of, 3–5, 200n9; as rejection of Whiteness and embrace of pan-African identity, 22–25; rhetorical mission of, 9, 11; role of resolving "double consciousness" of Black Americans, 21–22; and self-integration of Black Americans, 22; success of, 5–7, 44, 198; tie to Black nationalism, 140; and understanding of Black identity, 5; as universal versus as political, 2; use of Black English, 26, 105–6; as at war with America, 19; and White assumption of Western aesthetics as universal, 20; Whites as audience, 48, 49, 50–51. *See also* specific art forms

Black Arts Movement: Literary Nationalism in the 1960s and 1970s, The (Smethurst), 5, 200n2

"Black Arts Movement and Its Critics, The" (Smith), 4

Black Arts poets and poetry: accessibility of, 7–8, 29; audiences of, 7–8, 32, 97, 204n1 (chapter 4); and *bad*man tradition, 139; and Beyoncé, 190; Black English used, 29, 74, 113, 115; and "Black is Beautiful," 115; categories of, 199n2; central rhetorical mission of, 5–6; as citizen-orators, 40–41, 81; as conversation, 13–14; educational interventions by individual, 107, 129; as extension of black music, 129; gender and inclusion in anthologies, 153, 169; as griots, 13, 38–39, 81, 124; influence of White aesthetics on, 28; influence on Smitherman of, 113; as instrument of Black nationalism, 12–13; and martyrdom of Malcolm X, 70–76; media and performance venues of, 32, 141; misogyny in, 58–59; paideic mission of, 39–40, 201n171; as politically impotent, 43–44; praise of Black aesthetics by, 74; purpose of, 103–104; rap and, 148–50; roots of, 105–106; as teaching tools, 113; use of

Index 225

Black Arts poets and poetry *(continued)* toasts by, 116–17, 120; violence of, on White culture and Western aesthetics, 54; women, 180–81, 186. *See also* Black Arts women poets, testifyin by. *See also* Black Arts women poets, signifyin by; poet-rhetors; specific poets; specific works

Black Arts Repertory Theater/School (BART/S), 15–16, 32, 70

Black Arts women poets, signifyin by: to argue against restrictive conceptions and prejudices, 155; "constructive destruction" function of, 153, 157; and cultural nationalists' gender roles, 165–168; elder generation's lack of Black consciousness, 181–82, 183; importance of inclusion of all Black people, 172–74, 176–77; motherhood role, 169–72; rhetorical goals, 154; sex as revolutionary act, 171–72, 175; types of poems used in, 155; use of heavy, 156–57

Black Arts women poets, testifyin by: complex experiences as Black women, 158; individual as representing collective, 178–79; lyric nature of, 155, 178; motherhood role, 180–82; nurturing individual and collective strength of nationalists, 182–83; types of poems used in, 155; women as activists and nurturers, 183–84; to women's historic role in African American community, 177–78

Black Back: Back Black (Fabio), 5–6, 92–93

"Black Back" (Fabio): Black consciousness in, 94, 96–97; Black English used in, 93–94; repetition in, 92–94; testifyin in, 92–93; tonal semantics in, 92–93

Black consciousness: achievement of, 21; and BAM, 5, 7, 49, 74, 198; and Beyoncé's Super Bowl Halftime Show (2016), 190–91; and Black aesthetics, 115; Black Arts women poets signifyin on lack of, 181–183; in "Black Back," 94, 96–97; Black poetry to develop, 12; and Black Pride, 116; and Black versus Negro mentality, 69, 126–27; and Brooks, 89, 91–92; conveyed through use of Black English, 114; "double consciousness" and, 21–22; duty of Black Artists to praise, 124–25; and Fabio, 6; and freeing Blacks from White values, 53–54; and functionalism of Black art, 21; griots and, 38; and involvement in revolution, 63; as leading to Black nationalism, 54; literature to inspire, 39–40, 201n17; and love of community, 22; and move from violence to, 68–70; as necessary precondition to political action, 51, 144–45; and pan-Africanism, 16, 23–24, 37, 135–36; and power of nommo, 37; and Public Enemy, 143–47; and rejection of White culture and values, 22–23, 56, 135–36; relationship to revolution, 131–32; and self-love, 22, 92; and strategic essentialism, 49–50; and testifyin, 87; and toasts, 120, 129–32; and Western standards of beauty and morality, 20, 80–81

"Black Creativity: On the Cutting Edge" (Gates), 2–3, 200n7

Black Dialogue, 30

Black English: and BAM, 26, 105–6, 180–81; and Black aesthetics, 82–83; and Black consciousness, 114; and "black difference" in works, 105; and "Black is Beautiful," 115; codification and valorization of, 155–156; defined and characteristics of, 103, 156; grammar, 82; and Harlem Renaissance writers, 26, 104; Henderson's definition of, 103; in institutions of formal education, 108–9, 111–13; insular rhetorical modes of, 102–3; language and style of, 110–11; and linguistic imperialism, 108; linguistic legitimacy of, 109–10; modes of discourse in, 28–29, 33–36, 114; as mother tongue of Black Americans, 93; and music, 27, 28–29; "muthafucka" in, 118, 165–68; other terms for, 201n9; and rap, 141; recoding of words and images in, 93–94, 96; rhetoric effectiveness of, 156–57; in signifyin, 131, 204n1 (chapter 4); as systematic and rule-governed language, 107; toasts'

intended audience and use of, 119; used with Standard English, 85; use of, by early writers, 115; use of, by Malcolm X, 74; and writers of Harlem Renaissance, 26
"Black English Case" (1979), 111–12
Black Enterprise, 31
Black Experience, The (television program), 177
Black Feeling, Black Talk (Giovanni), 132–33
Black Feminist / Womanist Movement, 187
Black Fire (Baraka and Neal), 153
"Black is Beautiful": acceptance of as first step in revolution, 80; beauty of dark skin and Black physicality, 129; and Beyoncé's Super Bowl Halftime Show (2016), 190; in "Black Back," 94–96; and Black English, 115; Brooks's conversion to, 88–89; and cultural nationalists, 107; and exploitative economic and social institutions, 97–98; as message of poet-rhetors, 81; origin of, 78; and truth of people's history, 103; and vernacular theory of Black literature, 106
Black Judgement (Giovanni), 133
Black literature: Afro-American novel, 106; Bell's periodization of, 199n5; Gates's periodization of, 3; Henderson's definition of, 103; and tradition of beautiful talk, 104; vernacular theory of, 100–106; Western/ White aesthetic of earlier, 25
Black Lives Matter (BLM) movement, 189, 192–96, 199n1, 205n3
Black nationalists and nationalism: acceptance of Blackness as necessary for, 67; African revolutions as model for, 24; as being redefined by BLM, 193; Black Arts movement tie to, 140; Black Power movement as "the revolution ," 13; and capitulating "Negroes," 22–23; as collective struggle, 132; criticism of acceptors of White values, 181–82; in "Ego Tripping," 135–36; and emphasizing and hierarchizing differences among Black Americans, 174–75; as failed movement, 43; family as microcosm of community,

184; "Formation" as representative of history of women in, 191; and gender roles, 159, 160–62, 165, 168–69; as homophobic, 162, 175–77; hubs of, 135–36; and Last Poets, 141–143; literature to inspire, 39–40, 201n17; "Negro" as term imposed on Blacks, 64; and "Niggers are Scared of Revolution," 142; poetry as instrument of, 12–13; and Public Enemy, 144; role of culture as distinguishing factor among, 14, 200nn3–4; strains of, 14, 200n2; and strategic essentialism, 50; use of sex, 171–72; and "we a baddDDD people," 87; women with prominent roles in, 164. *See also* cultural nationalists and nationalism
Blackness: acceptance of, as necessary for revolution, 67; as aesthetic literary value, 100; in Black aesthetics, 21, 90–91; Black English as vehicle for celebrating, 81–83; Brooks's "conversion" to, 6; celebrated in "Black Back," 94–96; celebrated in "we a baddDDD people," 87; and freeing Blacks from White values, 53–54; as inherent element of text, 100; as inner attribute and not skin color, 98–99; intersectional dynamics of, 194; need to re-aestheticize, 80–81; poetry as best art form to convey, 101; in pre-Black consciousness, 78–79; shift of semantic significance of, 79; and Western standards of beauty and morality, 20, 78–81. *See also* Black consciousness
Black Panther Party for Self-Defense (BPP): Beyoncé's homage to, 189–90; gender roles, 160; platform of, 205n5; and Rodgers, 200n4; role of culture in revolution, 14, 200n3; women with prominent roles in, 164, 187
"Black Poetry—Where It's At" (Rodgers), 153–54
Black Poets, The (Randall), 118–19
Black Poets Speak Out (BPSO), 195–97
Black Power Movement: academic assessments of, 5; art as leading to, 54; BAM as "aesthetic and spiritual sister" of,

Black Power Movement *(continued)*
  12, 200n1; Beyoncé's homage to, 189–90; *Black Panther* newspaper, 195; defined, 13; fear of, and establishment of Black Studies programs, 202n3; federal government targeting of, 2–4; importance of use of "Black," 64; and sacrifice of multiplicity of Black identities, 50; and supporters of integration of Civil Rights era, 181. *See also* Malcolm X

Black Pride: defined, 116; and hip-hop, 144–46, 149; as Pan-African, 135; in rap, 140; toasts as underscoring messages of, 120, 122–23, 129–32, 135

Black Scholar, 29–30

Black selfhood. *See* Black consciousness

Black Studies programs: establishment of, and fear of Black Power movement, 202n3; and Fabio, 92, 107; and Sanchez, 82, 107; and vernacular theory of Black literature, 106

"Black Talk" (Fabio), 92

Black Woman, The (Bambara), 160–61, 169, 185

"Black Woman as a Woman, The" (Lindsey), 168–69, 185–86

Black Woman in America, The (Staples), 160

Black Woman's Role in the Revolution (Mumininas of the Committee for Unified Newark), 159

Black Women Novelists and the Nationalist Aesthetic (Dubey), 104–5

Black World, 30. *See also Negro Digest/Black World*

blame rhetoric: and aggressive descriptors, 52; Aristotle's definition of, 202n1; of BLM, 192–93; in lieu of physical violence, 49; and marginalized or radical groups, 44, 46–47, 76; in more hortatory poetry, 154; objectification, 51; as placebo politics, 51; rhetorical vilification in, 57–58; significance of, for Rhetorical Studies, 76; strategy of vilification, 52; and unification of Black communities, 58, 61; use of by revolutionaries, 49; violence of BAM, 49; in works of poet-rhetors, 41. *See also* "Black Art" (Baraka); "True Import of Present Dialogue: Black *vs.* Negro, The" (Giovanni)

Bland, Sandra, 193

"blk/rhetoric" (Sanchez), 123–24, 151

Blues, Ideology, and Afro-American Literature (Baker), 105

Blues for Mister Charlie (Baldwin), 205n4 (chapter 5)

blues music, 27–28, 105

Boal, Augusto, 195

Book of Rhymes: The Poetics of Hip Hop (Bradley), 138

Boss Soul (Fabio), 92, 93–94

Boxley, James Henry, III, 143

Bradley, Adam, 121, 138, 139–41

breaking/breakdancing, 138

Broadside Lotus Press, 31

Broadside Press, 30–31, 89, 133, 173

Brooks, Gwendolyn: audience for pre-1967 poetry of, 89; basic facts about, 87–89, 187; Black Writers' Conference (1967, Fisk University), 88; and BPSO, 197; "conversion" to Blackness, 6; *Negro Digest/Black World* issue dedicated to, 152–53; publisher of, 31; reevaluation of and conversion to "Black is Beautiful," 88–89; review of *Selected Poems*, 20; use of narrative sequencing by, 89–91; and "we a baddDDD people" (Sanchez), 87–88

"Brother Freedom" (Burroughs), 72

"Brother Malcolm: Waste Limit" (Major), 75

Brown, Elaine, 164

Brown, H. Rap, 121–22

Brown, James, 79

Brown, Jericho, 195–96

Brown, Mike, 195

Brown, Sterling, 115

Browne, Mahogany, 195–96, 198

Burroughs, Margaret: and Madhubuti, 128; and "Malcolm poems," 70, 72; need to re-aestheticize Blackness, 80–81

"But He Was Cool" (Madhubuti), 129–32, 204n1 (chapter 4)
Byerman, Keith, 104

Cade, Toni. *See* Bambara, Toni Cade
Callaloo, 1–2
call-response (communicative form), 34, 67
Cancer Journals, The (Lorde), 173
capitulating "Negroes," 22, 23
Carmichael, Stokely. *See* Ture, Kwame
Carter, Alprentice "Bunchy," 14
Chang, Jeff, 137, 143
change: art as primary rhetorical agent of, 17; in epideictic rhetoric, 45; and Last Poets, 141–42; need for self to, 67; poetry as instrument for, 12–13; as theme, 11–12
Chuck D (Ridenhour, Carlton), 143–47
citizen-orators, 40–41, 81
civil rights movement, vilification of leaders of, 57–58
Clarke, Cheryl, 12, 29, 205n4 (chapter 5)
Cleaver, Kathleen, 164
Clifton, Lucille, 197
Cohen, Hettie, 61
College Composition and Communication (CCC), 110, 155
Collins, Patricia Hill, 160, 162
Committee for Unified Newark (CFUN), 159, 204n3 (chapter 5)
Common, 149
communicative competence, 112–13
conservative nationalism, 14. *See also* Nation of Islam (NOI)
Cortez, Jayne, 162
coversoff poetry, 153–55
Crawford, Margo Natalie, 31–32
Crenshaw, Kimberlé, 185
Critical Inquiry, 200n7
Cullors, Patrisse, 192, 194–95
cultural nationalists and nationalism: art "to unbrainwash an entire people," 16; and BAM, 14, 200n3; and "Black is Beautiful," 107; and BLM, 192; change in values as preceding revolution, 41, 79–80; hip-hop as descendants of, 145; and Malcolm X, 15–16; political struggle as necessary next step, 131–32; as strain of Black nationalism, 14, 200nn2–3; and strict roles for women, 158–60, 163–64, 165–68; US Organization, 14, 51, 200n2
"Cultural Strangulation: Black Literature and the White Aesthetic" (Gayle), 20
Cunningham, Margaret Danner, 88

Derricotte, Toi, 197
Dillard University, 3, 200n8
DJing, 137
DJ Kool Herc, 137
Dogon people of Mali, 37
Don't Cry, Scream (Madhubuti), 11–12
"double consciousness," 21–22
Douglas, Emory, 195
Dove, Rita, 197
Drayton, William, Jr., 144
Dubey, Madhu, 104–5
Du Bois, W. E. B., 2, 21–22
du-wah poetry, 154

Eady, Cornelius, 197
Eardrum (Kweli), 149–50
Ebony Museum of Negro History and Art, 80
economic nationalism, 200n2
education: Afrocentric curriculum, 107, 129, 204n2 (chapter 4); art as instrument of political education, 6, 12–13, 16–17; in institutions of education, 108–9, 111–13; paideic mission of Black Arts poets, 39–40, 201n17; as part of poet's role, 40; rhetorical, of Isocrates, 40. *See also* Black studies programs
"Ego Tripping" (Giovanni), 133–37
Ego-Tripping and Other Poems for Young People (Giovanni), 133, 204n1 (chapter 4)
Ellison, Ralph, 204n7
English Journal, 112
"English Teacher, Why You Be Doing the Thangs You Don't Do?" (Smitherman), 113

epideictic rhetoric: belief in inherently conservative nature of, 44; focus on present of, 46–47; as foundation of values governing all other rhetoric, 45; as fundamental tool for revolutionaries, 47; social and political functions of, 45; strategic use of, 41. *See also* blame rhetoric; praise rhetoric

Equal Educational Opportunities Act (1974), 111

"Ethos of the Blues, The" (Neal), 28

Evans, Mari: basic facts about, 177; in September 1969, *Negro Digest/Black World*, 152; testifyin to women's historic role in African American community, 177–80

Everett, Ron. *See* Karenga, Maulana Ron

"Everything Man" (Kweli), 149–50

Executive Committee of the Conference on College Composition and Communication (CCCC), 109–10

Fabio, Sarah Webster: basic facts about, 92; and Black consciousness and revolution for Black self-determination, 6; and Black Studies program, 92, 107; chapbooks by, 92; codification and valorization of Black English, 155–56; and contemporary Black poetry's related to Black history, 100; destruction of Western category of "universality," 19; need for Black linguistic and aesthetic forms of expression, 19; poetry of, as bi- or tri-lingual, 93; recordings of poetry, 92–94. *See also* "Black Back" (Fabio)

Fanon, Frantz, 172

Farmer, Ashley D., 204n3 (chapter 5)

Fear of a Black Planet (Public Enemy), 144

"Fight the Power" (Public Enemy), 144–45, 204n5

Figures in Black: Words, Signs, and the "Racial" Self (Gates), 3

Fisk University Black Writers' Conference (1967), 6, 88

Flavor Flav, 144, 147

Floyd, George, 193

Folk Roots of Contemporary Afro-American Poetry, The (Bell), 105–106, 203n3

"For Brother Malcolm" (Spriggs), 75–76

For Malcolm: Poems on the Life and the Death of Malcolm X (Randall and Burroughs), 70

"For Malcolm" (Whitsitt), 72

"For Malcolm X" (Walker), 73

"Formation" (Beyoncé), 189–191, 205nn1–2

"Forms of Things Unknown, The" (Henderson), 100, 105

"For Our American Cousins" (Wilson), 72

"For Saundra" (Giovanni), 43

Freedomways, 30

Fuller, Hoyt: and "Black is Beautiful," 106; and *Negro Digest/Black World*, 19, 30, 201n12; sexuality of, 205n4 (chapter 5); on Western aesthetics when reviewing Black art, 20

functionalism of art: and BAM, 17, 21; in "Black Art," 61; music for Black community, 27

Furious Flower Poetry Center (James Madison University), 197, 205n4 (Coda)

Gabbin, Joanne, 197

Gadson, Jonterri, 195–96

Garner, Eric, 193

Garza, Alicia, 192

Gates, Henry Louis, Jr.: African American literary periods, 3; BAM and understanding of Black identity, 5; Black English and "black difference" in works, 105; criticism of Harlem Renaissance, 199n6; criticism of Henderson's criteria for identifying Black text, 104; critique of BAM, 3–4; eras of African American literature, 2–3, 200n7

Gayle, Addison, 18–21, 80, 107, 129

gender: and Black Panther Party, 187; equality and strength of Black struggle, 59; and inclusion in poetry anthologies, 153, 169; misogyny in Black Arts poetry,

58–59; overlapping roles as form of White oppression, 159; roles in Black nationalism, 160–62; roles in cultural nationalism, 158, 159–60, 163–64, 165–68; strict, roles as distraction to nationalism, 168–69; and toasts, 35–36

Gilyard, Keith, 36, 71

Giovanni, Nikki: basic facts about, 132–33; Black Writers' Conference (1967, Fisk University), 6; and BPSO, 197; Pan-African influence on, 133; poetry as politically impotent, 43; and Shakur, 148–49; signifyin by, 204n1 (chapter 4); women's rights, 187–88. *See also* "True Import of Present Dialogue: Black *vs.* Negro, The" (Giovanni)

Giuliani, Rudy, 190

graffiti and hip-hop, 138

grassroots activism, 15, 201n7

Greene, Talib Kweli, 149–50

Griffin, Richard, 143

griots and griottes: basic facts about, 37–38, 201n16; Black Arts poets as, 13, 38–39, 81; rapper as postmodern, 139; reinforcement of values through stories by, 125–28; roles of, 38

Guardian, 18

Hale, Thomas A., 38

Hall, Stuart, 50

Hamilton, Charles V., 13

"Hard Love Rock #II" (Lorde), 174–75

"Hard Rock Returns to Prison from the Hospital for the Criminal Insane" (Knight), 125–128, 204n1 (chapter 4)

Harlem Renaissance: audience of, 25–26; Gates's criticism of, 199n6; goals of, 25; as literary period, 3, 199n5; writers during, 25; writers' failure to use Black English, 26, 104

Harper, Philip Brian, 50–51

Harrison, Paul Carter, 33, 37

Hauser, Gerard, 45

Hayer, Talmadge, 72

"Heir" poets, 199n2

Henderson, Stephen: Blackness as aesthetic literary value, 100; criteria of Black poetry, 101–102; importance of, 100; poetry as best art form to convey Blackness, 101; purpose of Black Arts poetry, 103–4; saturation of Black poetry, 102, 104; structure of Black poetry, 102–3; theme of Black poetry, 101–2

heroes: in hip-hop, 138, 143, 145; importance of folk, 122–24; merger of teller and, in toasts, 120; in rap, 138–39; in toasts, 36, 122–23, 127–28, 134–35, 137. *See also bad*man (hero)

hip-hop: and African rhetorical tradition, 147; Blackalicious's hip-hop version of "Ego Tripping," 136; and Black Pride, 149; as call for collective political activity, 144–45; as continuation of Black Arts mission, 117; elements of, 137–38; elements of toasts in, 117, 136, 137, 146–47, 150; emergence of, 137–38; failure to develop as movement, 148; hero in, 138, 143, 145; as text of resistance, 137–38; and toasts, 137, 146–47. *See also* rap music

"Hip Hop Nation" (Smitherman), 148

Homecoming (film), 191

Home Coming (Sanchez), 171–72

homosexuality: BAM as homophobic, 59, 162, 203n10, 205n4 (chapter 5); and Black Lives Matter, 193, 205n3; and Black nationalism, 162, 175–77; language of violence against, 22; as presence in Black nationalist movements, 191; as White pathology, 172–73

Huggins, Erica, 164

Huggins, John, 14

Hughes, Langston, 2, 26, 115

Hutchins Center for African and African American Research (Harvard University), 3–4

"I Am a Black Woman" (Evans), 152, 177–80

"In a Period of Growth" (Madhubuti), 79

Institute of Positive Education (IPE), 129
intersectionality, 185–86, 193
"I Sing of Shine" (Knight), 28, 118–19, 204n1 (chapter 4)
Isocrates, 40
"It Is Deep" (Rodgers), 182–84

Jackson, Jesse, 157
Jackson, Michael, 205n2
Jaeger, Werner, 39
jazz poetry, 154
"Jesus was Crucified" (Rodgers), 180–82, 205n5
Jewish Americans, 60–62. *See also* anti-Semitism
Jihad Productions press, 159
Joans, Ted, 73–74
Johnston, Amanda, 195–96
Joiner, Charles, 111–12
Jones, Claudia, 185
Jones, LeRoi. *See* Baraka, Amiri
Jordan, June, 197
Journal of Black Poetry, 30, 136
Jujus/Alchemy of the Blues (Fabio), 92
Jujus & Jubilees (Fabio), 92

Kaimowitz, Gabe, 112
kairos, 40–41
Karenga, Maulana Ron, 21; basic facts about African rhetoric, 36–37; categories of Black nationalists, 200n2; criteria for Black art, 17–19; cultural revolution as necessary before political action, 51; definition of nommo, 37; gender roles, 159; on need for Black aesthetics, 17; and Pan-African ideology, 24–25; rhetorical aims of BAM, 44
Kawaida philosophy, 159
"Keep on Pushin': Rhythm & Blues as a Weapon" (Touré), 27
Kgositsile, Keorapetse, 27, 40–41, 51
Killens, John Oliver, 132
King, Peter, 190
King v. Ann Arbor (1979), 108

Knight, Etheridge: basic facts about, 124; duty of Black Artists, 124–25; "I Sing of Shine," 28, 118–19, 204n1 (chapter 4); and Randall, 124
Knowles-Carter, Beyoncé, 189–92, 205nn1–2
Kweli, Talib, 149–50, 204n8

language: of educated elite versus, of "Black masses," 28–29; meaning of "Black" versus "Negro," 23–24; need for Black linguistic and aesthetic forms of expression, 19–21; of violence, 22; of Whites as norm, 109. *See also* Black English
Language Behavior in a Black Urban Community (Mitchell), 157
"Last M.F., The" (Rodgers), 165–68
Last Poets, 141–43, 149
Lee, Don L. *See* Madhubuti, Haki
legitimation, 51
Lewis, Kenneth, 112
Liberator, 30, 201n14
"Life of Lincoln West, The" (Brooks), 89–92
Lincoln, Abraham, 72
Lindsey, Kay (S.), 168–70, 185–86
Locke, Alain, 25
Lorde, Audre: "Black is Beautiful" and exploitative economic and social institutions, 97–98; and BPSO, 197; need to define and danger in defining Black community, 173–74; as outsider, 173; signifyin by, on need to include all Blacks regardless of sexuality, 176–77; signifyin by, to critique Black nationalists' homophobia, 172–73, 175–76
Lotus Press, 31
Love Poems (Giovanni), 148–49
love poetry, 154–55
Lynn, Lonnie Rashid, Jr., 149

MacLeish, Archibald, 54
Madgett, Naomi Long, 31
Madhubuti, Haki: on *Annie Allen*, 89; audience of Harlem Renaissance writers, 25–26; basic facts about, 128; Black Arts

poets' central rhetorical mission, 5–6; and Black integration, 24; Blackness as inner attribute, 98–99; Blackness in pre-Black consciousness, 78–79; Black writers' use of vernacular, 26; and BPSO, 197; and Karenga's theories, 18; poetry as extension of Black music, 129; poetry as politically impotent, 43–44; rhetorical mission of BAM, 11–12; schools with Afrocentric curriculum, 107, 129, 204n2 (chapter 4); and Smitherman, 113; and Third World Press, 30–31, 128, 165; toast extolling Black Pride, 129–32; women's role, 18

Magic of Juju: An Appreciation of the Black Arts Movement, The (ya Salaam), 200n9

Mailloux, Steven, 42

Major, Clarence, 75, 153

"Malcolm" (Sanchez), 74–75

"Malcolm poems," 70, 71–76

Malcolm X: assassination of, 70, 71; audiences of nationalist rhetoric of, 73–74; and Baraka, 15, 16; Beyoncé's tribute to, 189; "Black" as opposed to "Negro," 23–24; and cultural nationalism, 15–16; difference between "Negro" and "Black" revolutions, 64; as example of generative possibilities of change, 71; as martyred paragon of Black consciousness and Black Power politics, 70, 71–76; rhetorical ability of, 73; right of Black Americans to use force, 71; signifyin by, 157; use of Standard and Black English, 74

Marcuse, Harold, 42

Martin, Trayvon, 1, 193, 199n1

Martin Luther King Junior Elementary School Children v. Ann Arbor School District Board (1979), 111–12

"mascon" words, 103

MCing, 137–38

"Memorial 3. rev pimps" (Sanchez), 171–72

millennial nationalism, 14. *See also* Nation of Islam (NOI)

Mirror: A Soul. A Two-Part Volume of Poems (Fabio), 93

"Mister Toussan" (Ellison), 204n7

Mitchell-Kernan, Claudia, 107, 156–57

"Modernist" poets, 199n2

Mosaic, 196

Moynihan, Daniel Patrick, 163, 182, 184

Moynihan Report, 163, 182, 184

Muhammad, Elijah, 23, 64

mulattos, 58, 202n8

Mullen, Harryette, 59

Mumininas of the Committee for Unified Newark (CFUN), 159, 204n3 (chapter 5)

Murray, Sonny, 32

music: BAM as originating from, 27; Black Arts poetry as extension of Black, 129; as Black community ritual, 27; and Black English, 27, 28–29; blues, 27–28, 105; and call-response communicative form of Black English, 34; as communicative ideal, 27; as foundational to Black Arts poetry, 105–106; poetic forms inspired by, 154; relationship to poetry, 27; role of, in Black community, 27–28; and tonal semantics communicative form of Black English, 34. *See also* hip-hop; rap

"My Ace of Spades" (Joans), 73–74

My Own Thing (Fabio), 92

mythication, 51

narrative sequencing (communicative form): testifyin, 35, 86–87; "The Life of Lincoln West," 89–91; toasts, 35–36

National Council of Teachers of English (NCTE), 110

Nation of Islam (NOI): as conservative or millennial nationalist organization, 14; and gender roles, 160; and Neal, 200n4; as religious nationalist organization, 200n2; and Sanchez, 200n4

Neal, Larry: audience of Harlem Renaissance writers, 26; and BAM, 15; BAM as "aesthetic and spiritual sister" of Black Power movement, 200n1; on Black aesthetics, 17; characteristics of poets of revolutionary movements, 116; gender and inclusion

Neal, Larry (continued)
   in *Black Fire*, 153; ideal poet-performer, 191; importance of Black folk heroes and history in raising Black consciousness, 122–23; influence of Malcolm X, 15; and Karenga's theories, 18; and NOI, 200n4; poetry in Black English, 29; and RAM, 200n4; role of music in Black community, 27–28; self-integration of Black Americans, 22; Uptown Writers Group, 200n4; Western aesthetics as "dead form," 25
"Negro" (Hughes), 115
Negro Digest/Black World, 2, 17, 19, 30, 152–53, 177, 201n12
Negro(es): capitulating, 22–23; challenged as preferred term of racial identity, 64, 69, 203n12; death of, mentality as necessary to realize Black consciousness, 69; as disparaging term, 23, 56–57; as enemy, 22–23, 67–69, 142; "literary," 25; mentality as being correctable, 56–57; mentality of Blacks versus mentality of, 126–127; in "The True Import of Present Dialogue," 64–65
Negro Family: The Case for National Action, The (Moynihan Report), 163, 182, 184
"Negro Youth Speaks" (Locke), 25
New Ark (Newark), New Jersey, 135–36
New Black Poetry, The (Major), 153
New Black Womanhood, 159–65
New Concept School, 129
"New Integrationist, The" (Madhubuti), 24
New Negro Movement: goals of, 25; as literary period, 199n5; writers, 3
New Negro Renaissance, 2, 5
New Rhetoric, The (Perelman and Olbrechts-Tyteca), 44
New York Head Shop and Museum (Lorde), 173–75
New York Herald Tribune Book Week, 20
New York Times Magazine, 59–60
nommo: defined, 37; harnessing power of, 37; power of, 104; as used by Black poets, 104
Norman, George, 71–72

objectification, 51
Ogotommêli, 37
Okpewho, Isidore, 37
Olbrechts-Tyteca, Lucie, 44–46, 49
100 Best African American Poems, The (Giovanni), 148
On Rhetoric (Aristotle), 45–47
Organization of African Unity, 16
Organization of Afro-American Unity (OAAU), 16, 70–71
Organization of Black American Culture (OBAC), 128, 165, 200n4
Outside the Black Arts Movement, 199n2

paideia, 39–40, 201n17
Pan-African ideology/identity: artifacts of, 130; BAM embrace of, 23–24; and Baraka, 24; and Black consciousness, 16, 23–24, 27, 135–36; and Black Pride, 135; and cultural nationalism of US Organization, 14, 200n2; form and content of "Ego Tripping," 133; and Giovanni, 133, 135; and Karenga, 24–25; rejection of Whiteness and embrace of, 22–24, 135–36
panegyric rhetoric. *See* praise rhetoric
Patterson, Louise Thompson, 185
Perelman, Chaim, 44–46, 49
"Pill: Genocide or Liberation, The" (Bambara), 160–61
Pindar, 47
Pisstained Stairs and the Monkey Man's Wares (Cortez), 162
Pluck! The Journal of Affrilachian Arts and Culture, 196
"Poem" (Lindsey), 169–70
"A Poem for Black Hearts" (Baraka), 16
Poems from Prison (Knight), 124, 125–28
"Poem to Complement Other Poems, A" (Madhubuti), 11–12
Poetics (Aristotle), 48
poet-rhetors: Beyoncé as, 190–91; "Black is Beautiful" as message of, 81; defined, 8, 12; as descendants of traditional Western rhetoric and African rhetoric, 8, 41;

indictment of Whites by, 44, 52; praise of Blackness and Black community by, 44, 52; use of Standard English by, 83–86; use of toasts by, 117

poetry: audience, 204n1 (chapter 5); connection between life and, 54–55; as source of epideictic rhetoric, 47–48

Poetry, 1

political education: aesthetics' relationship to, 1–2; art as instrument of, 6, 12–13, 16–17, 18

political nationalism. *See* Black Panther Party for Self-Defense (BPP)

"Political Poetry Is Hot Again" (Smith), 195

Pough, Gwendolyn, 140, 148

"Power of the Rap: The Black Idiom and the New Black Poetry, The" (Smitherman), 113–14, 204n1 (chapter 4)

"Practice of the New Nationalism" (Baraka), 136

praise rhetoric: amplification, 52–53, 202n4; and Beyoncé's Super Bowl Halftime Show (2016), 190–91; "Black Back" as, 94–96; as call for action, 74–76; conservative pull of traditional, 45–46; as duty of Black Artists to, 124–125; legitimation, 51; "Malcolm poems," 70, 71–76; in more lyric poetry, 154; mythication, 51; and unifying descriptors, 52; in works of poet-rhetors, 41

"Precursor" poets, 199n2

"Preface to Blackness: Text and Pretext" (Gates), 104

Professor Griff, 143

psogos rhetoric. *See* blame rhetoric

Public Enemy, 143–47, 204n5

"Public Enemy No. 1" (Chuck D), 145–46

pyramid poetry, 154

"Queen of Bounce," 191

"Race" (Cortez), 162

racism and assumption of Western aesthetics as universal, 20

Rainbow Signs (Fabio), 92

Randall, Dudley: *The Black Poets* anthology, 118–19; and Broadside Press, 30–31, 89; and Knight, 124; and "Malcolm poems," 70; and "we a badd DDD people" (Sanchez), 87

rap: and absence of political action, 140; and Black Arts poets' support, 148–50; and Black Pride, 140; and blame rhetoric, 140; and Public Enemy, 143–47; and resistance, 138; roots of, 139, 141; and song, 138; and toasts, 138

rappin poetry, 153–55

"Rap's Poem" (H. Rap Brown), 121–22

Re: Creation (Giovanni), 133

reception histories, 41–42

religious nationalists. *See* Nation of Islam (NOI)

repetition: in "Black Back," 92–94, 96; in call-response, 34; Gates on, 105; in "True Import of Present Dialogue," 67

Report from Part One (Brooks), 88

resistance rhetoric of toasts, 118–20

revolutionaries and revolutionary movements: Black consciousness as precondition to, 51, 54, 63, 144–45; and blame rhetoric, 44, 46–47, 76; and change in aesthetics of Blackness, 79; characteristics of poets of, 116; cultural revolution as necessary precondition of political, 51; Hard Rock as model of, 126, 128; and hip-hop, 137, 138; and "Niggers are Scared of Revolution," 142; poetry as first step in, 41; poetry as source of epideictic rhetoric, 47–48; purpose of rhetoric of, 62; rhetorical needs of, 46; rhetorical strategies central to rhetoric of, 52–53; rhetoric to justify claims and aspirations of, 49; role of art in, 53–54; sex and, 160–61, 169–72; as theme of Black poetry, 101–102. *See also* Black Power Movement

Revolutionary Action Movement (RAM), 14–15, 200nn2–4

"Revolutionary Dreams" (Giovanni), 187–88

"Revolutionary Theatre, The " (Baraka), 53–54

"Revolution Is One Form of Social Change" (Lorde), 173–74
Reynolds, Barbara, 194
rhetoric: ancient Greek, 39–41, 201n7; effectiveness of Black English, 156–57; needed by revolutionary movements, 46–47; power of, 202n3; and reception histories, 42. *See also* African rhetorical tradition; blame rhetoric; praise rhetoric
Rhetoric (Aristotle), 52–53, 202n4
rhetorical vilification, 57–58
Rhetoric of Black Revolution (Asante), 49
Rice, Tamir, 193
Richardson, Elaine, 36
Rickford, John: audiences of rap, 139; characteristics of toasts, 117; heroics in hip-hop boasts, 137; resistance rhetoric of toasts, 120; signifyin in toasts, 121
Rickford, Russell: audiences of rap, 139; characteristics of toasts, 117; heroics in hip-hop boasts, 137; resistance rhetoric of toasts, 120; signifyin in toasts, 121
Ridenhour, Carlton "Chuck D," 143–47
Rock, John Sweat, 78–79, 115
Rodgers, Carolyn: basic facts about, 165; and BPP,, 200n4; "constructive deconstruction" function of signifyin, 157; defiance of role of women by, 168; and OBAC, 200n4; signifyin lack of Black consciousness, 181–83; taxonomy of Black Arts poetry, 153–54; and Third World Press, 31, 128, 165; use of Black English, 180–81
Rodriguez-Sharpe, Sherina, 195–96
Rose That Grew from Concrete, The (Shakur), 148
Rountree, Clarke, 45–46, 202n1
Rowell, Charles Henry, 1–2, 6, 199n2

"Sambo," 126
Sanchez, Sonia: basic facts about, 82; Black English as vehicle for celebrating Blackness, 82–83; and Black Studies program, 82, 107; and BPSO, 197; and Cullors, 195; as griotte, 38; and Karenga's theories, 18; and Kweli, 150; and Last Poets, 143; need for Black heroes, 123–24, 151; and NOI, 200n4; paideia in works, 40; in praise of Malcolm X, 74–75; recognition of damaging utterances existing next to constructive ones, 194; signifyin on sex as revolutionary act, 171–72. *See also* "we a baddDDD people" (Sanchez)
San Francisco State University, 82
Schuyler, George, 2
Scott-Heron, Gil, 141
Selected Poems (Brooks), 20
"Self-Hatred of Don L. Lee, The" (Madhubuti), 98–99
self-love and Black consciousness, 92
self-reflective poems, 154–55
Senghor, Léopold, 17
sex: as essential human intimacy, 175; as rap theme, 138; as revolutionary act, 171–72
Shabazz, Ilyasah, 189
Shakur, Tupac, 148–49
Shine toasts, 118–20, 123
Shocklee, Hank, 143
shoutin (angry/ cathartic) poetry, 154
signifyin (communicative form): and audience, 34–35, 167; basic facts about, 34; Black English used, 131, 204n1 (chapter 4); characteristics of, 122; defining, 156, 157; Gates on, 105; point of "heavy," 156–57; and rap, 138, 141; as rhetorical mode, 186; in toasts, 121–22, 130–31, 135, 204n1 (chapter 4); and verbal dueling, 120–21. *See also* Black Arts women poets, signifyin by
Signifying Monkey: A Theory of African-American Literary Criticism, The (Gates), 105
Simone, Nina, 191–92
Simpson, Louis, 20
Sipiora, Phillip, 40
Smethurst, James: Black Arts poets as having conversation, 13–14; on development of BAM, 15, 201n7; issues with academic

assessments of Black Arts and Black Power movements, 5; strains of Black nationalism, 200n2
Smith, Arthur L. *See* Asante, Molefi Kete
Smith, David Lionel, 4
Smith, Tom W., 64, 203n12
Smith, Tracy K., 195
Smitherman, Geneva: absence of political action with rap music, 140; characteristics of signifyin, 122; and communicative competence, 112–13; connotations of "bad," 83, 203n1; definition of testifyin, 35; epic folk style of toasts, 117–18; hip-hop as text of resistance, 137; hip-hop's failure to develop as movement, 148; influence of Black Arts poetry on, 113; and linguistic imperialism, 108; and Mitchell-Kernan, 157; point of "heavy" signifyin, 156–57; rapper as postmodern griot, 139; sound and sense in use of tonal semantics, 93; storytelling as Black rhetorical strategy, 89; on structure of toasts, 119; testifyin as valorizing self and investing self in community, 87; toasts and "accomplishment against the odds," 36; on use of "hot," 132; use of term Black, 69
Smitherman, Geneva on Black English: codification and valorization of, 155–56; language and style of, 110–11; linguistic legitimacy of, 109–10; modes of discourse in, 28, 33–36, 114; as systematic and rule-governed language, 107; teaching in schools, 112–13; used in signifyin poetry, 204n1 (chapter 4)
Snellings, Roland. *See* Touré, Askia
Songs of a Black Bird (Rodgers), 165–68, 180–84, 205nn5–6
Sonny's Time Now (Murray), 32
"SOS" (Baraka), 203n2
Soul Ain't Soul (Fabio), 92
Soulbook, 30
Souls of Black Folk, The (Du Bois), 21
spaced (spiritual) poetry, 153–55
Spivak, Gayatri Chakravorty, 49–50

Spriggs, Edward, 75–76
Standard American English (SAE), 28
Staples, Robert, 160
"State/meant" (Baraka), 56, 62
Stephney, Bill, 146
storytelling as Black rhetorical strategy, 89
strategic essentialism, 49–50, 104–105
"Strivings of the Negro People" (Du Bois), 21
Strobert, Andrei, 143
Students' Right to Their Own Language declaration (1974), 108, 109–10
Super Bowl Halftime Show (2016), 189–92, 205nn1–2

Talkin and Testifyin: The Language of Black America (Smitherman), 33–36, 107–8, 110, 112
teachin poetry, 153–55
testifyin (communicative form): and Beyoncé's Super Bowl Halftime Show (2016), 190–191; in "Black Back," 92–93; defined, 35; as rhetorical mode, 186; secular, 158; as valorizing self and investing self in community, 87; in "we a baddDDD people," 86–87. *See also* Black Arts women poets, testifyin by
"Theatre of the Oppressed" aesthetic method, 195
Think Black! (Madhubuti), 78–79
Third World Press, 30–31, 128, 165
Thomas, Lorenzo, 38
Time (magazine), 2–3, 200n7
toasts (communicative form), 35–36; and African rhetorical tradition, 204n7; as antidotes to racist treatment of Black Americans, 119–20; and audience, 35, 119; basic facts about, 35–36; Blackalicious's hip-hop version of "Ego Tripping," 136; Black Arts poets' use of first person, 120; and Black consciousness, 120; in Black oral tradition, 117; characteristics of, 117; as common collective ritual, 131; defined, 117; elements of, in hip-hop, 117, 136–37, 146–47, 150; epic folk style of, 117–18;

toasts (communicative form) *(continued)*
extolling Black Pride, 129–32; heroes in, 122–23, 127–28, 134–35; "I am bad" assertion in, 133–34; importance of verbal artistry, 120; linguistic virtuosity of, 119, 122; and rap, 138; recorded, 136; resistance rhetoric of, 118–20; Shine, 118–20; signifyin in, 121–22, 130–31, 204n1 (chapter 4); structure of, 119; as underscoring messages of Black Pride, 135; use of, by Black Arts poets, 116–17; use of Black English, 119. *See also* badman (in toasts)
"To Be Young, Gifted, and Black" (Simone), 191–92
Together/To the Tune of Coltrane's Equinox (Fabio), 92
"To Malcolm X" (Norman), 71–72
Tometi, Opal, 192
tonal semantics (communicative form): basic facts about, 34; in "Black Back," 92–93; elements in, 34; in "we a baddDDD people," 86–87
Touré, Askia: description of role of griots by, 38–39; influence on BAM of, 15; and Karenga's theories, 18; music as communicative ideal, 27; paideia in works, 39–40; role of music in Black community, 27
"Toward a Definition: Black Poetry of the Sixties (After LeRoi Jones) " (Madhubuti), 129
"Towards a Black Aesthetic" (Fuller), 20, 106
"Transcendental Vision Indigo" (Touré), 38–40
tricksters (in toasts), 117
"triple oppression," 185–86, 193
"Tripping with Black Writing" (Fabio), 19
"True Import of Present Dialogue: Black vs. Negro, The" (Giovanni): ability to commit violence as opposed to actually committing, 68; all Whites as enemies, 65–66; in anthologies, 55, 200n6; calls to violence in, 65–66, 67; irony and injustice of Black soldiers fighting for democracy, 66–67; as secular sermon, 67–68

Truth Is On Its Way (Giovanni), 136
Ture, Kwame, 13, 64
Twentieth Century Literature, 113
"Two Poems" (Madhubuti), 43–44

Understanding the New Black Poetry: Black Speech and Black Music as Poetic References (Henderson), 100, 200n3
University of California, Merced, 200n8
"Untitled No. Hurt" (Rodgers), 184
Uptown Writers Group, 200n4
Uptown Writers Movement, 15
US Organization, 14, 51, 200n2

verbal dueling, 120–121
vernacular theory of Black literature, 100–106
Vietnam War, 66
vilification, 51
violence: against authority figures, 57–58; in BAM rhetoric, 49, 50–51; in "Black Art" by Baraka, 56, 62–64; of Black Arts poetry on White culture and Western aesthetics, 54; blame rhetoric in lieu of physical, 49; move from, to Black consciousness, 68–70; as rap theme, 138; rhetoric as counterpart to, 44; right of Black Americans to use, 71

Walker, Alice, 187
Walker, Jeffrey, 47–48
Walker, Margaret, 73
Washington Post, 194
Watani-Stiner, Larry, 14
Watts, Jerry Gafio, 203n10
We a BaddDDD People (Sanchez), 123–24
"we a baddDDD people" (Sanchez): as celebration of Blackness, 87; and Randall, 87; tonal semantics in, 86–87; use of Standard English in, 83–86; use of testifyin in, 86–87; valorization of Black expression, 82–84
"We Shall Survive, Without a Doubt" (Douglas), 195
West, Kanye, 149

Western art/Western aesthetics: and anti-Black racism, 91; Black English as outside, 26; and Black poetry, 153; and earlier Black writing, 25; hip-hop as music of resistance against, 137; Jews as synecdochic representation of, 60–62; rejection of, and embrace of Pan Africanism, 135; rejection of, as necessary, 21; as universal/ideal standards, 19–20; "universal" writing privileged over particularities of Black experience, 100; violence of Black Arts poetry on, 54; White values of beauty and goodness in, 20–21, 58, 78–79, 80–81, 91

"What Is Black?" (Fabio), 155

"What Shall I Tell My Children Who Are Black?" (Burroughs), 80–81

When They Call You a Terrorist (Cullors), 195

Whiteness: Black acceptors of values of, 181–82; Blackness as rejection of, 22–23; and concept of decency, 181; and Hard Rock, 126–27; and internal struggle of Black Americans, 21–22; racist stereotypes of Black men, 119; rejection of, and embrace of Pan-African identity, 22–24, 135–36; removal of, as necessary to develop Black consciousness, 56; and standards of beauty and morality, 20–21, 58, 78, 80–81; superficiality of aesthetics of, 119; violence of Black Arts poetry on, 54. *See also* Western art/Western aesthetics

Whites: all, as enemies, 65–66, 68; artists as part of oppressive political system, 19; attempts to control Black Americans culturally, 108; as audience of Harlem Renaissance, 25–26; as BAM audience, 48, 49, 50–51; blame rhetoric used to indict, 44, 52; as BLM's secondary audience, 192; fear of Black masculinity, 72; homosexuality as form of "degeneracy" of, 59; institutions of, as primary enemy, 186; Jews as representing racist, 60–62, 183, 205n6; language of, as norm, 109; literature as form of expression for, 27; overlapping roles as form of oppression by, 159; response to Beyoncé's Super Bowl Halftime Show (2016), 190–91; segregation and oppression of Blacks as unifier of, 176–77; as source of representation of Black Americans, 13

Whitsitt, Joyce, 72

"Who is The Black Woman?" (Bambara), 164–65

Wilson, Darren, 195

Wilson, Reginald, 72

womanism, 186–87

women: and BLM, 192, 193; criticism of, from Black nationalists and from White authorities, 181–182; denigration of, in Black Arts poetry, 58–59; feminism and Black nationalism, 185–88; "Formation" as representative of history of, in Black nationalism, 191; language of violence against agency of, 22; Madhubuti and role of, 18; matriarchal structure of Black American families, 163; motherhood role, 160–61, 169–72, 180–82; New Black Womanhood, 159–65; novelists of 1980s, 3, 199n5; strict roles for, in Black nationalism, 160–62; strict roles for, in cultural nationalism, 158–60

"Writers Symposium" *(Negro Digest/Black World)*, 2

ya Salaam, Kalamu: on development of BAM, 15, 201n7; and Karenga's theories, 18; as "participant and critic" of BAM, 200n9

Yo! Bum Rush the Show (Public Enemy), 145

"zero copulas," 84–85

Zimmerman, George, 199n1

www.ingramcontent.com/pod-product-compliance
Lightning Source LLC
Chambersburg PA
CBHW061724071225
36429CB00029B/490